Essays in Social Theory

Essays in Social Theory

STEVEN LUKES

First published 1977 by
THE MACMILLAN PRESS LTD
London and Basingstoke
Associated companies in New York Dublin
Melbourne Johannesburg and Madras

ISBN 0 333 19662 7 (hard cover)
      0 333 19693 7 (paper cover)

Printed in Great Britain by
THE CAMELOT PRESS LTD
Southampton

For Nina

Contents

Contents

Preface and Acknowledgements

These essays, written over the last fourteen years, doubtless have more in common than their author realises. Their general approach Polonius might have described as critical–analytical–conceptual–philosophical. Their subject-matter falls under no obvious label – which will annoy those with a taste for labels. I see no great point in, for instance, drawing a sharp line between the 'social' and the 'political', consigning the former to sociology and the latter to political science or political theory. Some of these essays are more sociological, others more political.

Certain perennial, evergreen issues recur – the distinction between empirical and normative theorising and the relations between them, and the bearing of theory on evidence and evidence on theory (themes dominant in Part 1); the alleged relativity of standards of rationality and of criteria of truth and validity (see Part 2); and the relation between 'individual' and 'social' factors, and the wide-ranging implications of different ways of conceptualising that relation (see Part 3). For some, such issues are best uprooted and weeded out; others tend them with loving care as prize exhibits in the academic flower garden. In my view, they form the roots of the tree of social-scientific knowledge. Those roots certainly need care and attention, but the tree's only fruit is explanatory theory, based on and vulnerable to evidence.

All the essays have previously appeared in journals or books, except the first, 'Power and Structure'. An earlier version of that essay was delivered at the British Sociological Association's Annual Conference in 1975, the present version at the American Political Science Association's Annual Meeting in 1976. Chapter 2, written with Graeme Duncan (whom I thank both for the pleasures of that collaboration and for his permission to reprint here), first appeared in *Political Studies*, vol. XI, no. 2 (1963); Chapter 3 in *Sociology*, vol. 9, no. 2 (May 1975); Chapter 4 in *Philosophy, Politics and Society*, 3rd series, edited by

P. Laslett and W. G. Runciman (Oxford: Blackwell, 1967); Chapter 5 in *The Socialist Idea: A Reappraisal*, edited by L. Kolakowski and S. Hampshire (London: Weidenfeld & Nicolson, 1974); Chapter 6 in the *European Journal of Sociology*, vol. 8 (1967); Chapter 7 in *Modes of Thought: Essays presented to E. E. Evans-Pritchard*, edited by R. Horton and R. Finnegan (London: Faber, 1973); Chapter 8 in the *Supplementary Proceedings of the Aristotelian Society* (1974); Chapter 9 in the *British Journal of Sociology*, vol. xix (1968); Chapter 10 in the *Observer* (4 June 1972); and Chapter 11 in the *New Statesman* (14 March 1975).

Oxford   S. L.
June 1976

Part 1

Politics and Society

Chapter 1

Power and Structure

This chapter is an attempt to address a fundamental and traditional problem central to the concerns of most philosophers, social scientists and historians, indeed to most of us at some time or other. It emerges at a number of levels. At the most general, metaphysical level, it takes the age-old form of the conflict between voluntarism and determinism. At the methodological level, it emerges as a dispute between theoretical frameworks, explanatory paradigms or problematics over whether the historical 'subject' has or has not an ineradicable and perhaps crucial explanatory role. This is an issue very much alive within contemporary Marxism, dividing so-called Hegelian 'historicists' and 'humanists' from their structuralist adversaries. It also underlies the division within contemporary sociology between, on the one hand, all those who are concerned to study social actors, their modes of symbolic interaction, their definitions of situations, their modes of constructing and negotiating social reality, and, on the other, those whose focus is upon systems and objective co-ordinates, on what Durkheim called 'social facts' and Marx 'definite relations that are indispensable and independent of [men's] will'.[1] And at the most common-sense and mundane level, the issue is simply this: to what extent and in what ways are social actors, whether individuals or collectivities, constrained to think and act in the ways they do? To what extent is an American President prevented from achieving desired outcomes by constraints, whether

external or internal?[2] What difference can a determined Cabinet
Minister make in a time of economic crisis, faced with the inertia of
the governmental system and obstructive civil servants?[3] Why did
Bukharin consistently fail to stand up to Stalin?[4] To what extent can the
elites of modernising societies conjoin possibility with will: to what
degree in any given case are they constrained to follow a single path
(*à la* Rostow) or a narrow range of possible paths (*à la* Barrington
Moore) or are able to cut out new paths?[5] Why have the increasingly
deradicalised Social Democratic parties of Western Europe made so
little impact on the balance of class advantages?[6] What enables social
movements, such as blacks in the United States, to transform objective
possibilities into concrete results?[7] I shall formulate this issue as that of
the relation between power and structure.

Let us look first at the concept of power. This concept, which looks so
simple and innocent, and which we all use all the time, actually carries a
considerable theoretical and ideological load. At its most general, it
simply means the capacity to bring about consequences, with no
restriction on what the consequences might be or on what brings them
about (or on whether or not the bringing about is seen as a causal
relation). However, when used in relation to human beings in social
relations with one another, it is attributed to persons or sets of persons.
Yet, clearly, talk of power in social and political life generally means
something more specific than that human beings can affect the world. In
applying this primitive notion to the understanding of social life,
something further is required: namely, that the affecting is seen as non-
trivial or significant.[8] Clearly, we all affect each other and the natural
world in countless ways all the time: the concept of power – and related
concepts, such as influence, authority, coercion, force, manipulation,
and so on – pick out ranges of such affecting that are held to be
significant in specific (and related) ways.

The question of how to define the concept of power is a notoriously
unsettled one, with different theorists offering different definitions and
ordinary language allowing for a wide variety of distinct, overlapping
and inconsistent usages. Indeed, I maintain that power is one of those
concepts identified by Gallie as 'essentially contested', which 'inevitably
involve endless disputes about their proper uses on the part of their
users'.[9] Thus any given way of conceiving of power (that is, any given
way of defining the concept of power) in relation to the understanding of
social life presupposes a criterion of significance, that is, an answer to
the question 'what makes *A*'s affecting *B* significant?'.

Some writers take an extremely general view. 'Power', wrote Bertrand Russell, 'may be defined as the production of intended effects'.[10] On this view the forms of affecting that will be significant in such a way as to count as power will be those that realise one or more agents' intentions. Note that the object of power here (*B*) may be either human (persons or sets of persons) or non-human. But not all ways of conceiving power tie it to intentionality, while most uses of 'power' – especially those involving the locution 'exercising power *over*' – restrict its object to persons or sets of persons. Disagreements exist about whether or not *A* must aim at or (partly or wholly) succeed in realising his will, intentions or desires; about whether there need be conflict between *A* and *B* (and, if so, whether it must be between their wills, preferences, interests, needs, and so on); whether there need be the threat of sanctions or deprivations, what the balance of costs and rewards to *A* and *B* must be; and about whether *B*'s interests, options, preferences, policies or behaviour must be affected for a given relation to count as power. For Max Weber, power (*Macht*) signified 'the chance of a man or a number of men to realize their own will in a communal action even against the resistance of others who are participating in the act'.[11] For Lasswell and Kaplan, power is 'the process of affecting policies of others with the help of (actual or threatened) severe deprivations for nonconformity with the policies intended'.[12] For Talcott Parsons, however, power excludes 'the threat of coercive measures, or of compulsion, without legitimation or justification' and applies definitionally to the 'generalised capacity to secure the performance of binding obligations by units in a system of collective organisation when the obligations are legitimized with reference to their bearing on collective goals and where in case of recalcitrance there is a presumption of enforcement by negative situational sanctions'.[13] By contrast, a contemporary Marxist definition is offered by Poulantzas, for whom power is 'the capacity of a social class to realise its specific objective interests'.[14] Again, power may be seen quite generally as being exercised when *A* affects *B* by limiting his liberty, that is by restricting his options; or it may be seen as being exercised when *A* affects *B* in a manner contrary to *B*'s interests (this last being the concept of power predominant in contemporary political science).

Two points are to be noted here: not only is there an endemic variety of concepts of power, depending upon different criteria specifying what is to count as significant affecting, themselves arising out of different social theories and moral and political perspectives; but also, any given *conception* of power (to use the Rawlsian distinction between concept and conception),[15] that is, any way of interpreting a given concept of power, is likely to involve further particular and contestable judgements – about, for example, what is going to count as 'severe deprivations' or 'collective goals', how relevant options are to be selected or how interests are to be identified.

One important point, however, seems clear in relation to all these concepts of power: that power is attributed to (individual or collective) human agents. Not all, as I have said, confine it to intentional agency; one may, for example, be held to exercise power through negligence, or routine action, or inaction, without considering those affected. They all, however, link the exercise of power to human agency. Human agents characteristically perform voluntary actions (of which intentional actions are a sub-class), these being actions done in the presence of open alternatives;[16] there is an openness between an agent's performing or failing to perform a voluntary action, and indeed to describe his action as voluntary is precisely to deny that there is a causal link between his want and his action.[17] Human agents exercise their characteristic powers when they act voluntarily on the basis of wants and beliefs which provide them with reasons for so acting. Such an exercise of the power of human agency implies that the agent at the point of action has the power to act otherwise, that is, at the least the ability and the opportunity both to act and not act: it is in his power to do either; there is 'an openness between performing or failing to perform the action',[18] and there is no set of external circumstances such that in those circumstances the agent will necessarily so act.

If all the foregoing is correct, then any given view of (that is, way of identifying) power involves two central claims. First, where power is exercised, it is always the case that the exerciser or exercisers *could* have acted differently. Second, where power is (as usually) seen as affecting other persons, then it is always the case that those affected by its exercise *would* have acted (using that term to include thought, wanted, felt) differently, but for the exercise of power.

What is important for the present argument is that, on this account, power – and cognate notions such as influence, authority, coercion, and so on – presupposes human agency. To use the vocabulary of power (and its cognates) in application to social relationships is to speak of human agents, separately or together, in groups or organisations, through action or inaction, significantly affecting the thoughts or actions of others. In speaking thus, one assumes that, although the agents operate within structurally determined limits, they none the less have a certain relative autonomy and could have acted differently. Compare the case of an employer who declares some of his workers redundant, in pursuance of a strategy to cut his costs, with that of an official government liquidator who declares an insolvent company bankrupt, thereby throwing its workers out of work. The first case is a simple case of power exercise on practically every definition; the second is not, just because we assume that the liquidator has no alternative (as liquidator – we may argue otherwise if we separate the man from his role). To talk of power implies that, if the future facing social actors is not entirely open, it is not entirely closed either (and indeed the degree of its openness is itself variable). To put it another way, in a world characterised by total structural determinism, imposing uniquely determining constraints upon action, there would be no place for power. Power, then, is exercised within structurally determined limits – which leads us to consider the notion of structure.

It follows fairly obviously from what I have so far said that structural factors, parameters or constraints in a given context will be those claimed to determine, that is, set limits to, the power of agents within· some assumed time period. I agree, of course, with Raymond Boudon when he says that 'the meaning of the concept of structure varies with the context in which it is employed'[19] and that a structural analysis of some object is simply the theory of that object viewed as a system (which will vary both with the nature of the theory and of the object). I further agree that 'structure' in its different uses variously connotes 'essence', 'totality', 'system of relationships', 'dependence of parts in relation to a whole', and so on, and contrasts with (for example) 'observable characteristics', 'aggregate', 'superficial system', 'conjuncture', and so on. However, it seems to me plain that the opposition between structure and agency picks out a basic feature common to the major sociological and anthropological conceptions of structure, and is compatible with others.

Consider the Marxian notion of 'the economic structure of society' (relations of production which are 'independent of [men's] will') and the 'legal and political superstructure' (note: super*structure*), Weber's economic and bureaucratic structures 'prescribing' the behaviour of individuals[20] and class structures determining life-chances, and Durkheim's social facts (characterised as external to, constraining upon and independent of agents) ranging from the morphological (the most 'crystallised') through institutionalised norms to *représentations* *collectives* and, at the extreme, free-floating currents of social life that have not yet taken a distinct form. Consider Radcliffe-Brown's concept of social structure as 'an arrangement of persons in institutionally controlled or defined relationships',[21] Nadel's as a 'role-system',[22] the Wilsons' definition of social structure as 'the systematic form of limitation by which eccentricities are checked and complementary diversities are preserved',[23] Lévi-Strauss's account in terms of underlying principles of organisation which are invisible and often unconscious – 'what is important is to find out when a given player can make a choice and when he cannot'.[24] Consider Merton's claim that the 'interdependence of the elements of a social structure limit the effective possibilities of change or functional alternatives. The concept of structural constraint corresponds, in the area of social structure, to Goldenweiser's "principle of limited possibilities" in a broader sphere',[25] Talcott Parsons's characteristic view that social structure 'focuses on the integration of the motivation of actors with the normative cultural standards which integrate the action system',[26] Blau's argument that social structure is defined by 'parameters' which specify the 'social positions that govern the social relations among their incumbents',[27] and Stinchcombe's claim that

> the core process conceived as central to social structure is *the choice between socially structured alternatives*. This differs from the choice process of economic theory, in which the alternatives are conceived to have inherent utilities. It differs from the choice process of learning theory, in which the alternatives are conceived to emit reinforcing or extinguishing stimuli. It differs from both of these in that . . . the utility or reinforcement of a particular alternative choice is thought of as socially established, as part of the institutional order.[28]

This basic opposition between structure and agency is, then, pervasive, although views differ about what constitute structural factors, about what sort of limits they set upon agency and about whether the limits they set curtail freedom or provide the condition of its effective exercise ('liberty', as Durkheim once said, being 'the fruit of regulation').[29] It underlies views of structure that focus upon ecological or morphological factors, institutional factors, stable systems of generalised role expectations, or cultural factors. It is in this sense that we speak of class structures, kinship structures, occupational structures, opportunity structures, age structures, but also of linguistic structures, thought structures,[30] structures of myths, and so on. This basic aspect of structure is also compatible with various further and familiar features of structure in its various applications – its persistence, its relative stability, its capacity to be hidden from agents and sometimes to be unconscious, and also the evident relativity of any attribution of structural determination to a theory of society, of the individual and of the relation between them presupposed by the attributor.

Now, just as I have argued that power is an essentially contested concept, and that any given empirical application of it carries a considerable theoretical load, so I claim exactly the same to be true of the concept of structure. Thus any given view of (that is, way of identifying) structural factors carries the following three implications. First, a (contestable) judgement about what is constraining upon agents, and the way in which it constrains them (more of this later). Second, a particular characterisation of those agents – that is, a way of identifying them counterfactually when asking the question 'could "they" have done such and such?' (Who are 'they'? Do 'they' include or exclude 'their' wants, beliefs, personality characteristics, commitments, and so on, and if so, *which* of these? More of this, too, later.) And third, the specification of a time period within which what is claimed to be structural is held to be so.

I turn now to consider a number of corollaries of these brief accounts of power and structure, before turning to the problem of the relation between them.

The first corollary is (somewhat surprisingly) that, on this account, the notion of a power structure becomes a self-contradiction, since power operates within structures. However, the matter is not so simple, since the possession and exercise of power by some can be a structural fact of the situation of others – so that what is structural with respect to the recipient(s) may not be so with respect to the exerciser(s). Again, structures may be created, maintained and destroyed by acts of power. The point, however, is that to the extent to which the explanation of a given outcome is structural, the claim being made is that to that extent the agents involved in bringing it about are powerless to act otherwise. (Compare, for example, Merton's theory of the structural sources of deviant behaviour, according to which there is a limited number of 'alternative responses open to individuals living in an ill-balanced social structure', when there is a 'dissociation between culturally prescribed aspirations and socially structured avenues for realising these aspirations'.)[31] In particular, if there is a conflict between the parties in a situation, *both* will tend to be seen as victims of the system, rather than one being held to exercise power over the other; it will not, for instance, be so much a question of, say, men choosing to exercise power over women, through voluntary actions on the basis of modifiable attitudes, as of a system of domination in which both men and women are caught up, albeit one serving the interests of the former at the expense of the latter.

The second corollary is that what is structural is *relative* – first, to a given time period (so that what is structural in the short term may not be so in the long term), and second, to specified or specifiable agents. Thus what is structural for one agent or set of agents (whether individual or collective) may not be so for another. What is structural for some Cabinet Ministers will not be so for others. What is structural for the Indian elite may not be so for the Chinese. Moreover, what is structural at the individual level may not be so at the level of groups of institutions. What is structural for a Cabinet Minister may not be so for the Cabinet as a whole. Indeed, groups or institutions will in certain respects *constitute* structures for their members.

The third corollary is that at certain periods of social transformation, what was structural ceases to be so and becomes subject to human agency, in the form of power, influence, authority, coercion, manipulation, and so on. This does not, however, apply only to periods of revolution. It could well be that the only distinctive feature of totalitarianism is the systematic elimination of certain structures, and, in particular, the State, by the power of a political elite, so that restrictions upon possibilities of action are destroyed.[32]

The fourth corollary is really a spelling out, in analytical fashion, of the nature of structural constraints. There are several distinctions that can be made here which, taken together, help to clarify the issues at stake. First, there is the distinction between external and internal constraints. *External* constraints typically will exclude options whatever the agents want, feel or believe. An example from the Crossman *Diaries*:

> I know I have the Prime Minister behind me. I also know that my housing programme is at the mercy not of any cuts [other members of the Cabinet] may wish to make but of economic forces which are threatening and pressuring and bullying this poor government.[33]

It is in this sense that we characterise as structural the geographical, technological or international political constraints facing the regime of a developing society. *Internal* constraints, by contrast, typically exclude options which are unacceptable to, beyond the capacity of or even inconceivable by the agents. Another example from the Crossman *Diaries*: he speaks of 'the pressures that are exerted on M.P.s in marginal constituencies ... appeasing industrialists or right-wing groups, churches or chapels'.[34] This example assumes a rational model of the M.P. calculating that certain actions will work against his interests, and ultimately prejudice the retention of his seat. Alternatively, the agent may be incapacitated for action, like 'poor Frank Soskice with his arthritis and his twisted shoulder and his amiability and his self-centredness. He is a disaster as Home Secretary and he has to deal with the hottest potato in politics – the problem of immigration'.[35] And of course, structural constraints can work at a deeper internal level still, in the form of ideological limitations, internalised values and beliefs, setting pre-set limits to what is even conceivable by agents. In general we may say that an *ability* is the absence of an internal constraint (that is, the presence of an internal permissive condition) and an *opportunity* the absence of an external constraint (that is, the presence of an external permissive condition).

A second distinction is that between positive and negative constraints: a *positive* constraint is an actual obstacle or preventing condition; a *negative* constraint an absence, such as a lack of resources, strength, skill or knowledge, that, equally, prevents a potential option from being realised.

As Joel Feinberg has remarked, these two distinctions cross-cut one another, creating four categories:

> There are *internal positive constraints* such as headaches, obsessive thoughts and compulsive desires; *internal negative constraints* such as ignorance, weakness, and deficiencies in talent or skill; *external positive constraints* such as barred windows, locked doors and pointed bayonets; and *external negative constraints* such as lack of money, lack of transportation, and lack of weapons.[36]

A third distinction is that between constraints upon ends and those upon means. The former limit the range of objectives that agents in a given context can seek: examples are Crossman's economic forces and constituency pressures. The latter set limits to the means of achieving a given objective: there is only a restricted number of ways to reduce a trade deficit, and of these some will be beyond the power of a government to implement, others unacceptable to it, and others inconceivable by it. Either of these types of constraint may be external or internal, positive or negative.

These distinctions have a certain value: they are clarifying and they help us avoid muddles often made. But any given way of drawing them is eminently contestable and question-begging. Thus, as I have already suggested, what counts as external or internal will be relative to and dependent on a particular model of the agent; as Feinberg has observed:

> How we make the distinction between 'internal' and 'external' constraints depends, of course, on how we draw the boundaries of the self. If we contract the self sufficiently so that it becomes a dimensionless non-empirical entity, then *all* causes are external. Other narrow conceptions of the self would attribute to its 'inner core' a set of ultimate principles or 'internalised values' or ultimate ends or desires, and relegate to the merely 'empirical self', or to a world altogether external to the self, all lower-ranked desires, whims and fancies.[37]

Moreover, most real cases are self-evidently mixed; the structural constraints of the market only apply to rational economic men who play by its rules, and normative constraints such as the law only set external limits to choosable options for so long as agents continue internally to accept the law as setting such limits. Again, the distinction between positive and negative constraints is relative to the way they are characterised; the presence of pressure is the absence of leeway, and to lack strength, skill or knowledge is to manifest weakness, incompetence and ignorance. And what counts as an end is always relative to a particular way of drawing conceptual boundaries; reducing a trade deficit can also be seen as a means.

There is, however, a further distinction which cuts both across these distinctions and deeper into the problem we are trying to address. That is the distinction between rational and structural constraints – that is, between constraints which operate through the agent's reasons and those which do not.

Rational constraints determine, that is, set limits to, the options of agents simply by providing them with relevant and sufficient reasons not to act in certain ways. The paradigm case of these is that of economic constraints, which by putting a price tag on certain options thereby render them ineligible; but, in general, the same applies to all cases where the choice situation is patterned by weightings which, given the agents' preference schedules, serve to determine or limit their choices. The key point here is that such constraints can be compatible with the agent's freedom to overcome them: the bayonets of the enemy, the threats of the dictator, the prospective verdict of the electorate no less than the antique dealer's price tag may simply provide me with good reasons for not acting in certain ways, which will be more or less compelling depending on the costs to me consequent upon so acting. Unless I am *unable* to do so, my acting as I do is both constrained and voluntary; on this view, I retain the freedom or power to act otherwise,[38] though, given that I have the wants and beliefs that I have, my actions have been determined. Rational constraints will not, therefore, be structural, that is limiting the power of agents; the agent is seen as retaining the power to overcome the constraint, however high the price.

By contrast, *structural* constraints do not operate through the agent's reasons, and they may indeed prevent certain reasons being reasons *for him*: that is, they may limit his capacity to have certain desires or to hold certain beliefs. Structural constraints limit the agent's freedom or power to act otherwise by precluding (rather than putting a price tag on) such a possibility. They may take the form either of a limit upon (internal) *ability* or upon (external) *opportunity*, they may be positive or negative and they may preclude the pursuit of ends or means (bearing in mind all the problems we have met with in considering these distinctions). Finally, they may be either *causal* (as, for example, when some psychological inability, like Frank Soskice's character, precludes a certain action, or the causal conditions for its performance, for example economic resources or technological conditions, do not exist), or else they may be what I can only call *conceptually necessary* (for instance, as a member of Kariera society, I cannot marry the daughter of my father's brother).[39]

One final remark in this connection: I have already suggested that judgements about what is constraining upon agents and the way in which they are so constrained has something to do with the way in which they are conceptualised. I shall later suggest that it has everything to do with this – that the two issues are deeply and intimately related.

The problem before us is this: how are we to think about the relation between power and structure? There are three clear-cut positions that can be adopted in relation to this issue.

The first is what we may call the *voluntarist*, anti-structural position.

On this view, the constraints facing choice-making agents are minimal –
and, in particular, the only structural constraints are external to the
choosing agent; internal constraints are always rational ones and can
always be surmounted. The opportunity to succeed in one's projects
may be lacking, but never the ability to think, choose and act otherwise.

One extreme exponent of this view is Sartre: for him the future facing
the subject is always open (the subject for the early Sartre being the
individual, for the later Sartre the 'group-in-fusion'), and all the acting
subject needs is moral integrity, sincerity, invention, imaginativeness.
There was for the early Sartre 'no human nature': man is 'what he
conceives himself to be . . . what he wills. . . . Man is nothing else but
that which he makes of himself.' He is 'not found ready-made; he makes
himself by the choice of his morality and the pressure of circumstances
is such that he cannot fail to choose one.' Thus Zola was wrong to show
the behaviour of base, weak, cowardly or evil characters as 'caused by
their heredity, or by the influence of their environment, or of society, or
because of psychological or organic determinism'; the existentialist, by
contrast,

> who portrays a coward, declares him to be responsible for his
> cowardice. . . . There is no such thing as a cowardly temperament
> . . . what produces cowardice is the act of giving up or giving way . . .
> the existentialist says that the coward makes himself cowardly, the
> hero makes himself heroic; and there is always a possibility for
> the coward to give up cowardice and for the hero to stop being a
> hero.[40]

For another version of this position, stressing the permanent
possibility of critical thought rather than of moral choice, consider Sir
Karl Popper, for whom 'it is necessary to recognise as one of the
principles of any unprejudiced view of politics that everything is
possible in human affairs'.[41] Popper writes elsewhere, attacking Kuhn:

> I do admit that at any moment we are prisoners caught in the
> framework of our theories; our expectations; our past experiences;
> our language. But we are prisoners in a Pickwickian sense: if we try,
> we can break out of our framework at any time. Admittedly, we shall
> find ourselves again in a framework, but it will be a better and
> roomier one; and we can at any moment break out of it again.[42]

Popper's 'central point' is 'that a critical discussion and a comparison of
the various frameworks is always possible' – and, from the context, he

clearly means that as an empirical generalisation, not a statement of *logical* possibility (hence the telling phrase 'if we *try*'). The contrary view, the so-called '*Myth of the Framework*' (the thesis that the framework cannot be critically discussed) he dubs 'in our time, the central bulwark of irrationalism'.[43]

The only structural constraints, on this first, voluntarist view, are external and upon action as opposed to thought or desire. This view is hostile to the notion of internal structural constraints; there are no limits to the exercise of moral choice or the operation of critical rationality. This anti-structural position may of course take an individualist or a collectivist form. We have considered two individualist versions, but one may see it in its collectivist form both among those, such as the Jacobins and the Fascists, who believe that the social order can be shaped and controlled at will by powerful political elites, and among those, such as the Blanquistes or syndicalists,[44] such as Sorel, who equally believe that political will is sufficient to achieve its revolutionary transformation.

The second position in relation to the issue of power and structure is the *structuralist* position, most clearly exemplified, in recent Marxist discussions, by Althusser and his followers. Thus Althusser writes:

the structure of the relations of production determines the *places* and *functions* occupied and adopted by the agents of production, who are never anything more than the occupants of these places, insofar as they are the 'supports' (*Träger*) of these functions. The true 'subjects' (in the sense of constitutive subjects of the process) are therefore not these occupants or functionaries, are not, despite all appearances, the 'obviousness' of the 'given' of naïve anthropology, 'concrete individuals', 'real men' – but the *definition and distribution of these places and functions. The true 'subjects' are these definers and distributors: the relations of production* (and political and ideological and social relations). But since these are 'relations', they cannot be thought within the category *subject*. And if by chance anyone proposes to reduce these relations of production to relations between men, i.e. '*human relations*', he is violating Marx's thought, for so long as we apply a truly critical reading to some of his rare ambiguous formulations, Marx shows in the greatest depth that the *relations* of production (and political and ideological social relations) are irreducible to any anthropological inter-subjectivity – since they only combine agents and objects in a specific structure of the distribution

16 *Politics and Society*

of relations, places and functions, occupied and 'supported' by objects and agents of production.[45]

Or as Balibar puts it, even more decisively, 'individuals are merely the effects' of 'the structure of social practices'; they 'do not appear in the theory except in the form of supports for the connexions implied by the structure, and the forms of their individuality as determinate effects of the structure'.[46]

Poulantzas has taken the same view. Thus he writes that 'the agents of production, for example the wage-earning labourer and the capitalist, as "personifications" of Wage-Labour and Capital, are considered by Marx as the *supports* or *bearers* of an ensemble of structures', and he goes on to say that 'everything happens as if social classes were *the result of an ensemble of structures and of their relations*, firstly at the economic level, secondly at the political level and thirdly at the ideological level'.[47] He attacks Miliband for failing to comprehend

social classes and the State as *objective structures*, and their relations as an *objective system of regular connections*, a structure and a system whose agents, 'men', are in the words of Marx, 'bearers' of it – *Träger*. Miliband constantly gives the impression that for him social classes or 'groups' are in some way reducible to *interpersonal relations*, that the State is reducible to interpersonal relations of the members of the diverse 'groups' that constitute the State apparatus, and finally that the relation between social classes and the State is itself reducible to interpersonal relations of 'individuals' composing social groups and 'individuals' composing the State apparatus.[48]

It is true that Poulantzas writes of the class struggle, and indeed now claims that 'social classes, although objectively determined (structures) . . . only exist within and through the class struggle (practices)', which he describes as 'the production, reproduction and transformation of "forms"'.[49] But his epistemological standpoint stands opposed to 'the problematic of agents as subjects' and that of 'class based on agents',[50] and he consistently treats structural analysis as central and primary, and questions of agency as quite distinct and secondary.[51] This is most explicit in relation to individual agency. He ridicules the 'humanist and historicist' charge of granting insufficient importance 'to the role of concrete individuals and creative persons; to human freedom and action; to free will and to Man's capacity for choice; to the "project" against "necessity"', claiming that 'everything there is to say on this subject has already been said', declining to answer the charge and seeing it as 'a reiteration in modern terms of the kind of objections that bourgeois idealism has always opposed to Marxism of whatever stripe'.[52] As for collective agency (and specifically that of classes), his main tendency is to dissolve it into structural determination.[53] Thus, in particular, he specifically *defines* power in terms of structural determination, as '*the capacity of a social class to realise its specific objective interests*',[54] arguing that this concept 'specifies the effects of the ensemble of [the levels of the structure] on the relations between social classes in struggle'.[55] Power, on this account, is 'an effect of the ensemble of the structures'.[56]

It is of course true that Althusser and Poulantzas have much to say about 'relative autonomy', but it is not agents, whether individual or collective, who are relatively autonomous but rather determining levels. As Ernesto Laclau has well put it, it is not a matter of 'autonomy conceived in terms of freedom': 'For Poulantzas . . . the "*relative*" character of an autonomy indicates that it belongs to a world of structural determinations, and it is only within this, as a particular moment of it, that the concept of autonomy must be elaborated.' Thus, with respect to the alleged relative autonomy of the State:

> From the Poulantzas viewpoint this relative autonomy would be in turn a structural element, that is to say, the result of a particular articulation between the instances corresponding to the mode of production under consideration; in that sense, one more objective determination of the system as a whole.[57]

In brief, this second, structuralist position maintains (at its most extreme) that structural constraints – operating at different levels (economic, political and ideological) and both externally and internally – are uniquely determining and totally explanatory (hence the irrelevance of the problematic of agents as subjects).

The third position *vis-à-vis* the issue of structure and power is what I shall call the *relativist* position, which simply holds that there are just different points of view, or levels of analysis, or problematics, and there is no way to decide between them. One can either take a voluntarist position, stressing responsibility and seeing individuals or collectivities as always exercising reason, choice and will, engaging in strategies and making a difference to history; or one can see them as wholly determined, acting out roles, and indeed being not merely influenced but actually constituted by ever pre-given structures of a system that operates upon them and through them. One can either adopt what Poulantzas calls 'a problematic of *social actors*'[58] or one can adopt what Miliband calls 'structural superdeterminism', according to which 'the structural constraints of the system are so absolutely compelling as to turn (for example) those who run the state into the merest functionaries and executants of policies imposed upon them by "the system"'.[59] This relativist position gets a considerable additional boost from the epistemological doctrine (common, incidentally, both to Bachelard, Althusser's mentor, and to writers such as Feyerabend and Kuhn) that there are no theory-independent facts, so that there is no possibility of appealing to evidence to resolve the issue, for any piece of evidence will already be interpreted from within a particular problematic. Laclau states this position clearly: 'modern epistemology asserts', he roundly asserts, that 'the concrete facts are produced by the theory or problematic itself – the problematic creates its own objects'.[60] From this, the third, relativist position, accounts in terms of power and agency and accounts in terms of structural determinism are simply incommensurable and there is no way of choosing between them or relating them to one another.

In my view none of these three positions is satisfactory: all three fail, in fact, to address the very problem at issue, namely, that of the relation between power and structure. Indeed, all three deny that there *is* a problem. The first position denies that there are structures (except minimally); the second denies that there are human agents; and the third refuses to relate them to one another.

One central claim implicit in the argument of this chapter is that the problem of where structural determinism ends and power begins is a real and important problem, about which disputes are endemic, but about which rational argument is possible and to which evidence can be brought to bear. Such disputes may occur between different observers (say, historians or social scientists), or between participant agents, or between observers and agents. Let us consider two examples.

Why, from the mid-1920s until his wretched end, did Bukharin, unlike Trotsky, systematically fail to resist Stalin, apart from occasional private and cryptic gestures of dissent and opposition? Why was it that 'driven by outraged contempt for Stalin and his policies, he remained throughout a restrained, reluctant oppositionist'?[61] Obviously, many complex and elaborate explanations may be devised, but we may here consider three broad possibilities.

The first is suggested by Lenin's characterisation of Bukharin:

> We know how soft Bukharin is; it is one of the qualities for which we love him and cannot help loving him. We know that more than once he has been called 'just like soft wax'. It appears that any 'unprincipled' person, any 'demagogue', can make an impression on this 'soft wax'.[62]

Bukharin was like 'soft wax' in Stalin's hands, and, after acting as his zealous henchman during the latter's rise to power, he lacked the *ability* to escape his control. One might add that, as with Rubashov in Koestler's *Darkness at Noon*, this inability was further compounded by his deep internalisation of loyalty to party unity and party discipline which had taken so deep a hold as to inhibit the option of resistance. Thus Solzhenitsyn has written of Bukharin:

> above all he feared expulsion from the Party! Being deprived of the Party! Being left alive but outside the Party! . . . Bukharin (like all the rest of them) did not have his own *individual point of view*. They didn't have their own genuine ideology of opposition, on the strength of which they could step aside and on which they could take their stand.

Bukharin manifested 'sincerity and honesty . . . devotion to the Party . . . human weakness . . . lack of moral strength needed to fight back', because he lacked an '*individual* position'.[63] This line of analysis is, in part, also taken by Cohen: Bukharin's reluctance to appeal to popular sentiment

> derived from the Bolshevik dogma that politics outside the party was illegitimate, potentially if not actually counter-revolutionary. . . . [He] was restrained by another consideration as well. In Marxist eyes, the social groups thought to be most receptive to his policies, notably peasants and technical specialists, were 'petty bourgeois' and thus unseemly constituencies for a Bolshevik. . . . Here again Bukharin was trapped by Bolshevik assumptions. . . . His reluctance to carry the fight against Stalin to the party-at-large derived from similar inhibitions. . . . By 1929 Bukharin had come to share most of Trotsky's criticisms of the party's internal regime. Unlike Trotsky, however, having sanctioned its development, he was its prisoner. . . .

Bukharin's duty, as he saw it, was to his party, which meant 'party discipline', the pretence of unity and the gesture of repentance . . . he retained faith in the revolution and the party, and thus was wed, psychologically and politically, to the system. . . . Given his special status, his loyalty to the party and the revolution, Bukharin apparently saw little choice. A short time later, with obvious personal implication, he quoted Engels on the dilemma that Goethe had faced: 'to exist in an environment which he necessarily held in contempt, and yet to be chained to it as the only one in which he could function'.[64]

Thus, as another writer has put it, the Bukharinists were 'even sometimes involuntary accomplices of the Stalinism that eventually crushed them'. Bukharin himself 'could not escape . . . from the . . . slavishness of that time': 'Having always compromised with Stalinism, [Bukharinism] deprived itself of the power to mobilise, around a stated, coherent strategy, those Marxists who sought to change the course of the Russian Revolution.' Trotskyism by contrast 'has *fought* and has not made compromise a principle and capitulation a habit'.[65]

A second possibility is that Bukharin's failure to resist was due not so much (or only) to inability as to lack of *opportunity*. This was the explanation favoured by Trotsky, who compared Bukharin's later utterances to 'bubbles emitted by a drowning man'.[66] E. H. Carr endorses this view, arguing that Bukharin's cause was lost once the 'wager on the peasant' was defeated by 'the inherent impossibility in NEP conditions of inducing the peasant to part with his grain'. Thereafter, Bukharin was in Stalin's grip:

In the first months of 1928 Stalin, having routed Trotsky, knew that he had won, and no longer needed the support of Bukharin; and Bukharin became increasingly uneasy at the drastic and brutal course of Stalin's policies. Who first made the break? All that can be said with certainty is that it was Stalin who called the tune, and set the pace.[67]

The third possibility is to see Bukharin's later career as a series of misjudgements and of tactical and strategic mistakes, of 'sins of commission and omission'.[68] On this view, to some extent adopted by Cohen, Bukharin's failure to resist can be attributed less to structural than to rational constraints. One would speak of his 'unwillingness' rather than his inability and inhibitions, or lack of moral strength and of choice. One would speak of his calculations of consequences deemed unacceptable to himself and his supporters, of his rejection of available options which he could have taken up but chose not to.[69]

Let us consider a second example. Why did the second British Labour Government of 1929–31 not act in a less orthodox, conservative and ineffective manner? Why did it not seek to combat the economic crisis with a radical unemployment policy, with extensive public investment financed by budget deficits, tax cuts or even the redistribution of income, together with an expansionist monetary policy?

One view is that of Robert Skidelsky, for whom the Labour Party was *unable* to rise to the demands of that time. Why, he asks, did it fail to use the dissent from orthodoxy which existed, for the ends of a radical unemployment policy?

I have sought the answer in terms of the Party's commitment to a Utopian socialism which incapacitated it from effectively working the parliamentary system and prevented it from coming to terms with economic reality. It suffered in those days from a split personality: on the one hand it was committed to constitutionalism; on the other it lacked a social democratic or gradualist programme without which tenure of power was bound to be rather barren of achievement. It thought in terms of a total solution to the problem of poverty, when what it was offered was the limited opportunity to cure unemployment. It was a parliamentary party with a Utopian ethic. It was not fit for the kind of power it was called upon to exercise.

For what was at issue between 1929 and 1931, with unemployment rising to nearly three million, was not Socialism versus Capitalism. It was interventionist Capitalism versus *laissez-faire* Capitalism. The Labour Party's commitment to a nebulous Socialism made it regard the work of the 'economic radicals' such as Keynes as mere 'tinkering', when in fact it was they who were providing the real choice. It was the failure of the Labour Party to recognise that this was the choice that doomed it to failure and sterility in this crucial period.[70]

Skidelsky's view is therefore of 1929 as 'the major missed opportunity of the inter-war period',[71] but a detailed counter-argument has recently been advanced by Ross McKibbin[72] which maintains precisely the opposite: that there was *no such opportunity*. McKibbin contests Skidelsky's claim that international experience pointed to alternative reflationary policies, arguing that 'there were in fact, no such solutions abroad . . . deflation was almost universal. British policy, in relation to this, appears generous and almost unorthodox.'[73] As for the situation in Britain:

> it is too easy to underestimate the barriers to fiscal or merely financial manipulation. The structural problems of the economy . . . required large-scale shifts in investment patterns, and the way in which the government could force such shifts was highly problematical . . . there were real obstacles to an apparently simple measure like devaluation. . . . It can be argued that a developed multiplier theory would have provided the necessary intellectual support for some kind of counter-cyclical capital expenditure. In fact, no such theory existed and it may not have been the right answer even if it had.
>
> The absence of a mature reflationary economics was matched by the physical incapacity of the state. Budgets were too small and administrative traditions not flexible enough. . . . It must be concluded that the ability of the state before the Second World War to do more than marginally influence the economy was limited. Above all, the state had no way then, and scarcely has today, of determining investment rates.

Indeed, he argues, even if there had been a successful reflation, it would have required very wide state supervision of the economy and thus met decisive external structural constraints of a political kind:

> It is scarcely conceivable that a Labour Government would have been permitted to introduce such policies while the existing structure of power remained intact. The bureaucracy, the Bank of England and the banks, the great financial institutions, most of industry, the dead weight of conventional wisdom, were thrown against innovation . . . spending policies would have made 'socialism' a central problem. Since the Labour Party probably would not, and certainly could not, reorganise economic life through state intervention, it did about as well as a 'progressive' party could do in a mature capitalist economy that was showing no signs of cyclical recovery.[74]

In short, the only 'practicable' alternatives to Labour were drift and deflation[75] – and the latter was successfully avoided until the crisis of July–August 1931. Reflation generated by capital expenditure and an expansionary monetary policy were physically, psychologically and politically impossible.

Both these views contrast with a third, implicit in the title of an article written at the time by R. H. Tawney: 'The Choice Before the Labour Party'.[76] This view has recently been taken up again by Royden Harrison in an argument against the Skidelsky thesis: it was not the Labour Party's fixation with 'Utopian Socialism' that governed its actions but a *political choice* – politics being a matter of 'conflicts between distinct complexes of interests, purposes and ideas'.[77] For Tawney, the Labour Government was 'the author, the unintending and pitiable author, of its own misfortunes':

> When the Cabinet took office, two alternatives were open to it. It could decide to live dangerously, or to play for safety. It could choose a short life, and – if the expression be not too harsh – an honest one; or it could proceed on the assumption that, once a Labour Government is in office, its primary duty is to find means of remaining there. . . . The Labour Government chose the second course. . . . Once convinced that discretion was their cue, ministers brought to the practice of the golden mean a conscientious assiduity almost painful to contemplate. They threw themselves into the role of The Obsequious Apprentice, or Prudence Rewarded, as though bent on proving that, so far from being different from other governments, His Majesty's Labour Government could rival the most respectable of them in cautious conventionality.[78]

Here, then, are two examples of disputes about the extent to which and the way in which the options open to an agent (in the one case indvidual, in the other collective) were constrained. Where did the limits on their power lie? Of course, to discuss even these two cases properly, a number of further, finer distinctions must be drawn: for example, there are different descriptions under which the relevant options may be brought; there is, for instance, the difference between Bukharin's power to oppose Stalin and his power successfully to resist him; and the Labour Party might have retained the power to act, as Tawney put it, 'on its principles', but never had the power to cope with the economic crisis (or vice versa). The point, however, is that disputes of real importance occur over whether (specifiable) options were within (specifiable) agents' power or beyond it, and, if the latter, whether this was because of factors 'external' or 'internal' to the agents.

Such disputes can, as I have suggested, equally occur between agents, and between observers and agents. Powerful politicians characteristically appeal to structural constraints: they claim that what others count as possible courses of action are in fact precluded by external circumstances (for example economic constraints); while others allege that they are in fact *choosing* a particular package of actions together with their consequences, as opposed to others; and yet others will argue that the politicians have been so deeply imbued and socialised by the system that they cannot make the choice anyway. But the disagreement can work in the other direction too, as with the revolutionary left, say, in Allende's Chile, or Portugal in 1975, when the agent characteristically believes that there is available a wider range of choice than the observer, worldly-wise after the event, may, from a 'structural' analysis based on all the evidence, be prepared to allow.

Can disputes of this kind be resolved? Can one of the disputants be shown to have a better case than another?

All those, whether observers or agents, who deny structural explanations of outcomes, explaining them rather in terms of power, make counterfactual claims to the effect that some specified agent or agents could have acted[79] (that is, had the ability and the opportunity to act) in a certain way. My first move, therefore, is to say that empirical evidence can always be adduced (which must always, by nature of the case, be indirect and, especially from an empiricist point of view, lacking in certainty) to support (or to counter) any such counterfactual claims. One can, in particular, point to evidence of the same agent acting differently under relevantly similar circumstances, or of relevantly similar agents so acting. Of course, others will then object that either the circumstances or the agents, or both, are not relevantly similar, and a detailed argument can then ensue.

Such appeal to evidence and argument concerning counterfactuals is quite central to the explanatory enterprise. I have suggested that, by the nature of the case, it must always be indirect and ultimately inconclusive, but it can be more or less plausible. One can, as Cohen does, seek out what evidence there is of Bukharin's attempts to resist Stalin, or his perceptions of choices, or his deliberations about tactics. One can attempt to show that Bukharin did stand up to Stalin on those rare occasions when it was possible and showed some chances of success. The weight of such evidence can be disputed: for Carr, Cohen 'does his best for his hero, rather over-playing the gestures of dissent and resistance, always behind closed doors or in cryptic language accessible only to the initiated, and passing over the futile and sometimes almost farcical attempts at appeasement and compromise'.[80] And one could make comparisons with the actions of others similarly placed who either actually resisted or failed to capitulate. Even at the time of the show trials, Solzhenitsyn argues:

> there was a choice! The most farsighted and determined of those who were doomed did not allow themselves to be arrested. They committed suicide first (Skrypnik, Tomsky, Gamarnik). It was the ones who *wanted to live* who allowed themselves to be arrested. . . . But even among them some behaved differently during the interrogations, realised what was happening, turned stubborn, and died silently but at least not shamefully. For some reason, they did not, after all, put on public trial Radsutak, Postyshev, Yenukidze, Chubar, Kosior, and, for that matter, Krylenko himself, even though their names would have embellished the trials.[81]

On the other hand, one might argue, *for Bukharin* (Rubashov?) there was perhaps no choice: perhaps his life history and his character rendered him unable to do what they did.

Again, one could point to evidence of economically radical or interventionist elements in the Labour Party, of the courage or innovativeness of certain of its leaders, of its still-proclaimed ideology and its constitution. The weight of such evidence could certainly be disputed. Or again, one could point, as evidence of opportunities open to the Labour Party, to the alleged successes of Swedish socialism, which had 'clearly come to terms not only with economic reality but also with the parliamentary system',[82] and of the New Deal. But against that, one might argue, as does McKibbin, that '"active" policies of the later thirties, as in the United States, actually failed, or as in Sweden were hedged with ambiguity and doubt'.[83] And in any case, one might add, there were no such options open to the British Labour Party since it was differently placed and differently constituted.

However, a moment's reflection shows that all this adducing of evidence and deployment of argument about whether specified agents could or could not have acted otherwise than they did begs a crucial question: How are those agents to be characterised? The way in which we answer the question 'Could the agent have acted otherwise?' depends crucially on how the agent is conceptualised.

Let us take two extreme possibilities. If the agent is seen as including all his characteristics – his desires and beliefs, his attitudes, loyalties, commitments, purposes and goals, and relations with others – then, as Leibniz thought, all propositions about him will be analytic and the answer to the question 'Could he have acted otherwise?' is always going to be 'No'. (And a parallel analysis applies of course to collective agents.) If, however, taking the extreme opposite view, the agent is conceived as a sort of core, sovereign choosing self – always able to choose even what sort of an agent to be, without any kind of predetermining nature – then the answer is always going to be 'Yes'. Or, more precisely, it is always going to be true that the agent can choose to act differently, although external structural constraints will prevent certain outcomes being achieved.

It is worth pausing to consider this second extreme possibility, since it is, in fact, a view of the self which in one form or another underlies and pervades the entire thought structure of our Western, liberal–capitalist societies. It has been suggestively described by Iris Murdoch as picturing man as 'a brave naked will surrounded by an easily comprehended empirical world':[84] the will is seen as the essential centre of the self, as distinct from impersonal reason which, when properly exercised (as it always can be), yields knowledge. Morality, on this view,

> is assimilated to a visit to a shop. I enter the shop in a condition of totally responsible freedom, I objectively estimate the features of the goods, and I choose. The greater my objectivity and discrimination the larger the number of products from which I can select. (A Marxist critique of this conception of bourgeois capitalist morals would be apt enough. Should we want many goods in the shop or just 'the right goods'?) Both as act and reason, shopping is public. Will does not bear upon reason. . . . Reason deals in neutral descriptions and aims at being the frequently mentioned ideal observer.

This image is, Miss Murdoch rightly observes, behaviourist, existentialist and utilitarian:

> It is behaviourist in its connexion of the meaning and being of action with the publicly observable, it is existentialist in its elimination of the substantial self and its emphasis on the solitary omnipotent will, and it is utilitarian in its assumption that morality is and can only be concerned with public acts. It is also incidentally what may be called a democratic view, in that it suggests that morality is not an esoteric achievement but a natural function of any normal man.[85]

It is an image central to the liberal tradition, owing something to

Hume and to Kant, and to Hobbes and Bentham through John Stuart Mill. Miss Murdoch sees this picture of the individual as a free rational will as strikingly exemplified in the writings of Stuart Hampshire and Sartre. According to the former, she says, man is

> rational and totally free except in so far as, in the most ordinary law-court and commonsensical sense, his degree of self-awareness may vary. He is morally speaking monarch of all he surveys and totally responsibile for his actions. Nothing transcends him. His moral language is a practical pointer, the instrument of his choices, the indication of his preferences. His inner life is resolved into his acts and choices, and his beliefs, which are also acts, since a belief can only be identified through its expression. His moral arguments are references to empirical facts backed up by decisions. The only moral word which he requires is 'good' (or 'right'), the word which expresses decision. His rationality expresses itself in awareness of the facts, whether about the world or about himself. The virtue which is fundamental to him is sincerity.

And similarly in Sartre:

> the individual is pictured as solitary and totally free. There is no transcendent reality, there are no degrees of freedom. On the one hand, there is the mass of psychological desires and social habits and prejudices, on the other hand there is the will. Certain dramas, more Hegelian in character, are of course enacted within the soul; but the isolation of the will remains. Hence *angoisse*. . . . Again the only real virtue is sincerity . . . this powerful picture has caught our imagination. The Marxist critics may plausibly claim that it represents the essence of the Liberal theory of personality.[86]

Between these two extreme views of the agent, there is of course a whole range of intermediate possibilities. We may characterise the agent in terms of a dispositional account of how a person or collectivity behaves under 'normal' circumstances; in which case we may take Lenin's view of Bukharin, or Ralph Miliband's view of the Labour Party, as by nature a non-socialist party ('Cart-horses should not be expected to win the Derby').[87] Or we may base our conception of the agent's nature on a dispositional account of his or its capacities for rising to unusual or historic occasions, when perhaps 'he' or 'it' could act otherwise. Or again we may see the agent as defined by what in his context he could reasonably be expected to do – as determined by the generalised expectations of significant others, or as the consequence of a 'collaborative manufacture' involving social arrangements and supporting performances by people within them.[88] On this view, perhaps, Bukharin could not have acted otherwise – but what about Eichmann? Perhaps the self should be seen (at least by lawyers and moralists) as always including the capacity to do what an agent could be morally expected to do[89] (but then, if one is any kind of moral relativist, there will be as many versions of the self as there are moralities). Or perhaps the agent's self is seen as defined in terms of some rational-choice model; on this view, the agent can always do what, given the logic of the situation and the ends or interests he is pursuing, it is rational to do. And all the above applies, *pari passu* and with greater complexity, to collective agents. How are they to be conceived? Consider the apparently simple question 'Could a particular committee have decided differently?' What do we hold constant and what do we vary under the counterfactual conditions we need to imagine?

Now, one possible answer to the question of how the agent is to be conceptualised, currently favoured in philosophical circles, is that we simply identify the agent by referring to him, not by means of a set of characteristics, but rather by a name given to the entity which bears the appropriate causal relation with that which was named.[90] On this view, a person is simply a human being born of certain parents, of whom we may then ask: How might 'he' (thus defined) act in any given possible world we might imagine? We might then say that, for example, given such and such a desire, he would do x; given such and such a belief, he would do y; if he had such and such a life history or character, he would do z. But this approach leaves entirely unanswered the question: Could 'he' at any given moment have *had* that desire or belief? In the course of his life history an agent acquires a structured set of actual and possible desires and beliefs which precisely *constitutes* his character; and the nature of a collective agent is likewise given by its ideology and possible goals. But if we grant that, then we are accepting that a socialised person interacting with others has a 'substantial self', and that a party or a class has a determinate nature – and that to identify these *is*, in part, to identify a range of abilities and inabilities to desire, believe and act. Some inabilities will be essential to the agent's character or nature, others will vary with circumstances. We may express this view of the agent in either of two ways. We may either say that the agent, identified as such-and-such a causally continuous named entity, acquires a specific, structured character that renders that agent unable to choose certain options; or we may prefer to say that the agent, identified as having that character, could not have made that choice (this claim being a logical one for essential inabilities and an empirical one for inessential ones).

The broad picture I am seeking to sketch here is of agents as *consisting in* a set of (expanding and contracting) abilities, faced with (expanding and contracting) opportunities. Together these constitute structured possibilities which specify the powers of agents, varying between agents and over time for any given agent. On this view, both behaviourism and empiricism will fail as recipes for explanation: the former because it focuses exclusively on the narrow thread of actualised possibility, rejecting the unactualised as of no explanatory significance;[91] the latter, at least in its narrower forms, because it systematically devalues the explanatory role of counterfactuals and the value of the evidence needed to support them.

I have argued that to investigate the structural constraints upon the power of agents is, at the same time, in part to inquire into the nature of those agents; such an investigation is of its nature an inquiry into counterfactuals, for which evidence must always be indirect and ultimately inconclusive. It would, however, be fallacious to conclude from the in-built difficulties of such research that there is in principle no correct answer to the question of what is within and what beyond the power of agents, or indeed that there are not practical ways of ascertaining whether some proposed answers are better than others.

On the view I have advanced, social life can only properly be understood as a dialectic of power and structure, a web of possibilities for agents, whose nature is both active and structured, to make choices and pursue strategies within given limits, which in consequence expand and contract over time. Any standpoint or methodology which reduces that dialectic to a one-sided consideration of agents without (internal and external) structural limits, or structures without agents, or which does not address the problem of their interrelations, will be unsatisfactory. No social theory merits serious attention that fails to retain an ever-present sense of the dialectic of power and structure.

Chapter 2

The New Democracy

> One of the most salutary results of this vast accumulation of data on politics has been to discredit the older speculative theorists and utopia-makers (Charles Beard, 1908).

The fact that traditional political theory has been held recently in low esteem can be traced in part to the extension of scientific methods to the study of society. At times this has led to a wholesale rejection of the older subject as value-laden and unscientific.[1] But a number of more sophisticated political scientists have seen some value in the work of speculative political theorists and have condemned, not political theory as such, but a philosophical approach to questions which they thought could best be answered in a more scientific manner. After paying some homage to the older theory, they have argued that its abstract notions and principles misdescribe the ways in which men behave and societies function. As a result, attempts have been made to confront certain traditional theories with the facts of political life, and to carry through a substantial revision of these theories. Nowhere has this confrontation and revision advanced further than in the field of democratic theory, which has been examined from the new perspective afforded by research into voting behaviour. Armed with material from the voting studies, Bernard Berelson and others have hastened to declare that past democratic theory is in many respects an inadequate theory of democracy.[2]

Berelson, probably the most influential of these writers, has sought explicitly to confront normative theory with empirical research, to their mutual advantage. He suggests in particular that political theorists

> might explore the relevance, the implications, and the meaning of such empirical facts as are contained in this and similar studies. Political theory written with reference to practice has the advantage that its categories are the categories in which political life really occurs . . . empirical research can help to clarify the standards and correct the empirical presuppositions of normative theory.[3]

Such an aim sounds unexceptionable and, if fulfilled, might be expected to increase men's understanding of society. It is not our intention to deny that voting-behaviour research can be useful in this respect, although its results do seem to have been disappointingly meagre. But we do wish to argue that the actual revision of democratic theory that has been attempted has considerably less justification that Berelson's general statement might suggest. In the first place, the writers with whom we are concerned misunderstand the nature of eighteenth- and nineteenth-century democratic theories,[4] which were not, nor did they purport to be, descriptions of the way in which people actually behaved. Moreover, the older theories are not usually considered in sufficient detail to show which theorists are being subjected to criticism. In the second place, the new theory of democracy, which seems to be founded upon facts, has serious though hidden shortcomings. It is, as we hope to show in the second part, loosely formulated and sometimes superficial, and it rests upon a vague notion of equilibrium and *a priori* assumptions about the self-adjusting powers of the 'system'. In the face of the failure of men to meet the classical norms, it provides a new set of norms, the chief among them apathy, which are much closer to realisation in present-day America and Britain. Those whom we describe as theorists of the new democracy are not all equally inadequate and complacent, but they use similar arguments and the general direction of their thought is towards an easy acceptance of the existing order. This, as we will suggest in the final section, is partly due to their fear of ideology and resulting preoccupation with the supposed conditions of a stable and non-totalitarian political system, which leads them to reject outright the old democratic vision of a community of participating members, in its various forms. Not only are the stated reasons for such a rejection inadequate; it can still reasonably be argued that the realisation of this vision, in one form or another, remains a desirable goal of social and political activity.

There are a number of different strands in classical democratic theory and it cannot therefore be characterised simply. Its major exponents differ over both the institutional requirements for democracy and the arguments which can best be urged in its favour. It is true to say, however, that in general a democratic society is treated as one in which all the citizens (the people) continuously and actively participate in the various community affairs, and above all in political affairs.[5] A democratic society, whether conceived on the Greek model, as by Rousseau, or on a national basis, as by John Stuart Mill, is pre-eminently a society marked by wide discussion and consultation, so that the whole people know the reasons for political decisions through taking part directly or indirectly in their formulation. J. S. Mill, whom we choose as the central democratic theorist because of his concern with representative government, as well as for his clarity, put the argument for widespread participation clearly. He wrote that

> the only government which can fully satisfy all the exigencies of the social state is one in which the whole people participate; that any participation, even in the smallest public function, is useful; that the participation should everywhere be as great as the general degree of improvement of the community will allow, and that nothing less can be ultimately desirable than the admission of all to a share in the sovereign power of the state.[6]

Mill proclaimed the need for general participation in a wide variety of affairs, not all of which were specifically political, and related this to his ideal of self-development.

The extension of the franchise and frequent elections, which have been central demands at least in English and American democratic theory, were supported for a number of reasons: that only the vote can reveal the general interest of the community; that it is a natural right, or a right deriving from the rendering of services; that powerful groups or interests must be absorbed into society rather than driven into violent action against established institutions; that the vote is necessary for self-protection; and that it, along with other forms of participation in the life of the nation, elevates those who possess it.[7] The most important for the purposes of our analysis are the last two, which are also those least objectionable to modern democratic thinkers.[8]

The utilitarians, disturbed at the ease with which governments became the property of 'sinister interests', developed one of the characteristic democratic arguments. The most difficult problem for government (which arises naturally from their psychological premises) is that of 'restraining those in whose hands are lodged the powers necessary for the protection of all, from making a bad use of it'.[9] Assuming that self-preference is unrestrained by social feelings, the only means of bringing about a rough identity between the interests of community and ruler are 'artificial' – widening the electorate and limiting the duration of governmental power by frequent elections. J. S. Mill, who believed like his father in the natural tendency of rulers to misuse their power, traced this tendency to a deficiency of understanding rather than to mere ill-will and selfishness. Rulers are less ill-disposed than ignorant. Only the man himself can adequately judge and safeguard his own interests – 'in the absence of its natural defenders, the interest of the excluded is always in danger of being overlooked'.[10] Constant vigilance and general participation ensure that all interests will be considered and thus that greater justice will prevail in the settlement of claims.

For the younger Mill, however, the franchise was more than a weapon against arbitrary power and a means whereby each group could ensure that its claims were adequately considered. Although he feared that an enfranchised working class would misuse its powers and suggested certain safeguards to secure the authority of the enlightened, he had great faith in the civilising effects of political participation itself. He described the franchise as 'a potent instrument of mental improvement' and followed Tocqueville in explaining the conscientious citizenship of the Americans by their democratic institutions. Self-government is in this sense self-sustaining: through the possession of legal rights men become capable of properly exercising them and thus they approach that moral autonomy which is the true end of life.

Those who have, like Mill and Rousseau, gone beyond self-protection and the possibility of peaceful change as the chief advantages of the democratic form of government, have tended to speak in terms of man's realisation of some characteristic excellence. The democratic society is the good society, bringing out the best in men; democracy, as Lindsay said, is a theory of society as well as a theory of government. Rousseau, who idealises only direct or 'populistic' democracy, eliminates conflict, since when men rationally seek the common good, which is ascertainable, there are no possible grounds for disagreement between them; whereas Mill pictures a community of critical, restless, dissatisfied individuals, constantly questioning one another's principles in the pursuit of truth and the general happiness. They evaluate differently 'long debates, discussion and tumult'.

Voting, as the chief institutional means of participation, becomes of crucial importance. It is conceived, not as a spasmodic or casual act, but as one in which rationality and disinterestedness are manifest. Rousseau wrote that when the people are called to vote upon a law, what 'it' is asked 'is not exactly whether it approves or rejects the proposal, but whether it is in conformity with the general will, which is their will. Each man in giving his vote states his opinion on that point, and the general will is found by counting the votes.'[11] Mill had a similarly high conception of the act of voting, though it is not linked so strongly with the notion of an ascertainable common good. In his words, 'the voter is under an absolute moral obligation to consider the interests of the public, not his private, advantage and to give his vote, to the best of his judgment, exactly as he would be bound to do if he were the sole voter and the election depended upon him alone'.[12]

To the eighteenth- and nineteenth-century democratic theorists, voting was perhaps the citizen's most important act, in which the people as a whole were to reveal their political energy and virtue. It was to be the culmination of long, thoughtful, and fair consideration of the relevant issues. But these writers never claimed to be simply describing existing reality, for they were elaborating, at least in part, a set of ideals for a democratic society, which were also meant to be operative ideals for their own times. They have been taken to task, however, for 'utopianism' and for making demands on the ordinary man that are impossible and indeed undesirable. Research into voting behaviour – who votes, how and why? who does not vote and why not? – would seem to have confirmed abundantly the old impressionistic conservative arguments about the 'bovine stupidity' and the 'heavy, lumpish acquiescence' of the mass electorate and to have shown the democratic hope to be a mere delusion, based on false intellectualist assumptions about human nature.

The voting studies[13] generally agree in showing that the voters fail to satisfy most of the traditional requirements of democracy. This is, perhaps, not too surprising, but detailed documentation of voting behaviour by panel study is certainly of value in confirming suspicions. Berelson gives a composite list of the qualities demanded by the older democratic theorists and confronts them with the actual qualities as revealed in the opinion surveys. Involvement, participation, and the sharing of responsibility were held to be virtues; disinterest and apathy were not approved. In fact, the evidence, says Berelson, shows that less than one-third of the electorate is really interested in politics, many vote without real involvement, open discussion and motives for participation are almost non-existent. Secondly, knowledge and information are inadequate. 'One persistent conclusion is that the public is not particularly well-informed about the specific issues of the day.'[14] Even when voters are well-informed, their knowledge reinforces inclinations more than it contributes to a 'free' decision. Nor do voters seem to vote on principles, of whatever kind, which they have considered carefully, and the standards which they do use are often irrelevant to 'the major problems of the age'. Finally, voters do not seem to decide rationally, in any of the traditional senses of that porous term. The studies have noted the prevalence of selective perception and the way in which the campaign reinforces the influence of a whole set of environmental factors, so that in the end its function seems to be largely that of 'activating latent predispositions'. Furthermore, the voters showing the greatest degree of 'open-mindedness', that is, the changers or floaters, are, in some of the studies at least, shown to be the most cross-pressured, the least interested and the least politically capable.[15] In brief, the voter is shown to be deficient in most of the ideal qualities of traditional democratic theory.

Before detailed research into voting behaviour had ever taken place, several writers (for instance, Lord Bryce and Graham Wallas) had rejected much of the old and largely *a priori* account of the rational democratic citizen as a description applicable to the bulk of their fellow-citizens, yet they did not feel it necessary on this account to undertake a complete revision of democratic theory, as is now demanded.[16] Some more recent writers have, on the other hand, held on to the notion of the rational citizen as applicable, despite the evidence of the voting surveys. The impact of these has been lessened by the claim that the short-term questionnaire method is too clumsy to elicit the important truths about the voter.[17] Schumpeter suggests a distinction between rationality in thought and rationality in action. The latter 'may be present without any conscious deliberation and irrespective of any ability to formulate the rationale of one's action correctly. The observer, particularly the observer who uses interview and questionnaire methods, often overlooks this and hence acquires an exaggerated idea of the importance of irrationality in behaviour.'[18] Plamenatz draws a similar distinction between what men do and their awareness of the significance of their actions.[19] He suggests that voters may be condemned by inarticulateness or private language to seem less reasonable than they in fact are, at least in the present state of interview techniques. It is true that men's ability to put throughts into words and describe actions differs, and that there may be good reasons, of which the agent is unaware, for his doing what he does (for instance, many traditional forms of behaviour). It is almost certain that the survey methods used do give a distorted picture of the complex reality that they seek to describe. But, as so far stated, these objections can serve only as a general warning and, if pressed, may easily develop into a mystical faith in the good sense of the common man. This criticism of the panel surveys is not, in any case, central to our purposes. The authors with whom we are mainly concerned accept the soundness of the survey findings and demand in consequence a substantial revision of classical democratic theory.

Berelson writes: 'Perhaps the main impact of realistic research on contemporary politics has been to temper some of the requirements set by our traditional normative theory for the typical citizen.'[20] The clearest statement of the nature of the revision comes, however, from Robert Dahl. He writes that

> we must conclude that the classic assumptions about the need for citizen participation in democracy were, at the very least, inadequate. If one regards political equality in the making of decisions as a kind of limit to be achieved, then it is axiomatic that this limit could only be arrived at with the complete participation of every adult citizen. Nevertheless, *what we call 'democracy'* – that is, a system of decision-making in which the leaders are more or less responsive to the preferences of non-leaders – does seem to operate with a relatively low level of citizen participation. Hence it is inaccurate to say that one of the necessary conditions for 'democracy' is extensive citizen participation.[21]

Not only is Dahl's definition of democracy extremely loose (in what political system are leaders not more or less responsive to non-leaders?) but the rejection of the classical requirement of participation rests upon an obvious redefinition of democracy, in which what are taken for present-day facts supplant the ideal. Dahl's conclusion is an obvious *non sequitur*, involving a slide from 'what we call "democracy"' to 'democracy'. He suspects that it may have represented a 'kind of ideal limit', but in restating the requirements of the system he ignores this central element of the old democracy, which was defined and justified as a system in which all participate. Without further argument it is misleading to claim that facts can simply refute ideals and demand changes in the essential requirements of a normative theory, or to reject (for example) Mill's democracy by means of a tacit redefinition of the notion. It needs, moreover, to be established that the new democracy, 'what we call "democracy"', is democratic in a sense acceptable to traditional theory.

This brings us to the central point in the first part of our analysis: that although what may now be called 'democracies' may function with little rationality, interest or participation on the part of the majority of citizens, this cannot count simply as a refutation of largely normative theories, which were centrally concerned with the quality of men's social life and not only with the functioning of a 'political system'. Dahl again provides the most explicit statement:

> One of the most interesting developments of the past century is the full-blown contrast that has arisen between the assumptions of many of the older democratic theorists and what now appear to be the actual facts of political life. *Yet if classical theory is demonstrably invalid in some crucial respects*, it is not so clear how we are to go about constructing theoretical models to replace the older ones.[22]

To claim that sociological findings can show these older political theories to be demonstrably invalid is seriously to misunderstand the most basic features of much political theory, which often touches reality only at the edges, and is only at that point open to empirical refutation. 'Political theory' is a general term which covers different types of statements and theories which yield conclusions of different sorts in different ways, and are therefore open to objection in different ways.[23]

In this connection, a familiar distinction can be made at the most general level between 'normative' theories, which present and elaborate goals and ideals, and 'empirical' theories, which describe and explain political reality. A theory of the first kind involves some vision of the Good Life and the Good Society, resting ultimately on a view of human nature and on assumptions about human needs and potentialities: two obvious examples are Plato's republic and Rousseau's ideal community. These ideals almost always conflict with existing realities, though they need not do so (cf. the later Hegel). Empirical theories, however, start from a set of explanatory concepts and classifications, which are then employed, in a number of markedly different ways, in describing and explaining political reality. They are descriptions, concerned with given societies, and they are not *primarily* moral critiques of them.

This general distinction is, of course, a formal one: these kinds of theory are often intimately connected, with each closely dependent on the other. Few empirical theories avoid value-judgements, whether or not they are explicit, and the vision of a normative theory generally rests upon a particular assessment of the present and past. The ideal may involve a moral estimate of the explanatory concepts, particularly if the ideal is of a kind that is supposedly being progressively realised in history, while empirical study may put ideals in a new light, as when the discovery of trends or movements in existing societies curbs the utopian fancy.

Most of the traditional theories of democracy were largely, if not primarily, normative, and critical of the societies in which they were conceived. They were essentially concerned with the achievement in society of what were regarded as various desirable human ends – liberty, good government, responsibility, moral autonomy, self-realisation, and so on – and with the means, including the franchise and general participation in politics, but also education and wise leadership, which could best contribute to these ends. Rousseau and J. S. Mill had serious doubts about the feasibility of their ideals, because of the corruptibility of the multitude, or the power of vested interests, or the sheer extent of societies. Mill had some sympathy with those reformers who favoured despotism because of 'the impediments imposed to the most salutary public improvements by the ignorance, the indifference, the intractableness, the perverse obstinacy of a people, and the corrupt combinations of selfish private interests armed with the powerful weapons afforded by free institutions'.[24] He feared that the extension of democracy would endanger good government and relied upon a variety of institutional devices to secure a privileged position for the educated, hoping, like his father, that the influence of the wise would spread to the community as a whole. Rousseau, similarly, has a long list of the conditions for the realisation of his ideal community, and he was very pessimistic about most of the societies of his time. In choosing democracy the classical theorists were in general aware of the ease with which it could be forestalled and perverted, though they were not without illusions; and they were aware, too, of the capacity of undemocratic societies to survive. Their theories are a critique of reality in terms of a vision of human nature and possibilities, and for this reason cannot simply be refuted on the grounds that people do not satisfy the required standards and that *soi-disant* 'democracies' none the less survive. Their ideals can logically contrast with the facts without being invalidated by empirical research, which does not in any *obvious* way call for their general revision. The term 'democracy' may perhaps legitimately be used to describe political systems like that of the contemporary United States, but it is wrong to assume that the validity of that theory of democracy in which general participation is central to the very notion itself is thereby destroyed.

All this is not, however, to say that evidence can never force changes or modifications in theories which are largely normative.[25] If such a theory seems intolerably remote from reality, it may be charged with utopianism. It is an endemic danger of normative political theory that it will maintain what Dewey called 'an immune and monastic impeccability'. A particular ideal or set of ideals may, in the Marxist sense, be condemned by historical forces to sterility; it might be shown that it is realisable, but only at the cost of further consequences which violate it; it might itself be shown to be incompatible with other important values; it might be shown that the conditions of realisation of an ideal are too vast or unexpected for men to endure; or else it may be shown to be literally impossible to effect the changes demanded. All these means of casting doubt on the feasibility of ideals are legitimate weapons to be used by sceptics: the effectiveness of each is clearly open to dispute, particularly in the case of the last two. For men may disagree about the degree to which social circumstances affect attitudes and behaviour and thus about the extent to which any given traits are alterable. (To what extent, for example, is the lack of a sense of responsibility a function of a social situation?) Nevertheless, the use of any of these forms of objection needs to be fully and extensively pursued, and it needs to be shown exactly how and why the ideal is rendered improbable or impossible to attain. This has nowhere been done. Thus, when it is stated baldly that the old theory made impossible demands, this is more like the recognition of a complacent or despairing abandonment of an ideal than the proof that that ideal must needs be abandoned. And it should be realised that, unless one takes a crude historicist position, this proof could only be really convincing if one could show that traditional democratic theory made demands which men are by nature unable to satisfy. Only then would the ideal be literally *invalidated*, for it would have been shown that the obstacles to its realisation are irremovable. Such a demonstration would presumably come from social psychology, but it has certainly not been achieved, nor is it likely to be even possible until that study is very much further advanced. Only then could the facts (about human nature) even in principle serve to invalidate the old theories of democracy. Otherwise, one can certainly argue over its *feasibility* in the light of case studies – from Michels onwards. Even so, it seems that very little has been done to show that the classical democratic ideals are manifestly utopian. It is not, to repeat, our point that normative political theory is simply independent of sociological evidence: obviously, any theory of democracy must take into account the main features of actual societies. It is simply that empirical study and analysis can only in certain specified cases actually compel us to abandon the ideal or transform it out of all recognition.

Finally, it ought to be added that research into voting behaviour has performed the valuable service of destroying some popular myths about the actual functioning of elections – myths which exist at the level of public rhetoric rather than that of political theory. The 'mandate' theory, for example, has been damaged beyond repair by the voting studies (though by much else besides): as the authors of *The American Voter* put it, 'The thinness of the electorate's understanding of concrete policy alternatives – its inability to respond to government and politics at this level – helps explain why it is that efforts to interpret a national election in terms of a policy mandate are speculative, contradictory and inconclusive.'[26] Similarly, many of the studies have thrown into question the notion of the independent or 'floating' voter, a kind of rational jellyfish, preferably of the middle class, floating one way or the other to decide the issue. At these and probably other points the election studies have refuted or at least modified some simple and widely believed theories about what happens in elections; the 'business vocabulary' for describing actual elections has at least been purged. But these low-level and non-critical theories are open to support and objection in this simple way, whereas the old ideal of democratic man is not.

It has been generally agreed that the theory of the whole electorate as politically competent and interested, expressing these qualities in democratic elections, has not proved suitable as a basis for empirical analysis. The lack of realism in many of the older descriptive accounts of elections has led a number of political scientists to work with the so-called 'competitive theory of democracy'. Joseph Schumpeter, one of the leading exponents of this theory, has defined the 'democratic method' as 'that institutional arrangement for arriving at political decisions in which individuals acquire the power to decide by means of a competitive struggle for the people's vote'.[27] Voting, which provides the electors with the opportunity to change their leaders, and competition between candidates for office, are here the key institutional devices of democracy. If 'democracy' is taken to be a political system defined institutionally in this way, empirical analysis then concentrates on the conditions for its successful operation, while the chief problem of policy becomes that of ensuring that these conditions in fact exist. The main requirement seems to be effective competition between leaders: this, in Plamenatz's view, ensures that the electorate is not 'manipulated' by the active ruling elite. (This view that freedom is guaranteed by free competition between elites derives ultimately from Mosca.) When there is no effective competition, the system ceases to be one in which the leaders are responsive to the independent wishes of non-leaders. Thus Dahl, for example, sees the main problem of democracy as that of regulating the 'great political oligopolies' – which is much as it seemed to the early utilitarians.

This 'competitive model' is adopted with variations by the writers with whom we are concerned. It is a general model useful as a point of departure in the description of existing democracies. The general picture is one of energetic and competing minorities at the top and a relatively apathetic majority, whose role is essentially that of exercising a very generalised control during the election, which is seen as a process of selecting and rejecting candidates in competition for public office. It should be seen clearly that such a model is not necessarily inconsistent with most traditional theories of democracy (except Rousseau's), for it clearly recognises that an election in a large society can only produce clear-cut and satisfactory results in this sort of way. As Schumpeter writes:

> even if the opinions and desires of individual citizens were perfectly definite and independent data for the democratic process to work with, and even if everyone acted on them with rationality and promptitude, it would not necessarily follow that the political decisions produced by that process from the raw material of those individual volitions would represent anything that could in any convincing sense be called the will of the people.[28]

The competitive model need not be incompatible with traditional notions of democracy, and it is just because classical democracy was *not* defined institutionally as a 'system of decision-making' that this is so. For, as we have seen, democracy in the traditional sense involves a great deal more than the correspondence of individual wills and collective decisions; it involves, for example, political equality, active consent about the form of government and the 'rules of the game', widespread discussion and participation, political and otherwise, through all kinds of activities and channels. To take a particular and relevant example, a study by Janowitz and Marwick,[29] which explicitly uses this competitive model, attempts to distinguish between a process of genuine consent and manipulation. The authors emphasise the importance of the quality of the voting decision, pointing out that high turnout does not necessarily reflect the process of consent. They write in words of which John Stuart Mill would have approved:

> The underlying belief in a democracy that everyone ought to vote is indeed such a deep-seated belief that it must be regarded as a utopian goal. Reforms have been suggested above that are designed to enhance the quality of the vote by modification of the social structure. Yet in terms of practical political reform, the crucial problem is to improve the quality of competing political leaders and to increase voter competence.[30]

The theorists of the new democracy, however, are less concerned to make the competitive 'democratic system' more democratic in the traditional sense than to justify it as an efficient and stable system, depending on compromise, 'pluralism' and a general background of apathy and political incompetence. In fact, their theory, which is intended to explain the 'democratic system', becomes in the end the new normative theory of democracy. We are driven to this conclusion by the form of their argument. The question arises: What implications have election studies for democratic theory? The conclusion is that that theory must be made more 'realistic'. The confrontation of classical democratic ideals with actual 'democratic systems' (what we call 'democracy') has no other result than the acceptance of the actual systems and their assumed conditions as entirely desirable. Electoral apathy, incompetence, and so on, which exist in most stable 'modern democracies' are now considered to be conditions of their successful functioning and are therefore taken to be the new democratic norms.

There are of course differences between the writers under consideration. The social scientists, for example Dahl and Parsons, are more concerned to produce a scientific theory of the system, whereas others, for example Plamenatz and Schumpeter, are much less ambitious, which is not to say that their caution is misplaced. The system is justified on a number of different grounds, and doubtless there are a number of important internal disagreements between these different writers. We can only examine a number of the most common arguments and assumptions, which may not be shared in detail by all of them.

The most notable feature of this recent democratic theory is the shift in emphasis from the needs and potentialities of the individual citizen to the requirements of the system. Despite inadequacies in individuals, the system works. In Berelson's vague words, 'The *system of democracy* does meet certain requirements of a going political organization. The individuals may not meet all the standards, but the whole nevertheless survives and grows. This suggests that where the classical theory is defective is in its concentration on the *individual* citizen.'[31] And again, in more exalted vein, 'Where the rational citizen seems to abdicate, nevertheless angels seem to tread.'[32]

It may be useful to look in some detail at Berelson's own account of the democratic system. He sees it pre-eminently as a system in equilibrium and he is followed in this by Talcott Parsons in an essay entitled '*Voting* and the Equilibrium of the American Political System'. (Parsons in fact attempts to integrate Berelson's picture into his own 'general theory of social systems'.) Berelson describes the system mainly in terms of 'balances' and the distribution of qualities in various dimensions. For political democracy to survive, the elements of the system must be distributed and related in a certain way. 'What seems to be required of the electorate as a whole is a distribution of qualities along important dimensions. We need some people who are active in a certain respect, others in the middle and still others passive.'[33] And, 'happily for the system', the voters are distributed along a smooth continuum. There must be a 'balance' between 'involvement and indifference', 'stability and flexibility', 'progress and conservatism', 'consensus and cleavage' and, finally, 'individualism and collectivism'. Low interest provides 'maneuvering room' ('only the doctrinaire would deprecate the moderate indifference that facilitates compromise') and heterogeneity produces a balance between strongly and weakly motivated actions. Also, apart from the many factors making for social stability, 'voters carry over to each new election remnants of issues raised in previous elections – and so there is always an overlapping of old and new decisions that gives a cohesion in time to the political system'. On the other hand, the least partisan are also functional to the system, making for 'flexibility' – 'for those who change political preferences most readily are those who are least interested, who are subject to conflicting social pressures, who have inconsistent beliefs and erratic voting histories. Without them . . . the system might prove too rigid to adapt to changing domestic and international conditions.'[34] There is, says Berelson, 'stability on both sides and flexibility in the middle' and once again 'an individual "inadequacy" provides a positive service for the society'. Finally, there is the essential requirement of 'pluralism', which 'makes for enough consensus to hold the system together and enough cleavage to make it move'. This social heterogeneity produces a 'cross-cutting and harmonious community interest' with a 'balance between total political war between segments of the society and total political indifference to group interests of that society'.[35]

There are a number of important objections to Berelson's account. To begin with, the description of the conditions claimed to be necessary and functional to the system all embody the basic assumption of a system in equilibrium. The use, explicit or otherwise, of equilibrium concepts in the social sciences is often open to serious methodological criticisms[36] and leaves its practitioners subject to the suspicion of having based conservatism upon a pseudo-scientific foundation. More specifically, the application of an equilibrium model to actual social situations does require either careful quantification of the relevant variables (ordinally or cardinally) or else a situation in which an equilibrium situation is directly visible (although, of course, the use of such a model may always lead to fruitful questions). Otherwise little specific sense can be made of the idea of 'balance' between elements. Yet Berelson speaks quite glibly of the balance between his various 'qualities', where neither of these conditions is fulfilled. Parsons, following Berelson, seems to accept these 'balances', translating them into his own terms as 'functional requirements'. He writes that, within a broad framework, 'if the political system is, in the relation between leadership and support, to be a relatively stable one that can integrate multifarious pluralistic interests and yet adapt to changing conditions, it must, *within broadly specifiable limits*, have certain characteristics'.[37] What we dispute is that any precise characterisation has been given of these 'broadly specifable limits' (by Berelson or by Parsons) such that we must accept their account of an equilibrium system with 'checks and balances' and the capacity for self-adjustment afforded by heterogeneity and apathy within the electorate. There is, in other words, no reason to agree that the 'democratic system' is in smoothly functioning equilibrium; and if we look hard at the assumptions behind this theory, we tend to be left with vague and questionable assertions about social harmony.

In the second place, the supposed requirements of the system are presented in an obviously value-laden and tendentious way. Berelson claims, in a rather obscure passage, that 'it turns out that this distribution itself, with its internal checks and balances, can perform the functions and incorporate the same values ascribed by some theorists to each individual in the system, as well as to the constitutive political institutions'.[38] Berelson here seems to be trying to have the best of both worlds. Not only is his theory of democracy realistic, describing actual societies, but the old individual values are somehow incorporated in it. Apart from the verbal peculiarity (how can a distribution of qualities incorporate the values ascribed to individuals?) the claim seems hardly to have been sustained in any detail. Both he and Parsons try to show that the *system* is rational – that is, its parts are co-ordinated and it develops smoothly – but this is not rationality in any of the senses normally ascribed to individuals. Some people are active, interested and competent; others are not. Does the distribution itself, rather than any individual, incorporate these values? If this is what Berelson means, it is a roundabout and deceptive way of putting the view that, though Americans as a whole are not ideal democratic citizens, a few people do possess the required qualities and, moreover, the political system does not disintegrate.

Thirdly, the system's supposed requirements are stated very loosely – often too loosely for the validity of the account to be assessed – and sometimes tautologously, with little descriptive content. What, for example, does the requirement that there should be a 'nice balance' between consensus and cleavage, reflecting the 'health of a democratic order', really amount to? It is true but uninformative to say that if there is *too much* cleavage a democratic system – or any other system – will disintegrate; one can scarcely disagree with Berelson when he writes, 'Political parties in a democracy should disagree – but not too much, too sharply, nor too fundamentally.' Yet how can one measure these qualities to find out whether they are in balance (and what is so sacrosanct about this notional equilibrium point in any case?). This is not to say that the ideas of consensus and conflict are analytically useless; it is simply that here they are being misused, for, given that there is a measure of basic or 'higher-order' consensus, there is room for wide dispute over the nature and degree of cleavage that is tolerable or desirable (and, as Lipset shows, cleavage may itself be a factor making for consensus). And it does not help to speak of 'pluralism' as a 'kind of glue' which holds the system together when threatened by cleavage. Does this mean anything precise? What, for instance, is one to make of the following obscure passage from Berelson? 'The multiplicity and heterogeneity of identifications and associations in the great society develop an overlapping, pluralistic social organization which both sharpens and softens the impact and the consequences of political activity.'[39]

Finally, there is no warrant for saying that the features isolated are requirements of the system – unless, of course, they are included definitionally as parts of it. The clearest and most important instance is that of apathy. Apathy serves, says Berelson, as a ' "cushion" to absorb the intense action of highly-motivated partisans'. Apathy, it is claimed, helps the democratic system to function smoothly by facilitating change and reducing the impact of fanaticism, thus guarding against the danger of 'total politics'. Also, in Parsons's words, there is the 'indifference reaction', among the apathetic and incompetent floaters, which is the 'element of flexibility necessary to allow sufficient shift of votes to permit a two-party system to function effectively without introducing unduly disruptive elements into the system'.[40] Yet what is the basis for this claim that apathy must exist to hold the system together and give it flexibility, while cushioning the shock of disagreement and change? The theoretical framework seems hardly adequate to allow the role of apathy as an element of the system to be described in this way. That is to say, arguments about the necessity of apathy may always be confronted with the suggestion that any given society with democratic institutions or a democratic temper can in certain conditions tolerate an appreciably higher degree of participation than these theorists allow. The evidence, such as it is, does not in any way prove or even confirm the theory of the necessity of apathy to the survival of democracy.

Yet many of the writers under discussion support this theory, either on the basis of the equilibrium model criticised above or more generally on the basis of the evidence of scattered historical cases of differing degrees of participation. For example, Tingsten makes the point, on the basis of interwar election figures in Austria and Germany, that 'an exceptionally high voting frequency may indicate an intensification of political controversy which may involve a danger to the democratic system'.[41] His conclusion is that high political participation *may* not be a sign of the health of a democracy, but he also points out that it is misleading to speak of participation as though it were one thing whatever the community or circumstances: in other countries 'a high degree of participation cannot be judged in the same manner'.[42] Moreover, in the cases mentioned, high participation seems less a cause than a consequence of deeper-rooted social conflicts – high participation may mark some periods of crisis but it does not explain their origins. All that the evidence shows is that a high degree of electoral participation has sometimes been a symptom of crises in democracy and not even, as Lipset says, misinterpreting Tingsten's point, that 'political apathy may reflect the health of a democracy'.[43] The historical examples need careful handling – one might well argue, for instance, that the Weimar Republic fell chiefly because of apathy about the regime. In any case, neither apathy nor participation can profitably be considered in abstraction from historical contexts; apathy in the Weimar Republic can scarcely be identified with that of the affluent society of contemporary America, while increased participation, if it means a sudden 'intrusion of the masses into politics' in an artificial way, is hardly equivalent to the classical prescriptions for heightened general participation in the political and other activities in the life of the community. In brief, it has nowhere been shown that apathy is either necessary or functional to democracy.

To sum up, our conclusion is that no adequate empirical theory, still less a 'scientific' theory, of institutional 'democracy' has been provided. Apart from incidental insights, the notion of a stable equilibrium system is misleading as an account of 'what we call democracy' and is deceptively presented as a development of traditional theories of democracy. Furthermore, the 'requirements' of the 'democratic system' – in particular, apathy – have certainly not been proved to be necessary to the survival of a democratic society.

It is evident that the theorists of the new democracy share a number of contemporary preoccupations which have blinded them both to the possible development and to the possible diversity of democratic societies and have led them to describe apathy as a central requirement of the functioning of such societies. Essentially, these preoccupations centre on a basic distinction between totalitarianism and liberal democracy, which underlies a great deal of recent sociological and political writing. This dichotomy, historically explicable though it is, has in our view distorted much recent thinking about politics among Western intellectuals. It has led to an exaggerated fear of 'ideology' and the celebration of its supposed end in the modern affluent Western society, and, in addition, the familiar 'argument from the concentration camp' has often been used to condemn traditionally democratic and radical ideas which really have no necessary connection with totalitarianism. In general, this argument takes the form of isolating a particular idea or policy from its context, either theoretical or historical, and then indicating its putative affinity with totalitarian ideas and practices. One may well question not only the specific interpretations, but also the belief that political ideas can, in any case, be more or less clearly divided into the liberal-democratic and totalitarian categories. In times of great uncertainty conservatism has a natural appeal and the advantages of stable societies are apt to be greatly exaggerated. The political system is seen as an exquisitely fragile mechanism and all possible dangers to its stability are jealously guarded against. Hence the general contemporary concern with the conditions of a stable, non-totalitarian political system and the resulting desire to avoid anything which might lead to a dangerous involvement of the masses in politics. Such a development, it is claimed, would threaten both the smooth functioning of the system and the freedom and privacy of the individual.

This background helps to explain the new directions of democratic theory. The early democratic theorists, hating the tyranny of the old regime of monarchs and aristocrats, stressed the role of vigilance and participation in protecting hard-won rights against predatory 'sinister interests'. Political participation especially was to safeguard society, protect individuals and groups and develop individual qualities as well as men's control over their social lives. The theorists of the new democracy tend to see widespread participation, interest and conflict as substantial dangers to democracy and like to refer to the fraudulent claims of those totalitarians who see themselves as the real practitioners of democracy and the true representatives of the people. There are thus these twin dangers of 'total politics', which may disrupt the system, and totalitarian politics, which may eliminate freedom and privacy. This explains their eagerness to define the new political role of democratic man very narrowly. Meanwhile all the more radical features of the democratic tradition are abandoned in favour of a timid conservatism.

A characteristic piece of writing in this connection is W. H. Morris-Jones's article, 'In Defence of Apathy',[44] which is often referred to in the literature and has had some measure of influence. The explicit purpose of this article is 'to suggest that many of the ideas connected with the general theme of a duty to vote belong properly to the totalitarian camp and are out of place in the vocabulary of liberal democracy'.[45] But the discussion proceeds less by detailed argument than by a process of contamination; from ideas which are part of the liberal-democratic tradition the slide is made to allegedly connected notions which are clearly totalitarian. 'Political interestedness', says Morris-Jones, is the 'mark of the elect' and the obligation to vote is a dangerous idea, for 'it needs no demonstration that a totalitarian view of life easily involves an obligation not only to vote, but to do much more – and to do it, moreover, in the right direction.'[46] The trick is transparent. There is really no connection between the obligation to vote and the obligation to act in the right direction; any idea can be simply contaminated in this way by detaching it from the theory within which it was advanced and then showing that some people have held it alongside genuinely nasty views. Apart from this, Morris-Jones advances the positive argument that parliamentary democracy should be seen less as a 'system of government resting primarily on participation and consent' but rather as 'a manner of dealing with business, a way of going about things'. In this case, the presence of the apathetic is a 'sign of understanding and tolerance of human variety' and has a 'beneficial effect on the tone of political life . . . [being] a more or less effective counterforce to those fanatics who constitute the real danger to political democracy'.[47] The implication is obvious: to advocate widespread and general political participation is to advocate the development of intolerance and doctrinaire fanaticism.

This inference is frequently drawn in contemporary political theory and it is usually carried further, to the totalitarian conclusion that men are to be made purely political, privacy and liberty is to be invaded, and all the good things of civilised life destroyed. Examples of this kind of argument are to be found in Morris-Jones's article, in Hogan's book on *Election and Representation*,[48] in Talmon's critique of Rousseau[49] and in Berlin's *Two Concepts of Liberty*.[50] On the one hand, the connection is claimed to be established between the desire to participate and the totalitarian result. Berlin, for example, writes:

The desire to be governed by myself, or at any rate to participate in the process by which my life is to be controlled, may be as deep a wish as that for a free area for action, and perhaps historically older. But it is not a desire for the same thing. So different is it, indeed, as to have led in the end to the great clash of ideologies that dominates our world.[51]

On the other hand, apathy is held to be valuable because it shows the 'limitations of politics', that men are more than political creatures and can if they wish ignore politics entirely. In Hogan's words, 'Viewed in this light, the apathy and caprice for which political democracy has been blamed is seen to be rather to its credit than otherwise. It means at any rate that people are free to interest themselves or to disinterest themselves as they please in political affairs.'[52] This argument in terms of an ideal of freedom is deeply misleading. What is in question is not the right of men to be apathetic (and thus the enforcement of a duty to vote) but whether a society in which men concern themselves with political matters, as well as with many other matters, is likely to be more desirable than one marked by widespread apathy. If the vast majority of men were quite uninterested in politics and full general participation were demanded of everybody immediately, it is perhaps natural to infer that only constant coercion could achieve the desired result – and even more so if the desired result were unanimity. But it should hardly need saying that the ideal of general political participation is quite compatible with liberal safeguards and the rejection of coercion for partisan political goals, for instance, 'voting in the right direction'. It may be urged, with no totalitarian overtones whatsoever, that men ought to play some part in politics for their own good and for the good of society. The old democratic ideal sees apathy as dangerous because men cannot rely on others to protect their own interests and because the holders of power are likely to exercise it with too little concern for the general body of the people and for minority interests. It also considers politics to be a proper concern of the citizen and one of the fields of human excellence. In doing this, the classical theorists were very far indeed from urging constant and active participation at the behest of totalitarian masters, Stalinist Russia is as far removed from their ideals as it is from those of these modern anti-totalitarians.

As for coercion, this was the very thing that the classical theorists of democracy were concerned at all costs to avoid. The new theorists may argue that the old ideals must lead to this result, but we see no compelling reason to believe them. The now familiar dichotomies between totalitarianism and liberal democracy, between positive and negative liberty, between 'utopianism' and piecemeal pragmatism, have achieved something like a stranglehold over political theorising. No middle way is conceded between the concentration camp and a cautious conservatism. Talmon remarks characteristically of the 'early totalitarians' that they refused 'to take the people as it was for granted; the people, that is to say the sum total of the given generation, the good and the bad, the advanced and the backward, with their wishes, enlightened or otherwise.'[53] The implicit bias of this kind of view is obvious: we must accept the existing situation in its entirety, so that the only political issue left is that of making the 'system' work more efficiently. Yet the refusal simply to accept the existing situation by no means implies the acceptance of coercion and minority domination, shaping the fabric of an existing society in the image of a utopia.

The voices of sanity and reason sound above all in times of crisis and rapid change, and their conservative tone is familiar. Edmund Burke similarly appealed to the proved virtues of stable societies against the widespread criticism of established institutions at the time of the French Revolution. The arguments of the writers we have discussed bear witness to a worthy concern with avoiding the real dangers of totalitarian politics, dangers which no one should minimise; but they have gone too far in the opposite direction. Preoccupied with stability and protecting the system against too much participation, they have in reality abandoned, without realising it, a whole tradition of political thinking – a tradition which they claim to be developing and revising. Their arguments are, in any case, too loose to convince and too complacent to excite. This is not to say that the older democratic theories are not in need of any revision. But they have survived these particular attacks and retain their central interest and value. In particular, general political participation has not been destroyed as a desirable goal for democratic societies, nor are the new ideals that have been offered to us imposed upon us by the facts of contemporary political life.

Chapter 3

Political Ritual and Social Integration[1]

. . . questions of conventional and ceremonial behaviour in Britain, at least, have not attracted the attention of sociologists.[2]

. . . so far, social anthropologists and sociologists have not taken the study of modern political rituals very seriously. Are they generally rituals of conflict? On the whole, this does not seem to be so in Britain, a country in which ritual is important at various levels of the polity. Perhaps the induction of an American President shows more openly the balance of cohesion and conflict, between interests, parties and offices. But Americans tend to play down the rituals of formal office; does ritual reassert itself elsewhere in the complex structure of American life, through churches and through social orders? Is modern society as a whole becoming 'deritualized', as followers of Max Weber tend to assume? Or does ritual reassert itself somehow in all polities, as it did in Hitler's Germany and Stalin's Russia? The fair answer is that we do not know.[3]

This chapter is concerned with the role played by rituals in the politics of advanced societies. It is in part a polemic against a body of theorising about such rituals to which a number of sociologists have recently contributed, though it concludes with some positive suggestions. This is, as Professor Mackenzie's remarks suggest, a relatively uncharted and unexplored area, infested with theoretical difficulties and ideologically controversial issues, into which this is merely an exploratory foray. After extracting a working definition of ritual from the disputes of the social anthropologists, I will discuss a range of attempts that have been made by some sociologists to apply a particular theory of ritual – the Durkheimian theory – to the politics of modern societies. I will criticise these attempts and, finally, suggest an alternative approach which raises wider questions and promises a more satisfactory analysis of the role of ritual in political life.

The Definition of Ritual

It is social anthropology which has made this topic its own: as Mary Douglas has observed, 'we have got to the position in which Ritual replaces Religion in anthropologists' writings'.[4] There is, however, considerable dispute among anthropologists about how ritual is to be identified and interpreted. As Edmund Leach has written: 'even among those who have specialised in this field, there is the widest possible disagreement as to how the word ritual should be used and how the performance of ritual should be understood'.[5]

Most writers agree in seeing ritual as rule-governed – in the sense of being both patterned and usually involving normative pressure on its participants. They disagree about whether, on the one hand, ritual is definitionally to be linked with religion (or with religion and magic) and in particular with mystical or non-empirical or supernatural beings or powers;[6] or whether, on the other, ritual need not be inherently religious, so that relevant similarities between religious and non-religious rituals come into view.[7] There are two strong arguments in favour of the latter alternative. First, not all cultures make a clear distinction between the natural or empirical and the supernatural or non-empirical, nor do they all make it in the same way (and can it in any case be clearly drawn?). Accordingly, analysing their practices by means of a category which presupposes such a distinction could be distorting or even irrelevant. Second, there are practices which are, in all or most relevant respects, similar to religious rituals – such as the civic rites of the Greeks and Romans, or the ceremonies of Confucianism – but in which reference to the supernatural or mystical is either not central or else absent: in such cases there seems no good reason to withhold the label of ritual. And indeed, we are precisely interested in looking at modern political rituals, in which the mystical or supernatural often play little or no role.

Some anthropologists have traditionally stressed the irrational or non-instrumental character of ritual, others its expressive or symbolic nature. A modern instance of the former view is Jack Goody's definition in terms of 'standardized behaviour (custom) in which the relationship between the means and the end is not "intrinsic", i.e. is either irrational or non-rational'.[8] Leaving aside the question of specifying non-contestable criteria of rationality, this offers a useful account of how the anthropologist actually proceeds: for it is precisely the apparent irrationality of certain activities and beliefs which leads him to see them as symbolic. An activity, it has been suggested, is symbolic where the means 'appear clearly disproportionate to the end, explicit or implicit, whether this end be that of knowledge, communication or production'.[9] But what, then, does the symbolic nature of ritual consist in? It seems unduly loose to see it simply as the 'expressive, even dramatic' aspects of acts which have 'meanings' and involve 'mental associations',[10] or, quite generally, as the 'aesthetic' and 'communicative aspect of behaviour', that is, an 'aspect of almost any kind of action', that which '"says" something about the individuals involved in the action'.[11] On this view, all activities would be rituals. Here it would seem most profitable to follow Radcliffe-Brown in characterising the referents of ritual symbolism as having a special significance or social value within the relevant social group (a significance and value which the ritual itself serves to reinforce).[12] Such referents are objects, relationships, roles, situations, ideas, and so on, which have a special place in the life of the group and towards which at certain times, through the mediation of ritual, the attention of its participants is drawn, at different levels of consciousness and with varying emotional charge.

From the above, exceedingly condensed, discussion, I suggest we can extract the following definition of ritual: *rule-governed activity of a symbolic character which draws the attention of its participants to objects of thought and feeling which they hold to be of special significance.*[13]

There are a number of acute methodological problems involved in the study of ritual, chief among them being how to establish whether one interpretation of its symbolism is more valid than another. The observer cannot simply accept the actors' interpretations, the 'rationalizations of the devout';[14] indeed, these will themselves need to be interpreted. On the other hand, he cannot be completely uncontrolled in his interpretations. His task is to interpret the ritual within its context: the objects of thought and feeling which are the referents of the symbolism, and their special significance within a given social context, are matters that must be empirically established. On the other hand, and especially in so far as the symbolism is not explicit, he will find crucial explanatory clues by comparison with quite alien contexts and from general theoretical ideas he brings to bear. The observer's interpretation will, inevitably, be theory-dependent, but *his* theories can hardly be independent of native interpretations, whether of ordinary participants or of ritual specialists, or of their behaviour.[15] Thus reference to native accounts is both indispensable and non-definitive, and this poses real problems for verification and falsification in the interpretation of ritual. Probably the most one can hope for in this area is to achieve interpretations which can be compared with one another for plausibility and tested (supported and even sometimes refuted) in the light of new data.[16]

The arguments we are to consider follow the Durkheimian tradition in singling out the social reference of ritual symbolism, discounting or reinterpreting supernatural or mythical interpretations in social terms ('Behind these figures and metaphors, be they gross or refined, there is a concrete and living reality', namely, 'Society'),[17] and in seeing the effects of ritual as socially integrative. I shall, in fact, argue that, aside from their other failings, these views fail to exploit one crucial element in the Durkheimian theory of ritual. In order to support both that claim and my examination of these attempts to account for the meaning and functions of modern political rituals, I must, however, briefly refer to the source of these attempts, namely, the Durkheimian theory of religion and ritual.

The Durkheimian Theory

This has essentially three component elements: first a (causal) theory of how certain situations, those of 'collective effervescence', generate and recreate religious beliefs and sentiments, renewing *représentations collectives* which relate to sacred beings; second, an interpretation of religious beliefs and practices; and third, a (functional) theory of the consequences of those beliefs and practices.

Durkheim's interpretation of religious belief and ritual has, in turn, two aspects. He saw them as 'representing' social realities in two senses: first, as a cognitive means of interpreting the social world, rendering it intelligible, albeit in a metaphorical and symbolic idiom, so that religion is a sort of mythological sociology – 'a system of ideas with which the individuals represent to themselves the society of which they are members, and the obscure but intimate relations which they have with it';[18] and second, as a way of expressing and dramatising social realities, providing a 'flag', a 'rallying sign', a set of 'dramatic representations', analogous to 'games and the principal forms of art'.[19] Again, the consequences of religion operate at two levels: that of the individual and that of society as a whole: individuals are 'strengthened in their social natures', while 'the group periodically renews the sentiment which it has of itself and of its unity'.[20]

Durkheim maintained that certain features of religion, which he claimed to discern in its 'elementary' forms, were functional prerequisites of all societies. While religion was abandoning its cognitive role to science (including sociology) the function he saw ritual as playing in recreating and strengthening social integration was universal and indispensable. In this sense, he wrote, 'there is something eternal in religion which is destined to survive all the particular symbols in which religious thought has successively enveloped itself' – and he continued:

> There can be no society which does not feel the need of upholding and reaffirming at regular intervals the collective sentiments and the collective ideas which make its unity and its personality. Now this moral remaking cannot be achieved except by the means of reunions, assemblies and meetings where the individuals, being closely united to one another, reaffirm in common their common sentiments; hence some ceremonies, which do not differ from regular religious ceremonies, either in their object, the results which they produce, or the processes employed to attain those results. What essential difference is there between an assembly of Christians celebrating the principal dates of the life of Christ, or of Jews remembering the Exodus from Egypt or the promulgation of the decalogue, and a reunion of citizens commemorating the promulgation of a new moral or legal system or some great event in the national life?[21]

Durkheim was struck by what he saw as the pathological state of his own society, signified, as he saw it, by the very lack of public rituals. He saw this lack as an index of social pathology, of a transitional state of 'uncertainty and confused agitation',[22] which would be overcome; but a number of contemporary sociologists have argued, in particular with reference to Britain and the United States, that there is no such absence of ritual – that a Durkheimian analysis can be made of contemporary political rituals in these societies showing them to be important mechanisms of social integration. Let us look at some of these neo-Durkheimian arguments.

The Neo-Durkheimians

Edward Shils and Michael Young see their interpretation of the meaning of the British Coronation[23] as 'merely restating the interpretation, in a particular context of [Durkheim's] more general view'.[24] The Coronation was, they claim, exactly the kind of ceremonial of which Durkheim wrote, 'in which society reaffirms the moral values which constitute it as a society and renews its devotion to those values by an act of communion'.[25] The Coronation service itself was 'a series of ritual affirmations of the moral values necessary to a well-governed and good society'.[26] The service and the procession which followed it were 'shared and celebrated by nearly all the people of Britain' – 'in these events of 2nd June the Queen and her people were, through radio, television and press and in festivities throughout the land, brought into a great nation-wide communion'.[27] This popular participation through-out the country 'had many of the properties of the enactment of a religious ritual'.[28] There was 'the common sentiment of the sacredness of communal life and institutions . . . people became more aware of their dependence on each other, and they sensed some connection between this and their relationship to the Queen. Thereby they became more sensitive to the values which bound them all together.'[29] On sacred occasions – of which the Coronation is only one extremely 'august' form – 'the whole society is felt to be one large family, and even the nations of the Commonwealth, represented at the Coronation by their prime ministers, queens and ambassadors, are conceived of as a "family of nations".'[30] Shils and Young sum up their analysis of the Coronation's meaning as follows:

> A society is held together by its internal agreement about the sacredness of certain fundamental moral standards. In an inchoate, dimly perceived and seldom explicit manner, the central authority of an orderly society, whether it be secular or ecclesiastical, is acknowledged to be the avenue of communication with the realm of the sacred values. Within its society, popular constitutional

monarchy enjoys almost universal recognition in this capacity, and is therefore enabled to heighten the moral and civic sensibility of the society and to permeate it with symbols of those values to which the sensitivity responds. Intermittent rituals bring the society or varying sectors of it repeatedly into contact with this vessel of the sacred values. The Coronation provided at one time and for practically the entire society such an intensive contact with the sacred that we believe we are justified in interpreting it . . . as a great act of national communion.[31]

In a more recent study of public attitudes to the Monarchy, at the time of the Investiture of the Prince of Wales,[32] the authors conclude that their findings 'are more consistent with the religious analogy of the hold of the Queen on the imagination of her subjects than with the idols-of-mass-entertainment analogy'. It is, they write:

as if the Investiture brought to the fore a profound emotional commitment to the Monarchy, to the representatives of which the vast majority of people were prepared to extend an exceptional degree of respect. Most ordinary Englishmen were caught up in the spirit of the event to an extraordinary degree and communicated their enthusiasm to each other. The feelings about the Queen and Prince Charles which the Investiture evoked, managed to fuse personal with public concerns in a symbolic fashion that Durkheim would have understood.

Certain 'fundamental social values (family solidarity, national pride) were reaffirmed'; and indeed the whole occasion, in the authors' view, 'played the part of a ceremony, not only of rededication, but also of reconciliation'.[33]

For Lloyd Warner,[34] 'Memorial Day and similar ceremonies in the United States are one of the several forms of collective representations which Durkheim so brilliantly defined and interpreted in *The Elementary Forms of the Religious Life*'[35] The 'Memorial Day rites of Yankee City and hundreds of other American towns . . . are a modern cult of the dead and conform to Durkheim's definition of sacred collective representations'. They 'consist of a system of sacred beliefs and dramatic rituals held by a group of people, who when they congregate, represent the whole community' and they are 'sacred because they ritually relate the living to sacred things'.[36] Warner analyses 'the unifying and integrative character of the Memorial Day ceremony – the increasing convergence of the multiple and diverse events through various stages into a single unit in which the many become the one and all the living participants unite in the one community of the dead'.[37] The ceremony consists in 'the progressive integration and symbolic unification of the group'.[38] Warner summarises his own thesis as follows:

> Memorial Day ceremonies and subsidiary rites (such as those of Armistice or Veterans' Day) . . . are rituals of a sacred symbol system which functions periodically to unify the whole community, with its conflicting symbols and its opposing, autonomous churches and associations . . . in the Memorial Day ceremonies the anxieties which man has about death are confronted with a system of sacred beliefs about death which gives the individuals involved and the collectivity of individuals a feeling of well-being. Further the feeling of triumph over death by collective action in the Memorial Day parade is made possible by recreating the feeling of well-being and the sense of group strength and individual strength in the group power, which is felt so intensely during the wars . . . when the feeling so necessary for the Memorial Day's symbol system is originally experienced.[39]

Warner is here taking Durkheim's analysis very seriously. Following what he calls Durkheim's 'important theoretical lead', he argues that war provides that period of creative collective effervescence, of heightened 'interaction, social solidarity and intensity of feeling' which 'produce new sacred forms, built, of course, on the foundations of old beliefs'.[40] In brief, Memorial Day is 'a cult of the dead which organizes and integrates the various faiths and national and class groups into a sacred unity. It is a cult of the dead organized around the community cemeteries. Its principal themes are those of the sacrifice of the soldier dead for the living and the obligation of the living to sacrifice their individual purposes for the good of the group.'[41] Along with Christmas, Thanksgiving and the Fourth of July, it is part of the 'ceremonial calendar of American society' which 'functions to draw all people together to emphasize their similarities and common heritage; to minimize their differences, and to contribute to their thinking, feeling and acting alike'.[42] And Warner directly compares this ceremonial calendar with the seasonal alternation of secular and sacred ceremonial periods found among the Australian aborigines.[43]

Robert Bellah's discussion of 'Civil Religion in America'[44] applies the 'Durkheimian notion that every group has a religious dimension'[45] to

American society as a whole. He offers an analysis of Kennedy's Inaugural on the assumption that it indicates 'deep-seated values and commitments that are not made explicit in the course of everyday life'.[46] He argues that, distinct from personal religious worship and association:

> there are, at the same time, certain common elements of religious orientation that the great majority of Americans share. These have played a crucial role in the development of America's institutions and still provide a religious dimension for the whole fabric of American life, including the political sphere. This public, religious dimension is expressed in a set of beliefs, symbols and rituals that I am calling the American civil religion. The inauguration of a president is an important ceremonial event in this religion. It reaffirms, among other things, the religious legitimation of the highest political authority.[47]

From the earliest years of the Republic, Bellah writes, in a highly Durkheimian formulation, there has existed 'a collection of beliefs, symbols and rituals with respect to sacred things and institutionalized in a collectivity'.[48] The formative, creative periods, determining its sacred symbolism, were, first, the Revolution (seen as the final act of Exodus leading the American Israel from the old lands across the waters to the New Jerusalem) and then the Civil War (introducing, especially with Lincoln, a new theme of death, sacrifice and rebirth). It has, writes Bellah, 'its own prophets and its own martyrs, its own sacred events and sacred places, it own solemn rituals and symbols'.[49] Borrowing selectively from the religious condition, it has been able 'to build up without any bitter struggle with the church powerful symbols of national solidarity and to mobilize deep levels of personal motivation for the attainment of national goals'.[50]

Finally, I shall consider Sidney Verba's analysis of the popular reaction to the Kennedy assassination.[51] Citing Durkheim's theory that religious symbols represent society and are socially integrative, he suggests that 'this central symbolic role in a modern secular society is pre-empted by the political symbols that stand on the highest level for the society – in the American case by the Presidency above all'; 'political commitment in the United States contains a prime component of primordial religious commitment'.[52] 'The reactions to the assassination', Verba writes, the intense emotion, the religious observances, and the politico-religious symbolism – are evidence (though hardly proof) that such commitment exists. And the President is the appropriate focus of this commitment . . . he is . . . the symbol of the nation. and, as Durkheim stressed, the symbols of nationhood are more than particular objects that are made to stand for something larger; they are major constitutive elements of polities and societies.

But where does this central commitment to the symbols of nationhood – in this case the presidency – and to the nation thus symbolized originate? Early socialization of children is one source, but periodic ceremonies and collective events that allow the members of the society mutually to reinforce each other's commitment by collective activities are another way. In the relatively simple societies of which Durkheim wrote, this was accomplished by periodic reunions and ceremonials. In a complex and widely extended society like the United States, a society without the ceremonies of royalty, such reunions and common observances are somewhat rarer, though national elections and some national holidays may be examples of such events. The assassination crisis is important here because it is probably the nearest equivalent in a large modern nation-state to the kind of intense mutual rededication ceremony that is possible in a smaller and simpler society. There are several features that make it such a ceremony. The fact that it involved almost total participation is important. The figures on the universality of information and involvement are overwhelming as evidence of the ability of the mass media – television in particular – to link a large nation together. Furthermore, the media communicated not only information but shared emotion. . . . It was in many cases shared by families gathered around television sets, it was shared in church services and other community ceremonials, but it was intensely and widely shared through the media themselves. Not only were the emotions of individual Americans involved, but they were made clearly aware of the emotions of their fellow Americans.[53]

Verba lays very great stress on the integrative effects of the assassination (this must be the first conservative case for political assassination) and he sees this in essentially Durkheimian terms: the crisis was 'the occasion for an unexpected rededication ceremony',[54] which 'brought to the fore a pre-existing commitment – a commitment fundamental to the political community in the United States'.[55] He writes of 'traditional, religious and indeed somewhat magical aspects of political commitment' and suggests that this 'may be the kind of primordial emotional attachment that is necessary for the long-term maintenance of a political system'.[56] This may be 'what holds a complicated and pluralistic political society like the United States together'.[57] Thus 'many of the functions that religion and religious symbolism perform elsewhere in holding society together are performed in the United States by the central political symbols'.[58]

Criticism

What exactly do these neo-Durkheimian analyses claim to be the role of ritual in contemporary politics? They turn out on inspection to make a number of distinct claims: (1) political ritual is an *index* or *evidence* of (pre-existing) value integration (it indicates 'deep-seated values and commitments' and provides 'evidence' of 'primordial religious commitment'); (2) it is an *expression* of such integration ('society reaffirms the moral values which constitute it as a society'); (3) it is a *mechanism* for bringing about such integration (serving to 'mobilise deep levels of personal motivation for the attainment of national goals'); and (4) it itself *constitutes* such integration (consisting in 'the progressive integration and symbolic unification of the group' and functioning 'periodically to unify the whole community'). Thus these various relations are claimed to exist between ritual and value integration. It is further claimed, after the fashion of normative functionalism, that value integration is the central aspect of the integration of a society; value consensus maintains the equilibrium of the social system. Thus political rituals play a crucial part in the integration of modern industrial societies.

The first thing to be said about these analyses is that they conceptualise this latter integration in far too simple a manner. Shils and Young state baldly that a 'society is held together by its internal agreement about the sacredness of certain fundamental moral standards' – and as examples of such integrative moral values they cite 'generosity, charity, loyalty, justice in the distribution of opportunities and rewards, reasonable respect for authority [*sic*], the dignity of the individual and his right to freedom'.[59] (They never even consider the possibility that there might be divergences in the interpretation of such values within a society.) The other neo-Durkheimians make comparable assertions about the integration of society: hence, for instance, Verba's reference to 'what holds a complicated and pluralistic political society like the United States together'.

But 'what holds society together' – the so-called 'problem of order' – is an exceedingly complicated problem to which these writers propose an excessively simple answer.[60] The first question is whether, to what extent, and in what ways, a society *does* 'hold together'. That question must be answered first, before one can seek to determine what factors are responsible for its putative integration: specifying the *explanandum* must precede seeking explanations. In order to examine it seriously one must distinguish at least the following separable issues: (1) the continued participation of a society's members in its institutions and practices; (2) their conformity to its norms; (3) their sharing of a common consciousness and acting in concert; (4) the complementarity or reciprocity of their activities and roles; (5) the compatibility of their interests; (6) the degree of coherence of segments or parts of society; (7) the functional compatibility or 'degree of fit' between a society's core institutional order and its material base (the degree of 'system integration');[61] and (8) the persistence of structural features of the society over time. The writers we are considering – like normative functionalists in general – fail to separate these importantly different issues, and in fact focus mainly on (2). Moreover, the *explanation* they offer in terms of shared values is very partial, and can itself be seen as requiring further explanation. In short, value consensus takes one very little way indeed towards solving 'the problem of order', and, in so far as it exists, itself requires explanation.

But it is, in any case, empirically questionable how much value consensus there is, even in liberal democracies such as the United States and Britain. Reviewing the available evidence, Mann has argued that there is a very much lower degree of value consensus in such societies than consensus theorists seem to suppose.[62] If Mann is right, then the social cohesion of such societies cannot be attributed to a high degree of shared commitment to general values throughout their populations – though it may require such shared commitment among their elites.[63] Mann's thesis is that the compliance of subordinate classes is then to be explained, not by their participation in a value consensus, but in terms of their *lack* of commitment to a consistent set of values and beliefs that would translate their concrete experiences into radical politics. If we wish to explain that lack, 'we must rely to some extent on the Marxist theories of *pragmatic role acceptance* and *manipulative socialization*'.[64] On this view, the problem is not to explain why there is universal agreement over a set of internalised, integrative values and norms in terms of, say, political ritual and symbolism, but rather to explain the continuing compliance of subordinate groups in terms of their members' participation in activities, performance of roles and conformity to norms to which no realistic alternatives are perceived or imagined. I shall suggest below that an examination of political ritual could be highly pertinent to such an explanation.

It is not only arguable that the neo-Durkheimians, and consensus theorists generally, greatly overstate the degree of shared value commitments in liberal democracies; there are other societies which are, arguably, integrated (in a number of respects) in the *absence* of value consensus. Consider the case of Northern Ireland – which manifestly continues to 'hold together', in most of the ways specified above. That this is so clearly requires explanation, and that explanation can hardly avoid reference to the continuing functioning of the economic sub-structure. As the Northern Ireland Ministry of Commerce stated in an advertisement, at the height of the recent troubles: 'Every day tens of thousands of Northern Ireland Protestants and Roman Catholics work together, and, as the record shows, work hard. In the two years 1970 and 1971 manufacturing output rose 13 per cent (1970: 7·2 per cent – 1971: 6·1 per cent). Productivity in 1971 was up 6·7 per cent.'[65] And, of course, the explanation will equally refer to the exercise of power by the dominant groups, so visibly backed in this case by physical force. But the more general, and theoretically significant, point which emerges out of this example is that value consensus is not merely insufficient to ensure social integration; it is not even necessary. There are, to put it another way, functional alternatives to value consensus. The case of Czechoslovakia since 1968 demonstrates this with peculiar clarity.

So far, I have argued that the neo-Durkheimians have contributed virtually nothing to our understanding of the extent to which, and ways in which, modern industrial societies are integrated – first, because their conception of social integration is too simplistic, and second, because their assumption of value consensus is empirically questionable. I now wish to suggest that they make little contribution to our understanding of political rituals, because their approach (focusing on allegedly integration-strengthening rituals) is unduly narrow. That narrowness is revealed both by the selection of the rituals they analyse, and by the analyses they offer of the rituals thus selected.

Thus, in the first place, they select rituals which ostensibly support their view of social integration around a single value-system – that is, rituals which express a hegemonic ideology. But there are, of course, other contemporary rituals which express alternative and non-official attitudes and values. Consider, for example, the alternative Memorial Day parades staged in recent years in protest against the Vietnam War. Consider May Day parades in capitalist (as opposed to communist) societies. There are, indeed, interesting differences between these – both between different countries and within a given country. (Compare the communists' and the *gauchistes*' parades in France.) In general, such parades may promote consciousness and solidarity only to the level desired by the leaderships of working-class parties and trade unions. Consider the rituals of sport – both the games themselves (for example a Cup Final between Tottenham and Liverpool, symbolising North–South tensions) and the activities of spectators[66] (for example the community singing, the Royal Box to which the players proceed at the game's end at the Cup Final; or the behaviour of Welsh rugby crowds at Wales–England matches, or of black American boxing fans at black *versus* white fights, or of Czechs at ice hockey matches with the Russians). Again, strikes and other industrial actions can usefully be seen in this light. (On the other hand, these last cases, and to some extent those of sport, bring out an interesting feature which distinguishes them from, say, parades, or marches and demonstrations – namely, that they *are*, to some degree at least, what they symbolise: strikers *are* standing up to the bosses, it *is* black *versus* white in the ring, North *is* struggling against South, Wales against England, the Czechs against the Russians. What this shows is, perhaps, no more than that rituals may be more or less indirect; and, conversely, that 'direct action', and instrumentally orientated activities in general, may have their symbolic or ritual aspect, and that to identify this is not *eo ipso* to deny or debunk their non-symbolic aspect. To see them as rituals is to tell half the story.)

In this way, the neo-Durkheimian game can, no doubt, be played in reverse, to show how collective effervescences can serve to integrate and strengthen subordinate social groups, whether these are engaged in a struggle within the existing social order, or are aiming to challenge it, or at the extreme, overthrow it. (On the other hand, there are other, mixed cases, such as ethnic parades, as on St Patrick's Day, in New York, which express both the common consciousness of subordinate groups *and* the dominant, melting-pot ideology.)

An interesting example of the possibilities of such an analysis is provided by John Berger in an article written at the height of the French May Events of 1968.[67] Berger offers a highly Durkheimian analysis (though I have no evidence that he has read Durkheim) of the meaning and functions of demonstrations. Demonstrations, he writes, are 'rehearsals of revolutionary awareness'. A demonstration is 'a *created* event which arbitrarily separates itself from ordinary life'. The 'importance of the numbers invovlved is to be found in the direct experience of those taking part in or sympathetically witnessing the demonstration. . . . The larger the demonstration, the more powerful and immediate (visible, audible, tangible) a metaphor it becomes for their total collective strength':

> I say metaphor because the strength thus grasped transcends the potential strength of those present, and certainly their actual strength as deployed at a demonstration. The more people there are there, the more forcibly they represent to each other and to themselves those who are absent. In this way a mass demonstration simultaneously *extends* and *gives body* to an abstraction. Those who take part become more positively aware of how they belong to a class. Belonging to that class ceases to imply a common fate, and implies a common opportunity.

And Berger goes on to discuss the symbolism of the choice of the demonstration's location, as near as possible to some symbolic centre, either civic or national, rather than some strategic centre, thereby symbolising the capturing of a city or capital. The 'symbol or metaphor is for the benefit of the participants': they transform the areas they march through into a 'temporary stage on which they dramatise the power they still lack'. The demonstrators 'become corporately aware that it is they or those whom they represent who have built the city and who maintain it. They see it through different eyes. They see it as their product, confirming their potential, instead of reducing it.'[68]

Again, there are other contemporary political rituals, equally ignored by these writers, which, while expressing dominant values and interests, do so in societies in which value consensus is manifestly absent or minimal. Consider, for example, the Orange Order's rituals in Northern Ireland. Of these, Richard Rose has written that the 'most striking ceremony is an annual parade on the Twelfth of July, when Orangemen, wearing black bowler hats and orange collarettes, parade for hours through Belfast and other major centres, under banners commemorating major battles in the establishment of Protestant rule in Ulster three centuries ago'. Rose cites a letter in the *Belfast Telegraph* with an unconscious echo of Durkheim: 'Orangemen that day not only commemorate a very significant military and political victory, but a great deliverance from Roman slavery, in much the same way as the Jews each year commemorate their deliverance from bondage in Egypt.' 'In an exclusively Protestant state', writes Rose,

> such a ceremony would be an occasion expressing communal solidarity, as Independence Day is in America or in any ex-colonial nation. In a regime with divided authority, however, the parades of Orangemen – especially when they march through Catholic quarters of towns – intensify discord, for Catholics regard the marches as a show of force by those who have conquered them.[69]

In this case, collective effervescences serve not to unite the community but to strengthen the dominant groups within it. Ritual here exacerbates social conflict and works against (some aspects of) social integration. The same result may flow from rituals of subordinate groups at certain times and places: consider the Petrograd Soviet or the street demonstrations during the French May events. On the other hand, these cases may be contrasted with some of the other conflictual rituals mentioned above (parades, some but not all strikes, rituals of sport) which appear (*à la* Gluckman) to express and institutionalise, even exaggerate in ritual form, underlying social conflicts whose continued existence, together with the social order which contains them, is accepted as given and unchangeable by participants and observers. These rituals may be said to contribute to social integration but not to value consensus.

Thus the selection by the neo-Durkheimians of official and allegedly value integration-strengthening rituals is exceedingly narrow. But so also are the analyses they offer of these rituals. These analyses begin and end with the official interpretation and altogether fail to explore, not only different levels of symbolic meaning in the rituals, but also socially patterned differences of interpretation among those who participate in them or observe them. Such an investigation would, of course, immediately raise the question of the extent to which such official rituals succeed in promoting the value consensus which is their rationale.

This leads us to the final objection to the neo-Durkheimian view of ritual – namely that it is one-sided and uncritical. It fails, in other words, to raise a whole range of significant questions about the relations between ritual and society, between political symbolism, on the one hand, and social realities and possibilities, on the other.

Suggestions

In order to substantiate this claim, let us recall the definition of ritual proposed above: namely, *rule-governed activity of a symbolic character which draws the attention of its participants to objects of thought and feeling which they hold to be of special significance.* My main positive suggestion is that political ritual should be seen as reinforcing, recreating and organising *représentations collectives* (to use Durkheim's term), that the symbolism of political ritual *represents, inter alia*, particular models or political paradigms of society and how it functions. In this sense, such ritual plays, as Durkheim argued, a cognitive role, rendering intelligible society and social relationships, serving to organise people's knowledge of the past and present and their capacity to imagine the future. In other words, it helps to define as authoritative certain ways of seeing society: it serves to specify what in society is of special significance, it draws people's attention to certain forms of relationships and activity – and at the same time, therefore, it deflects their attention from other forms, since every way of seeing is also a way of not seeing. I suggest, in short, that we should go beyond the somewhat simplistic idea of political ritual expressing-producing-constituting value integration seen as the essence of social integration (which is the banal but widely applied aspect of Durkheim's theory) and take up instead the fertile idea that ritual has a cognitive dimension (this being, in any case, the central and original part of Durkheim's theory), though placing it (as Durkheim did not) within a class-structured, conflictual and pluralistic model of society. I believe this to be a more illuminating way of interpreting rituals than that of the neo-Durkheimians: it suggests that such rituals can be seen as modes of exercising, or seeking to exercise, power along the cognitive dimension. On this view, the *explanandum* ceases to be some supposed value integration, but is rather the internalisation of particular political paradigms or *représentations collectives*, whose role in political life requires investigation.

Once we see matters this way, we are in a position to ask various questions about political rituals which the neo-Durkheimians notably fail to ask – questions such as the following: Who (that is, which social groups) have prescribed their performance and specified the rules which govern them? Who (which social groups) specify the objects of thought and feeling they symbolise – specifically, certain forms of social relationship and activity – as of special significance? Who exactly holds them to be specially significant, and significant in what ways? In the interests of which social groups does the acceptance of these ways of seeing operate? And what forms of social relationship and activity are in consequence ignored as of less or no significance? Under what conditions are political rituals most effective in getting participants and observers to internalise the political paradigms they represent? How are such rituals used strategically by different groups, exerting or seeking power in society?

Such an approach would go well beyond the conventional study of politics, which, as Edelman puts it, concentrates on who gets what, when and how, on 'how people get the things they want through government', and focus instead on mechanisms through which politics 'influences what they want, what they fear, what they regard as possible and even who they are'.[70] It would explore the symbolic strategies used by different groups, under specifiable structural conditions, to defend or to attain power *vis-à-vis* other groups.[71] It would also examine the ways in which ritual symbolism can provide a source of creativity and improvisation, a counter-cultural and anti-structural force, engendering new social, cultural and political forms, involving what Turner calls 'liminality' and 'communitas', as, for instance, among millenarian and revivalist movements.[72]

Most significantly for the theme of this chapter, it would examine the cognitive dimension of social control within modern class-structured societies, revealing the manifold ways in which institutionalised activities, seen as rituals, can serve to reinforce and perpetuate dominant and official models of social structure and social change, of, say, the 'kingdom', the 'Empire', the Constitution, the Republic, the nation, the socialist state, of 'democracy', a 'free society', the 'rule of law', the 'public interest', 'socialism', 'socialist legality', the 'road to communism', of political order and political conflict, and indeed of the very nature and boundaries of 'politics'. That official ceremonies, such as the Coronation, Memorial or Independence or Bastille Day, the Presidential Inaugural, even the reactions to the assassination crisis, or the Lenin centenary, the October Revolution parades, and the mass visiting of the Lenin mausoleum in the Soviet Union, do this is plain enough. They draw people's attention, and invoke their loyalties, towards a certain, powerfully evoked representation of the social and political order. But many other institutionalised activities that are *not* primarily identified by their participants as rituals play an exactly similar role.

Most obvious of these are the elaborate and public forms of judicial and quasi-judicial activity. Indeed, the ritual and symbolic aspect of the law, maintaining and developing *représentations collectives*, has been far too little studied. 'The abstract ideals of the law', wrote Thurman Arnold, 'require for their public acceptance symbolic conduct of a very definite pattern by a definite institution which can be heard and seen.' They are dramatically presented and 'memorialized by particular ceremonies' and thereby become 'moving forces in society'.

Indeed,

> The institutions which throw about the law that atmosphere of reality and concreteness so necessary for its acceptance are the court and the law school. The one produces the ceremonial ritualistic trial; the other produces a theoretical literature which defends the ideal from attack by absorbing and weaving into its mystical pattern all the ideas of the critics.[73]

'The Law' is, from this point of view, a vast apparatus of ritual and symbolism, devoted to instilling the powerful vision of a social order in which justice is achievable through the following of regular and sanctified procedures. As Arnold has eloquently put it, the 'rule of law'

> ordinarily operates to induce acceptance of things as they are. It does this by creating a realm somewhere within the mystical haze beyond the courts, where all our dreams of justice in an unjust world come true. Thus in the realm of the law the least favoured members of society are comforted by the fact that the poor are equal to the rich and the strong have no advantage over the weak. The more fortunately situated are reassured by the fact that the wise are treated better than the foolish, that careless people are punished for their mistakes. The trader takes heart by learning that the law ignores the more profitable forms of dishonesty in deference to the principle of individual freedom from governmental restraint. The preacher, however, is glad to learn that all forms of dishonesty which can be curbed without interfering with freedom or with economic law are being curbed. The dissatisfied minority is cheered by the fact that the law is elastic and growing. The conservative is convinced that it is becoming more and more certain. The industrial serf is told that no man, not even his great employer, is above the law. His employer, however, feels secure in the fact that his property is put above ordinary legislative law by the Constitution, which is the highest form

of law there is. It protects us on the one hand from arbitrary power exercised without regulations. It saves us from the mob, and also from the dictator. It prevents capitalism from turning into communism, democracy from becoming the rule of an unthinking people. It gives all people an equal chance for success, and at the same time protects those who have been born in more favored positions of privilege and power.

In this way, the law is 'the greatest instrument of social stability because it recognises every one of the yearnings of the underprivileged, and gives them a forum in which these yearnings can achieve official approval without involving any particular action which might joggle the existing pyramid of power'.[74]

Consider, again, the activities of legislatures, such as debates, question-periods, committee investigations, and so on. Though these obviously have their 'efficient' or instrumental aspects of criticising, controlling and deliberating, there is much to be said for seeing them, with Crossman, as among Bagehot's 'dignified' and 'theatrical' elements of the Constitution, serving to 'excite and preserve the reverence of the population'.[75] As Beer has suggested, one central function of modern legislatures is to 'mobilise consent' – not merely to the views and policies of government, but to the parameters of the managed capitalist economy, with its many complex coercions. They define what the citizen takes for granted and thereby set limits to what it is realistic to change, by reinforcing the dominant definitions of the meaning of 'politics', of the nature of significant political divisions, and of the proper channels and permissible limits of political conflict.

A parallel analysis could be made of administrative activities in the United States, such as business regulation which, proclaiming values such as the public interest, fairness, the protection of rights, and so on, can be seen as symbolically creating and sustaining 'an impression that induces acquiescence of the public in the face of private tactics that might otherwise be expected to produce resentment, protest and resistance'.[76] Indeed, it is scarcely exaggerating to suggest that most of the regular activities of politicians, lawyers and administrators can be seen, aside from their manifest and instrumental functions, as symbolising to themselves and to the wider public the potent representation of a relatively well-ordered society in which justice broadly prevails and governments are responsive to citizens. Edelman puts this as follows:

To quiet resentments and doubts about particular political acts, reaffirm belief in the fundamental rationality and democratic character of the system, and thus fix conforming habits of future behaviour is demonstrably a key function of our persisting political institutions: elections, political discussions, legislatures, courts and administration. Each of them involves motor activity (in which the mass public participates or which it observes from a distance) that reinforces the impression of a political system designed to translate individual wants into public policy.[77]

This, indeed, makes it 'possible for men to believe that they live not in a jungle, but in a well-organized and good society';[78] or, at the very least, it presents the existing social order as relatively unalterable and sets severe limits to what can realistically be changed by political means.

But it is, undoubtedly, elections which are the most important form of political ritual in liberal democratic societies, partly because of their central place in the official ideology of such societies, partly because of the high degree of mass participation they involve. Likewise, ever since the 1936 Constitution, they have had a no less important role in the Soviet Union where the extremely high voting figures evidently have considerable symbolic significance. Participation in elections can plausibly be interpreted as the symbolic affirmation of the voters' acceptance of the political system and of their role within it. The ritual of voting draws their attention to a particular model of 'politics', of the nature of political conflict and the possibilities of political change. Moreover, it both results from and reinforces the belief, in which there is normally little truth, that elections give them an influence over government policy.[79] In this way, participation in elections – that minimal but most basic democratic activity – appears as the essence of 'democracy' and thereby contributes to the stability of both the liberal and the socialist democracies.

So the ritual of elections, alongside that within legislatures, law-courts and the administration, can play a significant role in legitimating and perpetuating the political paradigms or *représentations collectives* which contribute to the stability of the political system, by helping to define its very nature, and to define away alternatives to it. In this way, political rituals can be analysed as part of what has been called the 'mobilization of bias'[80] – that 'set of predominant values, beliefs, rituals [*sic*] and constitutional procedures ("rules of the game") that operate systematically and consistently to the benefit of certain persons and groups at the expense of others'.[81] And parallel analyses could be made of rituals that are not 'predominant' or hegemonic – whether these are subordinate and oppositional but posing no challenge to the existing social and political order, or else radically oppositional and representing a real challenge to the existing order.

In sum, then, I have argued a threefold case. First, I criticised the neo-Durkheimians for using too simplistic a notion of social integration, and for making too narrow a selection and offering too narrow an analysis of political rituals. Second, I further criticised their approach for closing off a whole range of significant and critical questions about political rituals – questions which bring out their cognitive role and the cognitive dimension of the exercise of power in class-structured, pluralistic and conflictual modern industrial societies. And third, I suggested that, once we ask these questions, we arrive at a view of many political rituals which pictures them, not as promoting value integration, but as crucial elements in the 'mobilisation of bias'.

Chapter 4

Alienation and Anomie[1]

Both Marx and Durkheim were profound critics of industrial society in nineteenth-century Europe. What is striking is the markedly different bases of their criticisms of the ills of their societies, which can best be brought out by a careful consideration of the different assumptions and implications that belong to the two concepts of alienation and anomie, which they respectively employed.[2] These concepts were elaborated by the two thinkers in their earliest writings and remain implicit as basic and integral elements in their developed social theories. Thus a study of the differing perspectives which they manifest should be fruitful. I shall argue: first, that they are both socio-psychological concepts, embodying hypotheses about specific relationships between social conditions and individual psychological states; second, that they differ precisely in the sorts of hypotheses they embody; and third, that this difference derives in part from a fundamental divergence in the views of human nature they presuppose. Fourth, I shall examine the nature of that divergence, and in particular the extent to which the dispute is an empirical one. I shall conclude by asking to what extent such approaches to the analysis of society remain relevant and important today.

First, however, I need to make the negative point that contemporary uses of the notions of alienation and anomie, while claiming to derive from Marx and Durkheim, are not for our purposes a useful starting-point. 'Alienation' in particular has achieved considerable and widespread contemporary currency, but it has become debased in consequence. Its evident resonance for 'neo-Marxist' thinkers, in both the West and the East, for existentialist philosophers and theologians, for psychiatrists and industrial sociologists, for *déraciné* artists and intellectuals and student rebels, has meant that it has been widely extended and altered in the interests of a number of contemporary preoccupations; as a result the core of Marx's concept has been lost.[3] 'Anomie' has been less widely used, but it too has achieved a new life within American social science. In particular, Robert Merton's paper 'Social Structure and Anomie'[4] (published 1938) has led to an extensive literature of conceptual refinement and empirical research, chiefly concerned with 'deviance' in all its forms.[5] But here too, much of the original meaning of the concept has been lost; in particular, most writers have followed Merton in discarding Durkheim's theory of human nature.

Furthermore, modern versions of these concepts vary widely in the range of their empirical reference. In the work of sociologists they are often taken as synonymous or else one is taken to be a sub-type of the other. Thus Nettler, Seeman and Scott in recent attempts to develop typologies of alienation count anomie as a variant, while Srole counts alienation as a variant of anomie.[6] Worse, there has been endless dispute in the case of both concepts about whether they are to be taken as sociological or psychological or as socio-psychological and, if the last, in what sense. Thus Merton defines 'the sociological concept of anomie' as 'a breakdown in the cultural structure, occurring particularly when there is an acute disjunction between the cultural norms and goals and the socially structured capacities of members of the group to act in accord with them',[7] and Robin Williams observes that 'Anomie as a social condition has to be defined independently of the psychological states thought to accompany normlessness and normative conflict'; while, for example, Riesman, MacIver, Lasswell and Srole take it to refer to a state of mind.[8] Similarly, 'alienation' is sometimes taken to refer to an objective social condition, which is to be identified independently of people's feelings and beliefs, as in the work of Lukacs and those who follow him: men live within 'reified' and 'fetishist' social forms and the task is precisely to make them *conscious* of their history, which is 'in part the product, evidently unconscious until now, of the activity of men themselves, and in part the succession of the processes in which the forms of this activity, the relations of man with himself (with nature and with other men) are transformed';[9] on the other hand, very many writers take alienation to be a state of mind (for example, existentialist writers, theologians, psychiatrists, American sociologists). One writer even takes alienation to be synonymous with frustration of any kind, arguing that it 'lies in every direction of human experience where basic emotional desire is frustrated'.[10]

Concepts can embody hypotheses and, in the case of these two concepts, when the focus is sociological there is frequently assumed to be a psychological correlate, and vice versa. Thus, for example, Merton classifies the psychological states resulting from sociological anomie, while others make assumptions about the social causes of psychological anomie; similarly, Marxist sociologists make assumptions about the psychological effects of alienated social forms, while, for example, Eric Fromm sees the psychological state of alienation as a function of market society.

A basic unclarity thus exists about the range of reference of each of these concepts and, even where the concepts are clearly used to embody hypotheses about relationships between social conditions and mental states, the very diversity of such hypotheses makes an analytical comparison of the concepts in their modern forms unmanageable in a short space. Where 'alienation' can mean anything from 'bureaucratic rules which stifle initiative and deprive individuals of all communication among themselves and of all information about the institutions in which they are situated'[11] to 'a mode of experience in which the person experiences himself as an alien',[12] and where 'anomie' can extend from the malintegration of the cultural and social structure to 'the state of mind of one who has been pulled up by his moral roots',[13] then the time has come either to abandon the concepts or return to their origins for guidance.

Marx distinguishes four aspects of alienated labour: (1) 'the relationship of the worker to the *product of labour* as an alien object which dominates him'. Thus, 'the more the worker expends himself in work the more powerful becomes the world of objects which he creates in face of himself, the poorer he becomes in his inner life, and the less he belongs to himself'; (2) 'the relationship of labour to the *act of production*', with the result that 'the work is *external* to the worker, that it is not part of his nature; and that, consequently, he does not fulfil himself in his work but denies himself, has a feeling of misery rather than wellbeing, does not develop freely his mental and physical energies but is physically exhausted and mentally debased. The worker, therefore, feels himself at home only during his leisure time, whereas at work he feels homeless. His work is not voluntary but imposed, *forced labour*. It is not the satisfaction of a need, but only a *means* for satisfying other needs'; (3) The alienation of man from himself as a 'species-being', from 'his own active function, his life-activity', which is 'free, conscious activity'. Man is thus alienated from 'his own body, external nature, his mental life and his *human* life'; (4) The alienation of man 'from other *men*. When man confronts himself he also confronts other men . . . in the relationship of alienated labour every man regards other men according to the standards and relationships in which he finds himself placed as a worker.' Social relations 'are not relations between individual and individual, but between worker and capitalist, between farmer and landlord, etc.' Further, men's lives are divided up into different spheres of activity, where conflicting standards apply: 'The nature of alienation implies that each sphere applies a different and contradictory norm, that morality does not apply the same norm as political economy, etc., because each of them is a particular alienation of man; each is concentrated upon a specific area of alienated activity and is itself alienated from the other.'

'Alienation' thus refers to the relationship of the individual to elements of his social and natural environment and to his state of mind, or relationship with himself. Marx contends that

> the division of labour . . . impoverishes the worker and makes him into a machine, [that] the division of labour offers us the first example of how . . . man's own deed becomes an alien power opposed to him, which enslaves him instead of being controlled by him. For as soon as labour is distributed, each man has a particular exclusive sphere of activity, which is forced upon him and from which he cannot escape.

In conditions where men must work for the increase of wealth, labour is 'harmful and deleterious'; the division of labour, which develops in such conditions, causes the worker to become 'even more completely dependent . . . upon a particular, extremely one-sided mechanical kind of labour'. All the aspects of alienation are seen to derive from the worker's role in production: his view of his work, his products, the institutions of his society, other men and himself. In general, the capitalist economic system 'perfects the worker and degrades the man'. Thus Marx's socio-psychological hypothesis concerning alienation is that it increases in proportion to the growing division of labour under capitalism, where men are forced to confine themselves to performing specialised functions within a system they neither understand nor control.

Durkheim uses 'anomie' in *The Division of Labour* to characterise the pathological state of the economy, 'this sphere of collective life [which] is, in large part, freed from the moderating action of regulation', where 'latent or active, the state of war is necessarily chronic' and 'each individual finds himself in a state of war with every other'. In *Suicide* it is used to characterise the pathological mental state of the individual who is insufficiently regulated by society and suffers from 'the malady of infinite aspiration': 'unregulated emotions are adjusted neither to one another nor to the conditions they are supposed to meet: they must therefore conflict with one another most painfully'. It is accompanied by 'weariness', 'disillusionment', 'disturbance, agitation and discontent', 'anger' and 'irritated disgust with life'. In extreme cases this condition leads a person to commit suicide, or homicide. It is aggravated by sudden crises, both economic disasters and 'the abrupt growth of power and wealth': with increased prosperity, for instance, anomie 'is heightened by passions being less disciplined, precisely when they need more discipline'. Anomie is the peculiar disease of modern industrial man, 'sanctified' both by orthodox economics and by extreme socialists. Industry, 'instead of being still regarded as a means to an end transcending itself, has become the supreme end of individuals and societies alike'. Anomie is accepted as normal, indeed 'a mark of moral distinction', and 'it is everlastingly repeated that it is man's nature to be eternally dissatisfied, constantly to advance, without relief or rest, toward an indefinite goal'. Religion, governmental power over the economy and occupational groups have lost their moral force. Thus 'appetites have become freed of any limiting authority' and 'from top to bottom of the ladder, greed is aroused without knowing where to find ultimate foothold. Nothing can calm it, since its goal is far beyond all it can attain.' 'The lives of 'a host of individuals are passed in the industrial and commercial sphere', where 'the greater part of their existence is passed divorced from any moral influence . . . the manufacturer, the merchant, the workman, the employee, in carrying on his occupation, is aware of no influence set about him to check his egoism'.[14]

'Anomie', like 'alienation', thus also refers first to the relationship of the individual to elements of his social environment and second to his state of mind. Durkheim initially thought that the division of labour itself has a 'natural' tendency to provide the necessary regulative force, that it produces solidarity because 'it creates among men an entire system of rights and duties which link them together in a durable way', for 'functions, when they are sufficiently in contact with one another, tend to stabilize and regulate themselves'. Anomie is prevalent because of the rapid growth of the market and big industry, for since 'these changes have been accomplished with extreme rapidity, the interests in conflict have not yet had time to be equilibrated'; also there is the harmful existence of 'the still very great inequality in the external conditions of the struggle'. Later he came to believe that it was primarily due to the lack of occupational groups which would regulate economic life by establishing 'occupational ethics and law in the different economic occupations': anomie 'springs from the lack of collective forces at certain points in society; that is, of groups established for the regulation of social life'. Both explanations are consistent with Durkheim's socio-psychological hypothesis concerning anomie, which is that it is a function of the rapid growth of the economy in industrial society which has occurred without a corresponding growth in the forces which could regulate it.

Alienation and anomie have in common the formal characteristic that they each have a multiple reference to: (1) social phenomena (states of society, its institutions, rules and norms); (2) individual states of mind (beliefs, desires, attitudes, and so on); (3) a hypothesised empirical relationship between (1) and (2); and (4) a presupposed picture of the 'natural' relationship between (1) and (2). Thus, whereas Marx sees capitalism as a compulsive social system, which narrows men's thoughts, places obstacles in the way of their desires and denies the realisation of 'a world of productive impulses and faculties', Durkheim sees it as a state of moral anarchy in the economic sphere, where men's thoughts and desires are insufficiently controlled and where the individual is not 'in harmony with his condition'. We will later notice how (3) is related to (4) in the two cases. Let us here concentrate on (3), and in particular on the difference between the hypotheses in question.

Compare what the two thinkers have to say about the division of labour. For Marx it is *in itself* the major contributing factor in alienation, in all its forms, and not just for the worker but for all men. All men are alienated under the division of labour (for, as he says, 'capital and labour are two sides of one and the same relation' and 'all human servitude is involved in the relation of the worker to production, and all the types of servitude are only modifications or consequences of this

relation'). Men have to enter into 'definite relations that are indispensable and independent of their wills', they are forced to play
determined roles within the economic system, and, in society as a whole,
they are dehumanised by social relations which take on 'an independent
existence' and which determine not only what they do, but the very
structure of their thought, their images of themselves, their products,
their activities and other men. Alienated man is dehumanised by being
conditioned and constrained to see himself, his products, his activities
and other men in economic, political, religious and other categories – in
terms which deny his and their human possibilities.

Durkheim sees the division of labour as being (when properly
regulated) the source of solidarity in modern industrial society: the
prevalence of anomie is due to a lag in the growth of the relevant rules
and institutions. Interdependence of functions (plus occupational
groups) should lead to growing solidarity and a sense of community,
although the division of labour in advanced societies is also (ideally)
accompanied by the growth of the importance of the individual
personality and the development of values such as justice and equality.
For Durkheim the economic functions of the division of labour are
'trivial in comparison with the moral effect it produces'. By means of it
'the individual becomes aware of his dependence upon society; from it
come the forces which keep him in check and restrain him'. When
educating a child, it is 'necessary to get him to like the idea of
circumscribed tasks and limited horizons', for in modern society 'man is
destined to fulfil a special function in the social organism, and,
consequently, he must learn in advance how to play this role'. The
division of labour does not normally degrade the individual 'by making
him into a machine': it merely requires that in performing his special
function 'he feels he is serving something'. Moreover, 'if a person has
grown accustomed to vast horizons, total views, broad generalities, he
cannot be confined, without impatience, within the strict limits of a
special task'.

By now it should be apparent that alienation, in Marx's thinking, is,
in part, what characterises precisely those states of the individual and
conditions of society which Durkheim sees as the solution to anomie:
namely, where men are socially determined and constrained, when they
must conform to social rules which are independent of their wills and
are conditioned to think and act within the confines of specialised roles.
Whereas anomic man is, for Durkheim, the unregulated man who needs
rules to live by, limits to his desires, 'circumscribed tasks' to perform

and 'limited horizons' for his thoughts, alienated man is, for Marx, a man in the grip of a system, who 'cannot escape' from a 'particular, exclusive sphere of activity which is forced upon him'.[15]

Whence does this difference derive? In part, obviously, from the fact that Marx and Durkheim wrote at different periods about different stages of industrial capitalism. Also it is clear that Marx was concerned chiefly to describe the alienated worker, while Durkheim saw economic anomie as primarily characterising employers. But there is also a theoretical difference that is striking and important: these concepts offer opposite and incompatible analyses of the relation of the individual to society.

Compare Marx's statements that 'it is above all necessary to avoid postulating "society" once again as an abstraction confronting the individual' and that communism creates the basis for 'rendering it impossible that anything should exist independently of individuals' with Durkheim's that society is 'a reality from which everything that matters to us flows', that it 'transcends the individual's consciousness' and that it 'has all the characteristics of a moral authority that imposes respect'. Marx begins from the position that the independent or 'reified' and determining character of social relationships and norms is precisely what characterises human 'pre-history' and will be abolished by the revolutionary transition to a 'truly-human' society, whereas Durkheim assumes the 'normality' of social regulation, the lack of which leads to the morbid, self-destructive state of 'non-social' or Hobbesian anarchy evident in unregulated capitalism. Social constraint is for Marx a denial and for Durkheim a condition of human freedom and self-realisation.

It is my contention that one can only make sense of the empirical relationships postulated between social conditions and individual mental states which are held to constitute alienation and anomie by taking into account what Marx and Durkheim see as the 'natural' (or 'human' or 'normal' or 'healthy') condition of the individual in society. Alienation and anomie do not identify themselves, as it were, independently of the theories from which they derive: witness the diversity of contemporary uses of the terms, discussed above. They are, in fact, only identifiable if one knows what it would be *not* to be alienated or anomic, that is, if one applies a standard specifying 'natural' states of institutions, rules and norms and individual mental states. Moreover, this standard must be external. That is, neither the individual mental states nor the social conditions studied can provide that standard, for they themselves are to be evaluated for their degree of alienation and anomie.

Thus, despite recent attempts to divest these concepts of their non-empirical presuppositions,[16] they are in their original form an inextricable fusion of fact and value, so that one cannot eliminate the latter while remaining faithful to the original concepts.

The standard specifying the 'natural' condition of the individual in society involves, in each case, a theory of human nature. Marx's view of man is of a being with a wide range of creative potentialities, or 'species powers' whose 'self-realization exists as an inner necessity, a need'. In the truly human society there will be 'a new manifestation of *human* powers and a new enrichment of the human being', when 'man appropriates his manifold being in an all-inclusive way, and thus is a whole man'. Man needs to develop all his faculties in a context where neither the natural nor the social environment are constraining:

> objects then confirm his individuality . . . the wealth of subjective human sensibility . . . is cultivated or created [and] the practical relations of everyday life offer to man none but perfectly intelligible and reasonable relations with regard to his fellow men and to nature.

With the end of the division of labour, there will be an end to 'the exclusive concentration of artistic talent in particular individuals and its suppression in the broad mass'. The 'detail worker of today', with 'nothing more to perform than a partial social function', will be superseded by 'an individual with an all-round development, one for whom various social functions are alternative modes of activity'.[17] Furthermore, with the end of the social determination of 'abstract' individual roles, man's relationship with man and with woman will become fully human, that is, fully reciprocal and imbued with respect for the uniqueness of the individual. As Marx says:

> the relation of man to woman is the most *natural* relation of human being to human being. . . . It also shows how far man's needs have become human needs, and consequently how far the other person, as a person, has become one of his needs, and to what extent he is in his individual existence at the same time a social being.

Thus Marx assumes that the full realisation of human powers and 'the return of man himself as a *social*, i.e. really human, being' can only take place in a world in which man is free to apply himself to whatever activity he chooses and where his activities and his way of seeing himself and other men are not dictated by a system within which he and they play specified roles.

Durkheim saw human nature as essentially in need of limits and discipline. His view of man is of a being with potentially limitless and insatiable desires, who needs to be controlled by society. He writes:

> To limit man, to place obstacles in the path of his free development, is this not to prevent him from fulfilling himself? But . . . this limitation is a condition of our happiness and moral health. Man, in fact, is made for life in a determinate, limited environment.

'Health' for man in society is a state where 'a regulative force' plays 'the same role for moral needs which the organism plays for physical needs', which makes men 'contented with their lot, while stimulating them moderately to improve it' and results in that 'calm, active happiness . . . which characterizes health for societies as well as for individuals'. Durkheim's picture of a healthy society in modern Europe is of a society that is organised and meritocratic, with equality of opportunity and personal liberty, where people are attached to intermediary groups by stable loyalties rather than being atomised units caught in an endemic conflict, and where they fulfil determinate functions in an organised system of work, where they conform in their mental horizons, their desires and ambitions to what their role in society demands and where there are clear-cut rules defining limits to desire and ambition in all spheres of life. There should be

> rules telling each of the workers his rights and duties, not vaguely in general terms but in precise detail [and] each in his sphere vaguely realizes the extreme limit set to his ambitions and aspires to nothing beyond . . . he respects regulations and is docile to collective authority, that is, has a wholesome moral constitution.

Man must be governed by 'a conscience superior to his own, the superiority of which he feels': men cannot assign themselves the 'law of justice' but 'must receive it from an authority which they respect and to which they yield spontaneously'. Society alone 'as a whole or through the agency of one of its organs, can play this moderating role'. It alone can 'stipulate law' and 'set the point beyond which the passions must not go'; and it alone 'can estimate the reward to be prospectively offered to every class of human functionary, in the name of the common interest'.

The doctrines of Marx and Durkheim about human nature are representative of a long and distinguished tradition of such doctrines in the history of political and social theory. The difference between them is also representative of that tradition (and parallel differences can be traced back to the Middle Ages). Doctrines of this general type can be seen to underlie, for example, the work of Hobbes, Rousseau, the Utopian Socialists and Freud; and it is evident that, in large measure, Durkheim sides with Hobbes and Freud where Marx sides with Rousseau and the Utopians. For the former, man is a bundle of desires, which need to be regulated, tamed, repressed, manipulated and given direction for the sake of social order, whereas, for the latter, man is still an angel, rational and good, who requires a rational and good society in which to develop his essential nature – a 'form of association in which each, while uniting himself with all, may still obey himself alone'.[18] For the former, coercion, external authority and restraint are necessary and desirable for social order and individual happiness; for the latter, they are an offence against reason and an attack upon freedom.

I want here to ask two difficult questions. First, how is one to understand Marx's and Durkheim's theories of human nature, and, in particular, what is their logical and epistemological status? And, second, how is one to account for their divergence?

Statements about human nature can be construed in many different ways. They commonly include such terms as 'need', 'real self', 'real will', 'basic desires', 'human potentialities', 'human powers', 'normal', 'healthy', and so on. Statements of this sort might be taken to refer to: (1) man as existing before or apart from society; (2) man considered analytically, with those factors due to the influence of society abstracted; (3) man considered in an *a priori* manner, that is, according to some *a priori* definition; (4) man considered from the point of view of features which seem to be common to men in all known societies; (5) man considered from the point of view of features which are held to characterise him in certain specifiable social conditions as opposed to others.[19]

My suggestion is that very often, and in particular in the cases I am discussing, the last is the most accurate way to read statements about human nature. It is, in general, not absurd to take statements about human needs, 'real' wants, potentialities and so on as asserting that individuals in situation S are unable to experience satisfactions that situation S_1 is held to make possible for them and which they would experience and value highly. Now, it is, in my view, not necessary that such statements refer to actual *discontents* of individuals in situation S: both Marx and Durkheim, for example, were clear that individuals could acquiesce in and even value highly their alienated or anomic condition. What is required is that, once they are in S_1, they experience satisfactions unavailable in S.

Thus far it is evidently an empirical matter. It is an empirical and testable question (1) whether the satisfactions in question are precluded in S; (2) whether they would be available in S_1; and (3) whether they would be actually experienced by individuals in S_1 and would be important and valuable to them. (1) can in principle be investigated directly. To take easy examples, it is not difficult to show that work on the assembly line precludes work satisfaction or that the life of the highly ambitious businessman precludes a mental condition of harmonious contentment. (2) and (3) can be investigated indirectly or directly. To do so indirectly would involve looking at evidence available in S and, indeed, in other societies, which provides a strong presumption in their favour. Thus Marx can write of what happens when 'communist artisans form associations'. When 'French socialist workers meet together', he writes, 'society, association, entertainment which also has society as its aim, is sufficient for them: the brotherhood of man is no empty phrase but a reality, and the nobility of man shines forth upon us from their toil-worn bodies.' And he writes in *The Holy Family* that one 'must be acquainted with the studiousness, the craving for knowledge, the moral energy and the unceasing urge for development of the French and English workers to be able to form an idea of the *human* nobleness of that movement'. Durkheim can appeal to countless examples of cohesive social groups – primitive tribes, medieval guilds, rural Catholic communities, the Jews, and to the evidence of, for example, differential suicide rates. He compares, for instance, the poor with the rich and argues that

everything that enforces subordination attenuates the effects of [anomie]. At least the horizon of the lower classes is limited by those above them, and for this same reason their desires are more modest. Those who have only empty space above them are almost inevitably lost in it.

Direct investigation of (2) and (3) can be pursued only by social experiment. Thus the final test for Marx's theory of human nature is the communist revolution; and that for Durkheim's is the institution of a kind of centralised guild socialism.

We have analysed statements about human nature as empirical statements (in this case, hypothetical predictions) about the condition of man in S_1. But our analysis is as yet incomplete, for they also involve the affirmation that this condition is privileged – that it is evaluated as preferable to all other conditions. How is one to analyse this evaluation: is it also empirical, that is, a ranking in accordance with what men actually want, or is it non-empirical – a mere exhortation to look at the world in one way rather than another?

If it is empirical, the question arises: by *whom* is the condition of man in S_1 said to be preferred – which men's wants are relevant here? If one believes, as Marx and Durkheim did, that man is largely conditioned by social circumstances, that new needs are generated by the historical process, that his very picture of himself and others is a function of his situation, then the problem becomes even more acute, for no one is in a position genuinely to compare and evaluate alternatives, like Mill's wise man deciding between higher and lower pleasures. An appeal to men in S_1 is self-defeating, for it carries the presumption that their evaluations are privileged, which is what is at issue. An appeal to men in S will not do either, for they would not ordinarily have the necessary evidence, and, again, why should their judgements be privileged? Worse still, what criteria are appropriate? If men in S_1 are satisfied, fulfilled, contented in certain ways, what is privileged about judgements which value these states rather than others?

Both Marx and Durkheim *thought* that they had found solid empirical ground upon which to base statements about human nature. They both had a picture of history as a process of the progressive emergence of the individual and both thought that man's potentiality for individual autonomy and for genuine community with others (both of which they envisaged differently) was frustrated by existing social forms. They thought that they had found conclusive evidence for their respective views of human nature in present and past societies; they assumed that, despite the continual generation of new needs throughout history, men's fundamental aspirations, more or less hidden, and the conditions of their ultimate happiness had always been and would continue to be the same. They were both impressed by the growth of industrialism and by the possibilities it had opened up for human fulfilment,[20] and they believed that men were, despite the present, and temporary, obstacles, increasingly becoming (and would continue to become) what they had it in them to be; one could identify *this* by looking at their miseries and sufferings, as well as their strivings and aspirations towards 'human' or 'healthy' forms of life, and at historical examples of societies or institutions in which alienation or anomie were less severe or even absent. Yet this evidence about men's wants is itself selected and interpreted, and that requires a prior perspective, providing criteria of selection and interpretation.

It would seem, therefore, that statements about human nature, such as those examined here, are partly empirical and partly not. One can often get a long way with support of the empirical part, for evidence of all kinds is relevant to the question of what men's lives would be like in alternative circumstances. The hypothetical prediction about S_1 may be verifiable; at least one would know how to verify it, and one could in principle point to evidence which strongly supports it. The claim, however, that life in S_1 is to be judged superior, though it may rest on an appeal to evidence about men's wants, is ultimately non-empirical, for that evidence has been selected and interpreted in the light of the claim. Which men's wants and which of their wants has already been decided. Moreover, the claim of superiority does not follow logically from the evidence: one must add the premise that certain wants and satisfactions are more 'human' or 'healthy' than others. In the end what is required is a perspective and an initial set of evaluations.

It is precisely here that Marx and Durkheim differed radically. Marx wrote that the 'socialist perspective' attributed importance to 'the wealth of human needs, and consequently also to a *new mode of production* and to a new *object* of production' as well as to a 'new manifestation of human powers and a new enrichment of the human being'. He began from an image of man in society, where a morality of duty would be unnecessary because irrelevant, an image in which *aesthetic* criteria were of predominant importance in assessing the quality of man's relationship with the natural and social world.[21]

Yet where Marx wrote in the *Theses on Feuerbach* from 'the standpoint of . . . human society', Durkheim argued in the *Rules of Sociological Method* that it was 'no longer a matter of pursuing desperately an objective that retreats as one advances but of working with steady perseverance to maintain the normal state, of re-estab-lishing it if it is threatened, and of rediscovering its conditions if they have changed'. He was haunted by the idea of man and society in disintegration. Here he appealed to the remedy of moral rules, defining and prescribing duties in all spheres of life, especially where men's anarchic and unstable desires had the greatest scope. This is a moral vision, for, as he said, 'the need for order, harmony and social solidarity is generally considered moral'.[22]

Where Marx valued a life in which in community with others 'the individual' has the means of 'cultivating his gifts in all directions', and where the relations between people are no longer defined by externally imposed categories and roles – by class and occupation – and they freely come together in freely chosen activities and participate in controlling the conditions of their social life, Durkheim held that 'we must contract our horizon, choose a definite task and immerse ourselves in it completely, instead of trying to make ourselves a sort of creative masterpiece', and hoped to see people performing useful functions in a rationally organised society, in accordance with clearly defined roles, firmly attached to relevant groups and under the protective discipline of rules of conduct at home, at work and in politics. They both sought liberty, equality, democracy and community, but the content which they gave these notions was utterly different.

What is the relevance of these concepts today? This question needs to be sub-divided into three more specific questions, which follow the lines of the preceding argument. First, how valid is the empirical hypothesis which each embodies? To what extent do they succeed in identifying and adequately explaining phenomena in modern industrial societies? Second, how plausible is the theory of human nature which each presupposes? What does the evidence from past and present societies, from sociology and psychology, suggest about the plausibility of their respective hypothetical predictions, and about the nature of the changes which men and institutions would have to undergo to attain the conditions they predict and advocate? And third, how desirable is the ideal, how attractive is the vision to which each ultimately appeals? How today is one to evaluate these ideals: what degree of approximation to either, or both (or neither), are we to think desirable?

These questions are challenging and far-reaching. Here I shall raise them and offer tentative suggestions as to how one might begin to answer them.

(1) One problem in answering the first question is to know at what level of generality it is being posed. How *specifically* is one to read Marx's account of alienation and Durkheim's of anomie? Marx and Durkheim identified certain features of their own societies and offered explanations of them. But they may also be seen to have identified features characteristic of a number of societies including their own;

indeed, one may even see them, to some extent, as having identified features which may be said to characterise any conceivable society. Is it a specific type of technology, or form of organisation, or structure of the economy, or is it the existence of classes or of private property, or the accumulation of capital, or the division of labour, or industrial society, or the human condition, which is the crucial determinant of alienation? Is it the lack of a specific type of industrial organisation (technical or administrative?), or the absence of appropriate occupational groups, or an economy geared to the pursuit of profit, or the cultural imperatives of a 'success ethic', or the fact of social mobility, or the erosion of a traditionally stable framework of authority, or social change, or industrial society, or the human condition, that is the major factor leading to anomie? Alienation and anomie are phenomena which have particular aspects, unique to particular forms of society or institution, other aspects which are more general and still others which are universal. We may attempt to identify new forms of these phenomena, using these concepts and the hypotheses they embody in the attempt to describe and explain them. They are in this sense concepts of 'the middle range'. They allow for specific new hypotheses to account for particular new forms, or they may account for them by means of the existing, more general hypotheses. In general, the contemporary forms of alienation and anomie are best approached on the understanding that their causes are multiple and to be sought at different levels of abstraction. A systematic investigation of alienation and anomie would range from the most particular to the most universal in the search for causes.

Marx and Durkheim attributed, as we have seen, certain types of mental condition (specified positively, in terms of what occurs, and negatively, in terms of what is precluded) to certain types of social condition. Marx pointed to meaninglessness of work and a sense of powerlessness to affect the conditions of one's life, dissociation from the products of one's labour, the sense of playing a role in an impersonal system which one does not understand or control, the seeing of oneself and others within socially imposed and artificial categories, the denial of human possibilities for a fully creative, spontaneous, egalitarian and reciprocal communal life. He attributed these, in particular, to the form taken by the division of labour under capitalism and, more generally, to the fact of class society. Durkheim pointed to greed, competitiveness, status-seeking, the sense of having rights without duties, the concentration on consumption and pleasure, the lack of a sense of community with others, of a feeling of limits to one's desires and aspirations, and of the experience of fulfilling a useful function and serving a purpose higher than one's own self-interest, and the denial of human possibilities for an ordered and balanced life, where everyone knows his station and its duties. He attributed these, in particular, to the industrial revolution and the failure of society to provide appropriate groups to adjust to it, and, more generally, to social disorganisation.

We are familiar with countless examples of these phenomena, though in many cases not all the features isolated by the concepts are necessarily present. Let me give just two examples.

Alienation is found today in perhaps its most acute form among workers in assembly-line industries, such as the motor-car industry, where, as Blauner writes in his sensitive study of workers' alienation:

> the combination of technological, organizational and economic factors has resulted in the simultaneous intensification of all the dimensions of alienation. [Here, in the extreme situation] a depersonalized worker, estranged from himself and larger collectives, goes through the motions of work in the regimented milieu of the conveyor-belt for the sole purpose of earning his bread . . . his work has become almost completely compartmentalized from other areas of his life, so that there is little meaning left in it beyond the instrumental purpose [and it is] unfree and unfulfilling and exemplifies the bureaucratic combination of the highly rational organization and the restricted specialist. In relation to the two giant bureaucracies which dominate his life, he is relatively powerless, atomized, depersonalized, and anonymous.[23]

Likewise, anomie is noticeably evident and acute among 'the Unattached', well described by Mary Morse, especially those in 'Seagate' – the drifting, purposeless and unstable teenagers, who felt no connection with or obligation to family, work, school or youth organisation, the children of *nouveau riche* parents, suffering from 'a sense of boredom, failure and restlessness' and refusing 'to accept limitations, whether their own or external'. Often there was 'a failure to achieve unrealistic or unattainable goals they had set for themselves or had had set for them'; also there was 'a general inability to postpone immediate pleasure for the sake of future gain', there was 'a craving for adventure', and 'leisure-time interests were short-spanned, constantly changing and interspersed liberally with periods of boredom and apathy'. Finally, they showed 'pronounced hostility towards adults', adult discipline was quite ineffective and, in general, 'all adults in authority were classed as "them" – those who were opposed to and against "us".'[24]

These are merely two instances, but they illustrate the general point made above. The causes of alienation and anomie must be sought at different levels of abstraction. At the most specific level, all sorts of special factors may be of primary importance. In a case of alienation, it may be the technical or organisational character of an industry or the structure of a bureaucracy; in a case of anomie, it may be a combination of personal affluence and a breakdown, rejection or conflict of norms of authority at home, at school and at work. But clearly, too, the nature of the wider society is of crucial importance. The extent and nature of social stratification, the structure of the economy, the character of the political system, the pace of industrialisation, the degree of pluralism, the nature of the predominant social values – all these will affect the nature and distribution of alienation and anomie. Again, one can plausibly argue that *some* degree of alienation and of anomie is inseparable from life in an industrial society, characterised as it is, on the one hand, by the ramifying growth of organisation and bureaucracy in all spheres of life, by economic centralisation and by the increasing remoteness and technical character of politics; and, on the other, by built-in and permanent social changes, by the impermanence of existing status hierarchies and the increasing role given to personal ambition and career mobility. And at the most general level, they may each be seen to relate to the most universal features of social structure and social change. In this sense, some alienation must exist wherever there are reified social relations, socially given roles and norms; while some anomie must exist wherever hierarchies disintegrate and social control is weakened.

(2) What about the plausibility of Marx's and Durkheim's theories of human nature? They each had definite views about men's needs, which they believed to be historically generated and empirically ascertainable. How plausible today is the picture of mutually co-operative individuals, each realising a wide range of creative potentialities, in the absence of specific role expectations, lasting distinctions between whole categories of people and externally imposed discipline, in conditions of inner and social harmony, where all participate in planning and controlling their environment? What, on the other hand, is the plausibility of the view of human happiness, in which people are socialised into specific roles, regulated, and to some extent repressed, by systems of rules and group

norms (albeit based on justice, equality of opportunity and respect for the individual), serving the purposes of society by fulfilling organised functions – all of which they accept and respect as constituting a stable framework for their lives?

These questions confront all those who hold versions of these ideals today. One cannot begin to appraise either, or compare them with one another, until one has come to some view about the likelihood of either being realised. What evidence is there that if the social conditions are constituted in the way Marx and Durkheim wanted, people would experience and would value highly the satisfactions of which they speak? Here one would, for example, need to examine all the accumlated evidence throughout history of experiments in community living and in workers' control, of communes, collective farms and *kibbutzim*, on the one hand, and of experience in 'human relations' and personnel management, of professionalism and of life in organisations, on the other. There is a vast amount of such evidence available, but it has never been systematically reviewed in this light.

Let us look at two examples in this connection. In the opinion of Friedmann the Israeli *kibbutz* represents 'an original and successful application, on a limited scale, of communist principles', nearer to 'the ethical ideal defined by the philosophy of Marx and Engels (for instance, with regard to the role of money, the distinction between manual and intellectual labour, family life)' than life in Moscow or on a *kolkhoz*.

> The kibbutz movement [he writes] despite its limitations and its difficulties, constitutes the fullest and most successful 'utopian' revolutionary experiment, the one which approximates most closely to the forms of life which communism has assigned itself as an aim. It is in the kibbutzim that I have met men of ample culture, and even creators, artists, writers, technicians, among whom the contradiction between intellectual and manual work, denounced by Marx, is truly eliminated in their daily life.

Friedmann goes on, of course, to qualify and elaborate this; in particular, he outlines the perpetual confrontation between the *kibbutzim* and the wider society, devoted to economic growth and 'imbued with models of abundance, where, with the development of the private sector, there is proclaimed a sort of material and moral New Economic Plan'.[25] He examines the attempts of the *kibbutzim* to reduce to a minimum the tensions and frustrations of community life and asks the crucial questions: whether the *kibbutz* will be able to adapt to the economic and technical demands of an industrial society, while retaining its essential values; and whether the wider society will evolve in a direction that is compatible or incompatible with these values.

Let us take a second example, which relates to the plausibility of Durkheim's ideal, the overcoming of anomie. Perhaps the best instance is the evidence accumulated and interpreted by the theorists of modern managerialism, concerned to remedy 'the acquisitiveness of a sick society'[26] and treating the factory, the corporation and the large organisation as 'a social system'. Particularly relevant are the writings of the 'organicists', whose aim is to promote 'the values of social stability, cohesion and integration'[27] and to achieve, within the 'formal organization' (the 'explicitly stated system of control introduced by the company') the 'creation and distribution of satisfactions' among the members of the system.[28] Selznick, who typifies the attempt to explore communal values within large corporations and administrative organisations, argues that the organisation requires 'stability' in its lines of authority, subtle patterns of informal relationships, 'continuity' in its policies and 'homogeneity' in its outlook.[29] Another writer describes its reification and normative significance for those who participate in it in the following terms – terms of which Durkheim might well have approved:

> One might almost say that the organization has a character, an individuality, which makes the name real. The scientist will not accept any such reification or personalizing of an organization. But participants in these organizations are subject to no such scientific scruples, and generations of men have felt and thought about the organizations they belonged to as something real in themselves.[30]

For Selznick, social order and individual satisfaction are reconciled when 'the aspirations of individuals are so stimulated and controlled, and so ordered in their mutual relations, as to produce the desired balance of forces'.[31]

I have merely suggested two areas in which one might look for evidence that is relevant to the plausibility of the hypothetical predictions which partially constitute Marx's and Durkheim's theories of human nature. Clearly there is much else that is relevant in, for instance, the work of industrial sociologists, social psychologists, in community studies and the writings of organisation theorists. It is also important to look at what evidence there is about the prevalence of existing tendencies in modern societies which favour or hinder the sorts of changes which would be necessary in order to approach these ideals. Here it would be necessary to look, for example, at the changes in the nature of occupations brought about by automation – the replacement of the detail worker by the more educated and responsible technician; at the effects of economic planning on small-scale decision-making; at the effects of the growth of organisations on status aspirations; at contemporary trends in consumption patterns. All this, and much else, is relevant to an assessment of the costs of approaching either ideal in our societies. Without these detailed inquiries, it is hardly possible to state firm conclusions, but it would appear that Durkheim's ideal is much nearer to and easier of realisation in the industrial societies of both West and East than is that of Marx.

(3) Finally, how is one to evaluate these ideals? To do so involves a commitment to values and an assessment of costs. Either may be seen to conflict with other values or may not be considered to be worth the cost of its realisation. Both sociological evidence and conceptual inquiry are relevant in the attempt to decide these matters, but in the end what is required is an ultimate and personal commitment (for which good or bad reasons may, none the less, be advanced). One may, of course, hold, as both Marx and Durkheim in different ways did, that one's values are, as it were, embedded in the facts, but this is itself a committed position (for which, again, good or bad reasons may be advanced).

This is no place to argue about these matters at the length they require. Let it be sufficient to say that these two quite opposite and incompatible ideals represent in a clear-cut form two major currents of critical and normative thinking about society, to be found throughout the whole tradition of political and social theory in the West and still very much in evidence.

It has been common for that tradition to be attacked, by the advocates of a 'scientific' social and political theory, as being rudimentary and speculative, and lacking in scientific detachment. It is all rather like Sir James Frazer's view of primitive religion as 'bastard science'. What is required, it is argued, is the abandonment of concepts which are internally related to theories of the good life and the good society. Evaluation of this sort should be kept strictly apart from the process of scientific inquiry.

Yet the desire for scientific rigour is not in itself incompatible with the sort of inquiry which is concerned precisely to put to the task of empirical analysis concepts which have the type of relation I have outlined to theories of human nature and thereby to prior evaluative perspectives. This type of inquiry is exactly what has primarily characterised social and political theory in the past (under which heading I include the writings of the classical and some modern sociologists). The case for eliminating it necessarily involves advocating the abandonment of the application of models of alternative and preferred forms of life to the critical analysis of actual forms. That case has yet to be made convincing.

Chapter 5

Socialism and Equality

. . . there is now, with the existence of a large amount of sociological research on inequality of opportunity and inequality of result, and with the resurgence of interest among moral philosophers in inequality, as manifested in John Rawls's work, the possibility of serious examination of social ideals and social reality in this area.[1]

Professor Coleman's remarks above raise three questions. First, what are the 'social ideals' of equality? What forms of inequality are undesirable and what forms of equality desirable, and on what grounds? Second, what are the 'social realities' of inequality? What is the upshot of all the research into inequality in contemporary societies? And third, what bearing does the answer to the second question have on that to the first? How does social reality affect social ideals? What is desirable, in the light of the actual and what appears possible? The importance of these questions needs no elaboration. The ideal of equality has always been central to the socialist tradition: thus Professor Taylor specifies 'greater equality in the conditions of life' as the first goal of 'any socialist in a Western country today'.[2] In assessing the contemporary viability of the socialist idea, then, the three questions raised above demand to be faced. First, why is 'greater equality in the conditions of life' desirable?[3] Second, how unequal are such conditions in contemporary industrial societies, capitalist and state socialist, and what explains these inequalities? And third, are these inequalities ineradicable, or eradicable only at an unacceptable cost? Clearly, I cannot begin to answer these momentous questions here. What I shall try to do is to offer some suggestions as to how they might be answered. Concerning the first (philosophical) question, I shall seek to suggest a modified Kantian ethical basis for the social, political and economic equalities that socialists have traditionally sought to establish. As for the second (sociological) question, I shall briefly sketch some of the evidence about actual inequalities and the range of explanations for them. And with regard to the third question I shall briefly consider a number of arguments for the inevitability of inequality. Having done these things, it will be clear to even the most sympathetic reader that everything remains to be done.

The Social Ideals of Equality

The ideal of equality has been made to seem absurd in either of two opposing ways. It has been interpreted as based either on the principle of absolute and unconditional equality – 'treat everyone equally in every respect' – or else on the empty formal principle, 'treat people equally unless there are relevant or sufficient reasons for treating them unequally'. In fact, few serious thinkers, let alone socialists, have advocated the former,[4] and all the interesting forms of egalitarianism have put content into the latter in two ways: negatively, by ruling out certain sorts of reasons as justifications for treating people unequally; and positively, by advancing, or presupposing, a set of reasons for treating them equally.

Historically, the fight for equality has taken the form of attacking specific inequalities and their alleged justifications: inequalities of privilege and power – legal and political, then social and economic – have been attacked as unjustifiable, because arbitrary, capricious or irrational. For example, it has been suggested that inequalities are unjustifiable unless they can be shown to satisfy one or more of the following criteria: (1) merit or deserts; (2) need; (3) social benefit (and on such a basis it would be hard to justify the present extreme inequality of inherited wealth in Britain).[5] But, quite apart from the difficulty of interpreting these criteria, especially the last, such an approach always presupposes a view of what is justifiable, that is, what are relevant and sufficient sorts of reasons for unequal treatment, and over this individuals, classes and cultures conflict. What, then, of the positive way?

One influential argument for treating people equally – and in particular for according them equal income and wealth – is the utilitarian argument for attaining the maximum aggregate satisfaction, on the assumption of diminishing marginal utility: as Dalton put it, an 'unequal distribution of a given amount of purchasing power among a given number of people is . . . likely to be a wasteful distribution from the point of view of economic welfare'.[6] In their recent important study of inequality, Christopher Jencks and his associates state their position as follows:

> We begin with the premise that every individual's happiness is of equal value. From this it is a short step to Bentham's dictum that society should be organized so as to provide the greatest good for the greatest number. In addition, we assume that the law of diminishing returns applies to most of the good things in life. In economic terms this means that people with low incomes value extra income more than people with high incomes. It follows that if we want to maximize the satisfaction of the population, the best way to divide any given amount of money is to make everyone's income the same. Income disparities (except those based on variations in 'need') will always reduce overall satisfaction, because individuals with low incomes will lose more than individuals with high incomes gain.[7]

But this assumption is questionable. Why assume that a given amount of purchasing power yields equal utility for everyone (assuming one could make the interpersonal comparison), and why assume that it diminishes as income or wealth increases?

In any case, egalitarians and socialists have not rested their case on this precarious basis alone: there is an alternative tradition of thought on the subject, of which Rousseau is the classical figure and Rawls the major contemporary exponent, which offers an alternative interpretation of equality and which appeals to deeper values than the utilitarian. This interpretation may be called the principle of equality of consideration or respect. On this view, all human beings have certain basic features which entitle them to be considered or respected as equals, and this is seen as implying practical policies for implementing substantial political, social and economic equality.[8]

What, then, are the basic features of human beings which command equal consideration or respect? For Christians the answer is that they are all children of God, for Kant that they are rational wills and thus members of the Kingdom of Ends, for classical liberals that they share 'common rights to which they are called by nature',[9] for many socialists and anarchists that they share a 'common humanity'. These are all transcendental answers, whether religious or secular. Others speak of man's 'inherent dignity', 'intrinsic or infinite value,' or 'human worth'. But in all these cases, no *independent* reasons are given for respecting people equally – or at least none that would convince a sceptic disposed to do so unequally, according to, say, birth or merit. But it is arguable that there are a number of empirical features which could provide such reasons, to which, throughout their history, egalitarian doctrines have, implicitly or explicitly, appealed. On the one hand, there are basic human needs – minimally, the means to life and health – without which they could not function in a recognisably human manner. On the other hand, there are certain basic capacities (of which more below), characteristic of human beings, whose realisation is essential to their enjoyment of freedom. It may be objected that, since people have these needs and capacities to different degrees, they are therefore worthy of unequal respect. But to this may it be replied that it is the existence of the needs and capacities, not the degree to which the former are met and the latter realised or realisable, that elicits the respect, and that respecting persons precisely consists in doing all that is necessary and possible to satisfy their basic needs and to maintain and enhance their basic capacities (and to discriminate between them in this regard is to fail to show them equal respect).

The principle of equal respect for needs tells against all humanly alterable economic and social arrangements which discriminate between individuals' access to the means of sustenance and health (and it is not irrelevant in contemporary Britain, where there are still marked class differences in the risks of death and infant mortality). But 'need' is a concept to which appeal cannot be made beyond this basic (if rising) minimum level: beyond that point, it becomes a question of individuals' entitlement to the means of realising certain basic capacities. Three such capacities appear to be of particular significance.

There is, first, the capacity of human beings to form intentions and purposes, to become aware of alternatives and choose between them, and to acquire control over their own behaviour by becoming conscious of the forces determining it, both internally, as with unconscious desires and motives, and externally, as with the pressures exerted by the norms they follow or the roles they fill. In other words, human beings have the capacity to act with relative autonomy and to be or become relatively self-determining, to become conscious of the forces determining or affecting them, and either consciously to submit to them or become independent of them. Obviously, not all exercise this capacity to an equal degree, but all, except the mentally defective or deranged, possess it.

Second, human beings have the capacity to think thoughts, perform actions, develop involvements and engage in relationships to which they attach value but which require a certain area of non-interference in order to have that value. Enjoyments and delights of all kinds, intellectual and artistic activities, love and friendship are examples: all these require a space free and secure from external invasion or surveillance in order to flourish. There is, of course, considerable room for differences about which of these activities and relationships are of most value and about what kind of value they have, and indeed about which of them people should be left alone to engage in. But what seems indisputable is that there is a range of such activities and relationships in some of which all persons have the capacity to engage and to which they attach value.

Third, human beings have the capacity for self-development. By this I mean that everyone has the capacity to develop in himself some characteristic human excellence or excellences – whether intellectual, aesthetic or moral, theoretical or practical, personal or public, and so on. Obviously, not everyone will be able to develop any given excellence to the same degree – and perhaps, *pace* Marx, not all will be able to develop them in a many-sided, all-round fashion. But all human beings share the capacity to realise potentialities that are worthy of admiration. What counts as worthy of admiration will be subject to moral disagreement and cultural variation, but it is arguable that there is a delimited range of human excellences which are intrinsically admirable, though the forms they take differ from society to society, and that all human beings are capable of achieving some of them to some degree.

I have argued that these three characteristics of persons are at least part of the ground on which we accord them respect. What, then, does that respect consist in? The unsurprising answer is that, whatever else it involves, respecting them involves treating them as (actually or potentially) autonomous, as requiring a free and secure space for the pursuit of valued activities and relationships, and as capable of self-development. That answer has, given certain further assumptions, far-reaching social, economic and political implications, and points towards a society with substantially reduced inequalities, both of material and symbolic rewards and of political power.

What, we may ask, constitutes a denial of such respect? We fail to respect someone by denying his autonomy not only when we control or dominate his will, but also when we unreasonably restrict the range of alternatives between which he can choose. Such control and restriction is as likely to be social and economic as political, and as typical of the work situation and the family and of opportunities for education and employment as of the relation between the state and the citizen. In this sense, Tawney saw a central aim of 'measures correcting inequalities or neutralizing their effects' as increasing 'the range of alternatives open to ordinary men, and the capacity of the latter to follow their own preferences in choosing between them'.[10] But we also cease to respect someone when we fail to treat him as an agent and a chooser, as a self from which actions and choices emanate, when we see him and consequently treat him not as a person but as merely the bearer of a title or the occupant of a role, or as merely a means to securing a certain end, or, worst of all, as merely an object. We deny his status as an autonomous person to the extent that we allow our attitudes to him to be dictated solely by some contingent and socially defined attribute of him, such as his 'merit' or success or occupational role or place in the social order – or what Tawney called 'the tedious vulgarities of income and social position'.[11] This denial of autonomy was what William Godwin had in mind when he urged universal and equal political participation on the grounds that 'Each man will thus be inspired with a consciousness of his own importance, and the slavish feelings that shrink up the soul in the presence of an imagined superior, will be unknown.'[12] It is what William Morris meant when he wrote of socialism as a 'condition of equality' in which a man 'would no longer take his position as the dweller in such and such a place, or the filler of such and such an office, or (as now) the owner of such and such property, but as being such and such a man'.[13] It is what Tawney intended when he wrote of an egalitarian society as one in which 'money and position count for less, and the quality of human personalities for more',[14] and what George Orwell was thinking of when he wrote of 'breathing the air of equality' in revolutionary Spain, with 'no boss-class, no menial-class, no beggars, no prostitutes, no lawyers, no priests, no boot-licking, no cap-touching'.[15] Respecting persons in this way, as Bernard Williams has well put it, implies that they be 'abstracted from certain conspicuous structures of inequality' in which they are found and seen, 'not merely under professional, social or technical titles, but with consideration of their own views and purposes', as 'conscious beings who necessarily have intentions and purposes and see what they are doing in a certain light'.[16] But more is involved in respecting autonomy than looking behind the surface of socially defined titles or labels and seeing the world (and the labels) from the agent's point of view. Social existence in part determines consciousness; and the most insidious and decisive way of denying the autonomy of persons is to diminish or restrict their opportunity to increase their consciousness of their situation and activities. It is for this reason that respecting autonomy points towards a 'single status society' and away from the ideal of a stable hierarchy, since

> what keeps stable hierarchies together is the idea of necessity, that it is somehow foreordained or inevitable that there should be these orders; and this idea of necessity must be eventually undermined by the growth of people's reflective consciousness about their role, still more when it is combined with the thought that what they and others have always thought about their roles in the social system was the product of the social system itself.[17]

Secondly, one manifestly fails to respect someone if one invades his private space and interferes, without good reason, with his valued activities and relationships (and above all with his inner self). Examples of where it can be justifiable so to interfere are in cases, say, of imprisonment or conscription during wartime – where it may be claimed that there is 'good reason' for interference and thus no denial of respect in so far as they are necessary infringements of a person's freedom, either to preserve the freedom of others, or his own and others' in the long run, or as the only way of realising other cherished values. But, in the absence of these justifications, such as an invasion or interference is clearly a denial of human respect. It is easy to think of extreme forms of such a denial, as in the prison camps described by Solzhenitsyn or total institutions described by Erving Goffman. But less extreme forms result from inequalities of power and privilege in all contemporary societies. Liberals characteristically attack such invasions of liberty, especially in non-liberal societies, when they take the form of political authoritarianism, bureaucratic tyranny, social pressures to conformity, religious and racial discrimination. But interference with valued activities and relationships occurs in other ways to which liberals are less sensitive – through class discrimination, remediable economic deprivation and insecurity, and what Hayek has called the 'hard discipline of the market',[18] where nominally equal economic and social rights are unequally operative because of unequal but equalisable conditions and opportunities.

Finally, one also importantly fails to respect someone if one limits or restricts his opportunities to realise his capacities of self-development. It is the systematic and cumulative denial of such opportunities to the less favoured citizens of stratified societies, both capitalist and state socialist, that constitutes perhaps the strongest argument against the structured inequalities they exhibit. That argument really has two parts. The first part is simply an argument against discrimination, against the failure to 'bring the means of a good life within the reach of all'.[19] Thus the principal argument against a discriminatory educational system is not that it creates social inequality (which, as Jencks shows, it scarcely does, serving 'primarily to legitimize inequality, not to create it'),[20] but rather that it blocks the self-development of the less favoured and thereby fails to respect them. Again, where it is possible to make certain types of work more challenging and require a greater development of skill or talent or responsibility, it is a denial of human respect to confine workers within menial, one-sided and tedious tasks. Furthermore, workers – and citizens in political society as a whole – are denied respect to the degree to which they are denied possibilities of real participation in the formulation and taking of major decisions affecting them, for they are thereby denied the opportunity to develop the human excellence of active self-government celebrated by Rousseau and John Stuart Mill and central to the various forms of classical democratic theory. The second part of this argument against structured inequalities is that they provide an unfavourable climate for the self-development of ordinary people. The assumption that this is so was well expressed by Matthew Arnold, who claimed that for

> the common bulk of mankind . . . to live in a society of equals tends in general to make a man's spirits expand, and his faculties work easily and actively; while, to live in a society of superiors, although it may occasionally be a very good discipline, yet in general tends to tame the spirits and to make the play of the faculties less secure and active.[21]

Tawney made the same assumption, arguing that 'individual differences, which are a source of social energy, are more likely to ripen and find expression if social inequalities are, as far as practicable, diminished'.[22] Individuals, Tawney argued, 'differ profoundly . . . in capacity and character' but 'they are equally entitled as human beings to consideration and respect, and . . . the well-being of a society is likely to be increased if it so plans its organization that, whether their powers are great or small, all its members may be equally enabled to make the best of such powers as they possess'.[23] His case was that establishing 'the largest possible measure of equality of environment, and circumstance, and opportunity' was a precondition for ensuring 'that these diversities of gifts may come to fruition'.[24]

I have argued, then, that certain basic human needs and capacities provide at least part of the ground for equality of respect, and give some content to that notion of 'respect', and I have further suggested that a society practising equal respect would be one in which there were no barriers to reciprocal relations between relatively autonomous persons, who see each other and themselves as such, who are equally free from political control, social pressure and economic deprivation and insecurity to engage in valued pursuits, and who have equal access to the means of self-development. Such a society would not be marked by inequalities of power and privilege (which is not to say that a society without such inequalities would necessarily practise equal respect).

However, I should conclude this section by noting an important tension between the notion of equality of respect, as discussed here, and that of 'equality of opportunity', as normally understood. In the context of public debate, especially about education, this latter principle is *not* generally taken to refer to equality of opportunity to develop individual powers or gifts, but rather equality of opportunity to achieve scarce social rewards. Thus understood, it comes into conflict with equal respect, since it focuses attention upon forms of differentiation and grading which carry status and prestige. It endorses and serves to perpetuate those very structures of inequality, characterised by competition and emulation, of which equality of respect makes light – and, practised seriously, would abolish. This distinction was well drawn by Tawney when he contrasted 'the claim for an open road to individual advancement' with the desire 'to narrow the space between valley and peak'.[25] The former aspiration has, of course, a central place in the history of socialism: it represents the meritocratic policy of widening the social base of recruitment to privileged positions, which has always been the central plank of social democracy. Thus C. A. R. Crosland wrote:

> The essential thing is that every citizen should have an equal chance – that is his basic democratic right; but provided the start is fair, let

there be the maximum scope for individual self-advancement. There would then be nothing improper in either a high continuous status ladder ... or even a distinct class stratification ... since opportunities for attaining the highest status or the topmost stratum would be genuinely equal. Indeed the continuous traffic up and down would inevitably make society more mobile and dynamic, and so less class-bound.[26]

By contrast, the egalitarian socialist focuses on equalising the rewards and privileges attached to different positions, not on widening the competition for them. In fact, of course, these two strands are often intertwined in socialist theory and practice. But, although there are well-known arguments (an example of which we shall consider) to the effect that unequal rewards, together with equal opportunity to reap them, have essential economic and social functions, they are in tension with the social, political and economic implications of the principle of equal respect, which, as we have seen, points towards greater equality in the conditions of life, that is, of wealth, income, status and power.

The Realities of Inequality

Contemporary industrial societies manifest structured inequalities of such conditions, and of much else besides, such as access to education, social services and other public benefits, economic security, promotion prospects, and so on. Some patterns of inequality appear to be common to all such societies, both capitalist and state socialist, others to the one system or the other, yet others to particular countries. But three myths, prevalent in recent times, are belied by the evidence. The first is that of 'convergence', according to 'the logic of industrialism'. This is misleading in so far as it suggests a continuing trend in the development of industrial societies towards greater overall economic equality, towards an ever-increasing consistency of stratification systems around the occupational order (for example towards the congruence of middle incomes and middle-class life style and status), and towards a uniform pattern of social mobility.[27] The second is that 'affluence' in capitalist societies has eroded inequalities of income, wealth and security of life and that the power of private capital has been tamed, from within by the 'managerial revolution' and the divorce between ownership and control, and from without by the growth of the state and/or a pluralistic diffusion of power among competing interest groups. The third myth is the official communist (especially Soviet) interpretation of state socialist societies, which, while acknowledging the existence of non-antagonistic classes (working class and peasantry) and the stratum of the intelligentsia, and the existence of inequalities of income, consumption goods, education, and so on, between rural and urban population and between occupational strata, maintains that these inequalities are in process of continuing decline (the so-called process of *sblizhenie*, or 'drawing together'), denies that there is a hierarchy of status and is silent about the hierarchy of power.

Of the patterns of inequality common to industrial societies, it appears broadly true to say that, in contrast with traditional or non-industrial societies, 'the occupational order comes increasingly to be the primary source of symbolic as well as material advantages';[28] thus

> The occupational structure in modern industrial society not only constitutes an important foundation for the main dimensions of social stratification, but also serves as the connecting link between different institutions and spheres of social life, and therein lies its great significance. The hierarchy of prestige strata and the hierarchy of economic classes have their roots in the occupational structure; so does the hierarchy of political power and authority, for political authority in modern society is largely exercised as a full-time occupation.[29]

As for income, there appears to be a remarkable similarity in capitalist and communist societies in the structure of earnings – more precisely, in the distribution of pre-tax money wages or salaries of fully employed male adult workers in all industries but farming.[30] There is a broad relationship between the hierarchy of skills and knowledge demanded by occupations on the one hand, and the hierarchy of material rewards on the other (though there is a narrower range of differentials under command than market economies), and, related to this, there are certain more specific trends: high rewards accruing to those in management and to the technically highly qualified and skilled, and a relative decline in the rewards of clerical work. As for status inequality (allowing for the 'softness' of the data and their paucity for socialist systems, except Poland), various studies suggest a common structure of occupational prestige. For example, according to Sarapata, the correlation between the occupational prestige hierarchies of Poland and the United States is 0·882, Poland and England 0·862 and Poland and West Germany 0·879.[31] As for inequalities of power, apart from the obvious differences, parallels can be seen in the differential distribution of power and authority (whether in the form of legal ownership or directive control) within 'imperatively co-ordinated associations', such as the industrial enterprise; conversely, a tendency towards political pluralism, albeit of a highly restricted and managed type, has been observed in communist systems.[32]

Of the inequalities charcteristic of capitalism, the most obvious is that of wealth. It has been justly said that 'capitalism produces extremely rich people with a great deal of capital, and this is the most striking difference between the two systems'.[33] Moreover, such capital 'means so much more than the income it provides: security, diminished pressure to save and (in very large quantities) political power'.[34] A recent study of the subject in Britain[35] estimates that the top 5 per cent of wealth holders own between one-half and three-quarters of the total personal wealth. There has, it is true, been a long-term trend towards a greater spread of such wealth, but this has mainly been from the top 1 per cent to the next 4 or 5 per cent (that is, to relatives and others), as a defence against taxation.[36] It has been estimated that, equally divided, the yield from private property would substantially change the overall income distribution, providing a married couple with something over £9·00 a week.[37] Similar (though less extreme) concentrations of property ownership are found in other capitalist countries. Its impact is considerable because it 'leads to unequal incomes, and concentrates control over the economy in a few hands':[38] this is

> accentuated by the fact that the very rich tend to hold their wealth in the form of company shares and real property yielding a higher return than the assets typically owned by small savers. The concentration of share ownership is even greater than that in the distribution of wealth as a whole, which is important since shares convey not only income but also rights of control, and even allowing for the increasing power of corporation managers these still remain of considerable significance.[39]

As for income inequality, after a temporary narrowing in the 1940s, it has remained relatively fixed and in some cases somewhat widened – both before direct taxation and (as far as one can estimate) after it. Over-all taxation appears to be almost neutral in relation to income and in certain cases (the United States, West Germany) directly regressive, while redistribution through the Welfare State, although it obviously aids the poor more than the rich in relative terms, is paid for by wage-earners themselves, and is mainly 'horizontal' rather than 'vertical' – that is, it takes the form of a 'life-cycle' transfer *within* social classes; moreover, these welfare facilities often tend to favour more privileged groups.[40] In general, the social democratic 'welfare approach' brings about little disturbance of the stratification system[41] – and some have claimed that there is increasing inequality at its base, with the growth of an underclass of unemployed and unemployables.[42] In capitalist societies that stratification system exhibits a cleavage between the manual and non-manual categories of occupation – not merely with respect to income (here, indeed, there is substantial overlap) but with respect to a whole range of privileges and advantages: white-collar workers have strikingly better sick pay and pension schemes, holidays and other fringe benefits, life-cycle promotion and career opportunities, long-term economic stability (including for many guaranteed salary increases), working environment, freedom of movement and from supervision, and so on. Non-manual workers 'even when they diverge are more like one another than they are like manual workers' and 'the big divide still comes between manual workers on the one hand and non-manual grades on the other'.[43] As for status inequality, such evidence as exists appears to point away from the thesis of an accommodative *embourgeoisement* of affluent workers and increasingly towards different forms of polarisation between what Kerr terms 'the managers' and the 'managed'.[44] Inequalities of political power in capitalist societies are of course manifest in the inequalities already considered, since these represent the power of the dominant class to command a disproportionate share of rewards and privileges *vis-à-vis* the subordinate class. A full consideration of this topic would also involve an examination of all the means available to the former to preserve its rewards and privileges, not only within governmental institutions, but within the administrative service, the educational system, industry, the law, mass communications, and so on, not only through coercive power but also through 'the mobilization of bias', operating anonymously through the structure of institutions (especially private property and the market), the rituals of social and political life, and ideological assumptions.[45]

The inequalities typical of state socialist societies display a different pattern. Property, in the sense of legal ownership, is, of course, largely absent: as Lane writes, 'the really significant difference in the system of social stratification compared to Western industrial societies is the absence of a private propertied class possessing great concentrations of wealth'.[46] On the other hand, following Djilas, one can argue that the white-collar intelligentsia, and the *apparatchiki* above all, exercise rights of control over the use and products of collective property and expropriate surplus value from the subordinate class. On the other hand, there is no direct inheritance of such rights, as with private property, although there is evidence of *de facto* inheritance of educational privileges. The analogy between 'legal' and 'sociological' ownership cannot be taken too far, but clearly there is a considerable hierarchy of monetary privilege and power based upon such authority roles and above all upon party membership. With respect to income inequality, this has gone through a number of phases in all socialist regimes. The general pattern is this: a highly egalitarian stage of 'socialist reconstruction', followed by a substantial widening of differentials (most pronounced in the Soviet Union with Stalin's attacks on 'equality mongering') in order to increase material incentives, followed by a subsequent move towards greater equality.[47] The current picture is one of a substantially narrower range of money incomes in socialist than in capitalist societies: thus, for example, the ratio of the lowest wage to the average in the Soviet Union is 60:112·6 and even the most extreme estimate of the total range is substantially less than what is widely accepted as true of the United States.[48] Moreover, apart from Yugoslavia, there is no structural unemployment. The stratification system has a different pattern from that in capitalist systems: social strata are distinguished by money incomes, consumption patterns, styles of life, education, use of the social services, housing, 'cultural level', but there appears to be no major 'break' or 'big divide', as under capitalism, between the manual and the non-manual strata. As Parkin suggests, in many state socialist societies highly skilled or craft manual workers enjoy a higher position in the scale of material and status rewards, and promotion prospects, than do lower white-collar employees.[49] Thus, for example, in both Poland and Yugoslavia skilled manual positions have higher occupational prestige than do lower routine, white-collar positions. Parkin suggests that the over-all reward hierarchy is as follows: '(1) White-collar intelligentsia (i.e. professional, managerial and administrative positions), (2) Skilled manual positions, (3) Lower or unqualified white collar positions, (4) Unskilled manual positions', and that the major break lies between the skilled and the unskilled.[50] Thus 'the most obvious break in the reward hierarchy occurs along the line separating the qualified professional, managerial and technical positions from the rest of the occupational order'.[51] Thus the status hierarchy does not appear to reflect and reinforce a dichotomous class structure on the Western capitalist model (though Machonin provides conflicting evidence on this point from Czechoslovakia).[52] Clearly, however, the most significant contrast between the systems lies in the hierarchy of political power. Here, despite the pluralistic tendencies identified by certain Western observers, the explicitly hierarchical, monistic and all-pervasive structure of party control, increasingly manned by the white-collar intelligentsia, is altogether distinctive.

Finally, brief mention should be made of inequalities characteristic of particular societies within these two broad systems. Thus, with respect to income inequality, the United Kingdom is more equal than the United States[53] and Norway is substantially more equal still, while the Soviet Union has carried income equalisation very far within the socialist bloc, especially through the redistributive effects of collective consumption,[54] whereas Yugoslavia has seen a marked widening of the span of incomes and life-chances, with the introduction of 'market socialism', as to a lesser extent did Czechoslovakia in the later 1960s. Other peculiarities relate to racial, religious and linguistic factors (the United States, Northern Ireland, Canada), where inconsistencies between income and status hierarchies are to be seen, and long-range historical factors, as for example in Britain, where the stratification takes a distinctive form and the concentration of wealth is especially high.[55]

The explanation of inequality can be approached in either of two ways. On the one hand, one may seek to explain why individuals attain different positions, rewards and privileges; on the other hand, one may seek to account for the allocation of rewards and privileges to different social positions. The first approach implies a focus upon inequality of opportunity among persons; the second upon inequality of reward among occupational positions. In the foregoing, I have implicitly concentrated on the second question and I have also implicitly suggested a range of explanations for inequality at different levels. Some such explanations will be historically and geographically specific. Examples are, say, the particular circumstances explaining the exceptionally high status of Poland's intelligentsia,[56] or the cultural factors in ethnically or religiously divided communities, or the long-range historical factors referred to above. Other factors explaining the differences between income distributions in different countries, and in the same country over time, are the activities of the central government

and local authorities in allocating taxes and distributing benefits, the
control of entry into occupations by professional associations and
unions, national rates of economic growth, level of unemployment, and
so on. Other explanations will be at the level of the economic system,
and will focus primarily on the institution of private property, and all
that protects and legitimates it, under capitalism; and on political
intervention, allocating rewards and privileges, in accordance with the
ruling elite's policy objectives, under state socialism. However, at the
next level, the constraints operating on both systems come into view:
the division of labour under advanced industrialism, it has been argued,
creates a certain role structure inevitably accompanied by differentials
of material reward, status and power, which are in turn perpetuated by
the nuclear family.[57] Some writers have sought explanations of
inequality at a higher level still: according to them social inequalities
arise from the functional prerequisites or basic features of all human
societies, or, more universally still, from the genetic, biological or
psychological differentiation of human nature itself.

The Realisability of Equality

This leads us naturally to the question of the alleged inevitability of
inequality. There are a number of such arguments (of which I shall cite
some typical contemporary examples), ranging from the 'hard' to the
'soft'. The hardest are those which appeal to biological and
psychological data which, it is argued, set sharp limits to the possibility
of implementing egalitarian social ideals: 'biology', writes Eysenck,
'sets an absolute barrier to egalitarianism'.[58] Then there are sociological
arguments which maintain that inequalities are functional to, or
inherent in, all possible social systems – or less strongly, in all industrial
societies. And finally, there are arguments of a different order, which
seek to show that the costs of implementing equality in contemporary
societies are unacceptably high, because they conflict with other values.

The hard-line approach to the realisability of equality is currently
taken by various participants in the contemporary debate about
genetics, environment and intelligence. Professors Jensen, Herrnstein
and Eysenck assert that 'intelligence' is mainly determined by heredity
– specifically that about 80 per cent of the variance in I.Q. scores is
genetically determined. Eysenck urges 'recognition of man's biological
nature, and the genetically determined inequality inevitably associated
with his derivation'.[59] Social class is 'determined quite strongly by I.Q.',

and educational attainment depends 'closely' on I.Q. 'talent, merit, ability' are 'largely innate factors'.[60] Eysenck maintains that 'regression to the mean' through social mobility and the redistribution of genes prevents social classes from calcifying into hereditary castes, and he concludes that a 'society which would come as near to our egalitarian desires as is biologically attainable would give the greatest scope possible to this social mobility'.[61] Herrnstein,[62] by contrast, ignores 'regression to the mean' and stresses the process of 'assortative mating' between partners of similar I.Q. levels, and foresees a future in which, as the environment becomes more favourable to the development of intelligence, social mobility increases, and technological advance sets a higher premium on intelligence, social classes will become ever more caste-like, stratifying society into a hereditary meritocracy. Finally, Jensen, observing that some racial groups, especially American whites and blacks, differ markedly in their distribution of I.Q. scores (the mean I.Q. differing from 10 to 15 points), concludes that, since no known environmental factors can explain such differences, their explanation must be largely genetic. In his recent book, he affirms the hypothesis that 'something between one-half and three-fourths of the average I.Q. difference between American Negroes and Whites is attributable to genetic factors, and the remainder to environmental factors and their interaction with the genetic differences'.[63] He attaches much importance to this conclusion, since he believes that I.Q. is a major determinant of success in our society.

These claims obviously cannot be adequately considered here, but a few remarks are worth making. First the estimate of 80 per cent genetic determination of I.Q. is controversial. Others suggest a substantially lower figure. According to Jencks it is something like 45 per cent: Jencks and his colleagues estimate that 'genotype explains about 45 per cent of the variance in I.Q. scores, that environment explains about 35 per cent, and that the correlation between genotype and environment explains the remaining 20 per cent'.[64] Moreover, the evidence with respect to genetic determination is far less univocal than these writers imply: 'different methods of estimating the heritability of test scores yield drastically different results' and 'studies of different populations yield somewhat different results'.[65] Again, children's test scores are not immune to considerable improvement by effecting changes in their environment. Eysenck suggests that 'Clearly [*sic*] the whole course of development of a child's intellectual capabilities is largely laid down genetically',[66] yet this is strikingly contradicted by a number of twin and adoption studies.[67] Second, psychologists notoriously differ about what I.Q. tests measure: some, such as Jensen, Herrnstein and Eysenck, believe it measures some basic property of the intellect; others believe that intelligence is multidimensional, that it cannot be measured by a single number, and (according to many authorities) that that number in any case measures educationally and culturally specific aptitudes with limited wider applicability. Third, and related to this last point, it has been established (at least for the United States) that (1) social class is not, *pace* Eysenck, 'determined strongly' by I.Q.; (2) educational attainment depends less on I.Q. than on family background; and (3) I.Q. is not a major determinant of economic and social success.[68] Fourth, the difference in average I.Q. test performance between blacks and whites is consistent with all three of the following hypotheses: that it is explained by genes, by environment, and by both.[69] Moreover, it appears indisputable that present data and techniques cannot resolve this issue. It certainly has not been established that one can extrapolate from genetic determinants of differences within a population to explain mean differences between populations. And it is worth observing that, in any case, genetic differences within races are far greater than those between them, accounting for 60–70 per cent of all human genetic variation. In general, it appears entirely reasonable to conclude with Jencks that it is 'wrong to argue that genetic inequality dictates a hierarchical society'.[70] This is so even if Jensen should turn out to be nearer the truth than Jencks, and heredity does substantially constrain the maximum achievable by different individuals in the best of all possible environments. For, as we have argued, the principle of equal respect requires, in Tawney's words, that society's organisation be planned so that 'whether their powers are great or small, all its members may be equally enabled to make the best of such powers as they possess'. Since this requires the equalisation of rewards and privileges, biological differences would correlate with social positions but not with unequal rewards and privileges attaching to those positions.

Sociological arguments for the inevitability of inequality are of two broad types. One is that inequalities are functionally necessary for any society, the other that they are inherent in the very nature of social life. A much-discussed example of the former is the so-called functionalist theory of stratification; an interesting instance of the latter is furnished by Ralf Dahrendorf.

Davis and Moore's 'functionalist theory of stratification' seeks to demonstrate 'the universal necessity which calls forth stratification in any social system'.[71] It advances the following propositions:

(1) Certain positions in any society are functionally more important than others.

(2) Adequate performance in these positions requires appropriate talents and training.

(3) Some such talents are scarce in any population.

(4) It is necessary (a) to induce those with the requisite talents to undergo the sacrifice of acquiring the appropriate training; (b) to attract them to the functionally important positions; and (c) to motivate them to perform in these positions adequately.

(5) To achieve these objectives, differential incentives must be attached to the posts in question – and these may be classified into those things which contribute to (i) 'sustenance and comfort'; (ii) 'humor and diversion'; and (iii) 'self-respect and ego expansion'.[72]

(6) These differential incentives (unequal rewards) constitute social inequality, which, in securing that the most talented individuals occupy and adequately perform in the functionally important positions, fulfils a necessary function in any society: 'Social inequality is thus an unconsciously evolved device by which societies insure that the most important positions are conscientiously filled by the most qualified persons.'[73]

Controversy over this theory has raged for well over two decades,[74] and it is fair to say that the balance of the argument has largely lain with the theory's critics. There is the evident difficulty of identifying the 'functionally important' positions, as distinct from those which a given society values as important (bankers or miners? elementary or university teachers?) and the dubious assumption that training for these positions is sacrificial (especially since there would, presumably, be no material loss in an egalitarian society). Also, it ignores the point that a stratified society itself restricts the availability of talent and the further point that an advanced industrial society is in principle able substantially to increase the availability of talent and training. A further weakness of the theory is its assumption that unequal rewards (defined in a most culture-specific way) are the only possible means of mobilising qualified individuals into adequately performing important jobs. It leaves out of account the intrinsic benefits of different positions, in relation to the expectations, aptitudes and aspirations of different individuals (potential surgeons being anyway attracted by practising surgery and potential carpenters by carpentry); and it fails in general to consider functional alternatives to a system of unequal rewards – such as intrinsic job satisfaction, the desire for knowledge, skills and authority, an ethos of social or public service and a diminution of acquisitiveness and status-seeking, the use of negotiation, persuasion or direct planning, changes in the organisation of work and decision-making, and so on. Finally, to the extent to which the thesis does remain valid, at least for contemporary industrial societies – that is, in so far as unequal rewards are needed so that certain jobs are adequately filled – this in no way implies a society-wide system of structured social inequality, linking wealth, income, status and power (indeed, it would probably imply the reverse); nor is it plausible to suggest that the range and scope of actual inequalities, such as those surveyed in the previous section of this chapter, can be explained in this beneficently functional manner. It is, incidentally, noteworthy that liberal reformers in East European countries have used arguments analogous to Davis and Moore's to justify the widening of income differentials (as did Stalin in the 1930s). But the Davis–Moore theory does not specify any particular range of inequality as functionally necessary – or rather, it all too easily serves to justify any such range which its proponents may seek to defend or establish.

Dahrendorf's theory seeks to demonstrate that 'inequalities among men follow from the very concept of societies as moral communities . . . the idea of a society in which all distinctions of rank between men are abolished transcends what is sociologically possible and has its place in the sphere of poetic imagination alone'.[75] The thesis is essentially this: that '(1) every society is a moral community, and therefore recognises norms which regulate the conduct of its members; and (2) there have to be sanctions connected with these norms which guarantee their obligatory character by acting as rewards for conformism and penalties for deviance',[76] from which Dahrendorf concludes that 'the sanctioning of human behaviour in terms of social norms necessarily creates a system of inequality of rank and that social stratification is therefore an immediate result of the control of social behaviour by positive and negative sanctions'.[77] But the conclusion does not follow from the premises. It does not follow from the mere existence of social norms and the fact that their enforcement discriminates against those who do not or cannot (because of their social position) conform to them that a society-wide system of inequality and 'rank order of social status' are 'bound to emerge'.[78] Dahrendorf slides unaccountably from the undoubted truth that within groups norms are enforced which discriminate against certain persons and positions (he cites the example of gossiping neighbours making the professional woman an outsider) to the unsupported claim that, within society as a whole, a system of inequality between groups and positions is inevitable. To support that claim he would need to show the necessity of society-wide norms whose enforcement necessarily discriminates between persons and social positions, and this he fails to do. Nothing he says rules out the empirical possibility of a society containing a plurality of norms, each conferring and withholding status and prestige (so that gossiping neighbours look down on professional women, and vice versa), without themselves being ranked within a single system of inequality or stratification.

Finally, I turn to the argument that inequality is eradicable only at an unacceptable cost. This argument has been voiced in many forms, by those both friendly and hostile to socialism. A forceful contemporary formulation is that of Frank Parkin, who argues:

> A political system which guarantees constitutional rights for groups to organise in defence of their interests is almost bound to favour the privileged at the expense of the disprivileged. The former will always have greater organizing capacities and facilities than the latter, such that the competition for rewards between different classes is never an equal contest. This is not merely because the dominant class can more easily be mobilized in defence of its interests, but also because it has access to the all-important means of social control, both coercive and normative. Given this fundamental class inequality in the social and economic order, a pluralist or democratic political structure works to the advantage of the dominant class.[79]

What this argument perhaps suggests, Parkin writes, is that

> socialist egalitarianism is not readily compatible with a pluralist political order of the classic western type. Egalitarianism seems to require a political system in which the state is able continually to hold in check those social and occupational groups which, by virtue of their skills or education or personal attributes, might otherwise attempt to stake claims to a disproportionate share of society's rewards. The most effective way of holding such groups in check is by denying them the right to organise politically or in other ways to undermine social equality.[80]

But historical experience of this approach has been pretty uniform:

gross abuses of constitutional rights, terrorism and coercion, and, even when these latter are relaxed, the continuance of party control over all areas of social life, including literature and the arts. As Parkin observes,

> The fact that the humanistic ideals central to the socialist tradition have found little, if any, expression in the European socialist states highlights an unresolved dilemma; namely, whether it is possible to establish the political conditions for egalitarianism while also guaranteeing civil rights to all citizens within a system of 'socialist legality'.[81]

Conclusions

Fortunately, this is not the place to enter into the whole question of the 'socialist transition'. I merely wish to conclude this chapter with three brief observations. The first is that the massive inequalities of power and privilege outlined in the second section are, for many socialists, intolerable mainly because they violate something like the principle of equal respect delineated in the first section – a principle which derives from liberal premises, but which takes them seriously. The second is that the arguments for the unrealisability of equality considered in the third section all fail to show that these inequalities are ineradicable, whether on psychological or sociological grounds. And the third is that the argument that the costs of implementing equality are too high is the most crucial facing any socialist today. And it is perhaps the inclination to see the accumulated weight of historical evidence for the apparent need to pay such costs – from the rise of Stalin to the fall of Allende – as a challenge rather than as a source of despair that is, in the end, the distinguishing mark of an egalitarian socialist.

Part 2

Rationality and Relativism

Chapter 6

Some Problems about Rationality[1]

In what follows I shall discuss a philosophical problem arising out of the practice of anthropologists and sociologists which may be stated, in a general and unanalysed form, as follows: when I come across a set of beliefs which appear *prima facie* irrational, what should be my attitude towards them? Should I adopt a critical attitude, taking it as a fact about the beliefs that they *are* irrational, and seek to explain how they came to be held, how they manage to survive unprofaned by rational criticism, what their consequences are, and so on? Or should I treat such beliefs charitably: should I begin from the assumption that what appears to me to be irrational may be interpreted as rational when fully understood in its context? More briefly, the problem comes down to whether or not there are alternative standards of rationality.

There are, of course, a number of different issues latent in the problem as I have stated it. In particular, it will be necessary to distinguish between the different ways in which beliefs may be said to be irrational. There are, for example, important differences and asymmetries between falsehood, inconsistency and nonsense. Also there are different sorts of belief; indeed there are difficult problems about what is to count as a belief. Let us, however, leave the analysis of the problem until a later stage in the argument.

First, I shall set out a number of different answers to it that have been offered by anthropologists and philosophers with respect to primitive magical and religious beliefs. In doing so I make no claim to comprehensiveness. These and related issues have been widely debated throughout the history of anthropology; all I aim to do here is to compare a number of characteristic positions. It is, however, worth stressing at this point that I do not pose the problem as a problem *in* anthropology but rather as a philosophical problem[2] raised in a particularly acute form by the practice of anthropology. It is raised, though in a less clear-cut form, by all sociological and historical inquiry that is concerned with beliefs.

Second, I shall try to separate out a number of distinct criteria of rationality which almost all discussions of these issues have confused. Finally, I shall make some attempt at showing which of these criteria are context-dependent and which are universal, and why.

Let us compare for plausibility five different answers to the problem.

(1) First, there is the view that the seeming irrationality of the beliefs involved in primitive religion and magic constitutes no problem, for those beliefs are to be interpreted as *symbolic*. Take, for instance, the following passages from Dr Leach:

> a very large part of the anthropological literature on religion concerns itself amost wholly with a discussion of the content of belief and of the rationality or otherwise of that content. Most such arguments seem to me to be scholastic nonsense. As I see it, myth regarded as a statement in words 'says' the same thing as ritual regarded as a statement in action. To ask questions about the content of belief which are not contained in the content of ritual is nonsense. . . . In parts of this book I shall make frequent reference to Kachin mythology but I shall make no attempt to find any logical coherence in the myths to which I refer. Myths for me are simply one way of describing certain types of human behaviour.[3]

And again,

> the various nats of Kachin religious ideology are, in the last analysis, nothing more than ways of describing the formal relationships that exist between real persons and real groups in ordinary human Kachin society.
>
> The gods denote the good relationships which carry honour and respect, the spooks and the witches denote the bad relationships of

jealousy, malice and suspicion. Witchcraft becomes manifest when the moral constraints of the ideally correct social order lose their force.[4]

Professor Firth argues, in a similar fashion, that judgement about the rationality of beliefs is irrelevant to the purposes of the anthropologist. It is, he writes, 'not important for an anthropological study whether witches exist or not . . . we are dealing here only with human relations'.[5] Religious experience

is essentially a product of human problems, dispositions and relationships. . . . In its own rather different way it is to some extent an alternative to art, symbolising and attributing value to human existence and human endeavour. . . . At the level of human dilemma, creative activity and symbolic imagery, indeed, religious concepts and values can be taken as real; they are true in their context. With the claim that their basic postulates have an autonomous, absolute validity I do not agree. But to us anthropologists the important thing is their *affirmation* of their autonomy, their validity, their truth – not the metaphysical question, whether they are correct in saying so. Basically, in an anthropological study of religion, as in studies of art, we are concerned with the relevance of such affirmations rather than with their ultimate validity.[6]

The most systematic recent statement of this position is by Dr Beattie.[7] According to Beattie, beliefs associated with ritual are essentially expressive and symbolic. Thus, '[f]or the magician, as for the artist, the basic question is not whether his ritual is true in the sense of corresponding exactly with some empirically ascertainable reality, but rather whether it says, in apt symbolic language, what it is sought, and held important, to say'.[8] More generally,

although not all of what we used to call 'primitive' thought is mystical and symbolic, some is, just as some – though less – of 'western' thought is. If it is 'explanatory', it is so in a very different way from science. Thus it requires its own distinct kind of analysis. No sensible person subjects a sonnet or a sonata to the same kind of examination and testing as he does a scientific hypothesis, even though each contains it own kind of 'truth'. Likewise, the sensible student of myth, magic and religion will, I think, be well advised to recognise that their tenets are not scientific propositions, based on experience and on a belief in the uniformity of nature, and that they cannot be adequately understood as if they were. Rather, as symbolic statements, they are to be understood by a delicate investigation of the levels and varieties of meaning which they have for their practitioners, by eliciting, through comparative and contextual study, the principles of association in terms of which they are articulated, and by investigating the kinds of symbolic classifications which they imply.[9]

Thus the first answer to our problem amounts to the refusal to answer it, on the grounds that it is nonsensical (Leach), or irrelevant (Firth), or misdirected (Beattie).[10]

(2) The second answer to the problem comes down to the claim that there are certain criteria which we can apply both to modern and to primitive beliefs which show the latter to be quite incomprehensible. (I leave until later the question of whether this claim is itself intelligible.)

As an example, take the following passage from Elsdon Best:

The mentality of the Maori is of an intensely mystical nature. . . . We hear of many singular theories about Maori beliefs and Maori thought, but the truth is that we do not understand either, and, what is more, we never shall. We shall never know the inwardness of the native mind. For that would mean tracing our steps, for many centuries, back into the dim past, far back to the time when we also possessed the mind of primitive man. And the gates have long closed on that hidden road.[11]

A similar view was expressed by the Seligmans about the tribes of the Pagan Sudan: 'On this subject [of magic] the black man and the white regard each other with amazement: each considers the behaviour of the other incomprehensible, totally unrelated to everyday experience, and entirely disregarding the known laws of cause and effect.'[12]

(3) The third answer amounts to the hypothesis that primitive magical and religious beliefs are attempted explanations of phenomena. This involves the claim that they satisfy certain given criteria of rationality by virtue of certain rational procedures of thought and observation being followed; on the other hand they are (more or less) mistaken and to be judged as (more or less) unsuccessful explanations against the canons of science (and modern common sense).

The classical exponents of this position were Tylor and Frazer, especially in their celebrated 'intellectualist' theory of magic. Professor Evans-Pritchard has succinctly summarised their standpoint as follows:

They considered that primitive man had reached his conclusions about the efficacy of magic from rational observation and deduction in much the same way as men of science reach their conclusions about natural laws. Underlying all magical ritual is a rational process of thought. The ritual of magic follows from its ideology. It is true that the deductions of a magician are false – had they been true they would have been scientific and not magical – but they are nevertheless based on genuine observation. For classification of phenomena by the similarities which exist between them is the procedure of science as well as of magic and is the first essential process of human knowledge. Where the magician goes wrong is in inferring that because things are alike in one or more respects they have a mystical link between them whereas in fact the link is not a real link but an ideal connection in the mind of the magician. . . . A causal relationship exists in his mind but not in nature. It is a subjective and not an objective connection. Hence the savage mistakes an ideal analogy for a real connection.[13]

Their theory of religion was likewise both rationalistic and derogatory: Frazer in particular held religion to be less rational (though more complex) than the 'occult science' of magic because it postulated a world of capricious personal beings rather than a uniform law-governed nature.[14]

There has recently been elaborated a highly sophisticated version of this position on the part of a number of writers, who have stressed the explanatory purport of primitive magical and religious beliefs. In a brilliant paper,[15] Dr Robin Horton treats traditional African religious systems as theoretical models akin to those of the sciences, arguing that many of the supposed differences between these two modes of thought result, more than anything else, from differences of idiom used in their respective theoretical models. He is less interested in the contrasts revealed by the content of the two sorts of theories than in the continuities to be found in their respective aims and methods. In both cases there is: (i) a quest for explanation by seeking unity underlying apparent diversity, simplicity underlying apparent complexity, order underlying apparent disorder, regularity underlying apparent anomaly; (ii) the placing of things in a causal context wider than that provided by common sense; (iii) the playing of a complementary role to common sense; (iv) the variation of theoretical level according to context; (v) explanation by means of abstraction, analysis and reintegration; (vi) the use of analogy between puzzling observations to be explained and already familiar phenomena; (vii) the restriction to only limited aspects of such phenomena; and (viii) the development of theoretical models obscuring the original analogies.[16] As an example, Horton takes the case of the diagnosis of disease in traditional Africa, which, though reference is made to spiritual agencies, usually identifies 'the human hatreds, jealousies, and misdeeds, that have brought such agencies into play':[17] he even argues that such diagnosis often offers highly plausible social-cause explanations of sickness, both bodily and mental. More generally, his aim is to break down the contrast between traditional religious thought as 'non-empirical' and scientific thought as 'empirical':

> In the first place, the contrast is misleading because traditional religious thought is no more nor less interested in the natural causes of things than is the theoretical thought of the sciences. Indeed, the intellectual function of its supernatural beings (as, too, that of atoms, waves, *etc*) *is* the extension of people's vision of natural causes. In the second place, the contrast is misleading because traditional religious theory clearly does more than postulate causal connexions that bear no relation to experience. Some of the connexions it postulates are, by the standards of modern medical science, almost certainly real ones. To some extent, then, it successfully grasps reality. . . . Given the basic process of theory-making, and an environmental stability which gives theory plenty of time to adjust to experience, a people's belief-system may come, even in the absence of scientific method, to grasp at least some significant causal connexions which lie beyond the range of common sense.[18]

Horton's case is not that traditional magico-religious thought is a variety of scientific thought but that both aim at and partially succeed in grasping causal connections. He also, of course, maintains that 'scientific method is undoubtedly the surest and most efficient tool for arriving at beliefs that are successful in this respect'[19] and examines the different ways in which traditional and scientific thought relate to experience; his case is that these can ultimately be traced to the differences between 'closed' traditional cultures 'characterised by lack of awareness of alternatives, sacredness of beliefs, and anxiety about threats to them' and 'open' scientifically orientated cultures 'characterised by awareness of alternatives, diminished sacredness of beliefs, and diminished anxiety about threats to them'.[20]

Thus the third answer to our problem involves the application of given rational criteria to *prima facie* irrational beliefs which show them to be largely rational in method, purpose and form, though unscientific, and more or less (for Tylor and Frazer, entirely; for Horton, less than we thought) irrational in content. Durkheim put this case, with customary clarity, as follows:

> it is through [primitive religion] that a first explanation of the word has been made possible. . . . When I learn that *A* regularly precedes *B*, my knowledge is enriched by a new item, but my understanding is not at all satisfied with a statement which does not appear rationally justified. I commence to *understand* only when it is possible for me to conceive *B* in a perspective that makes it appear to me as something that is not foreign to *A*, as united to *A* by some intelligible relationship. The great service that the religions have rendered to thought is that they have constructed a first representation of what these intelligible relationships between things might be. In the circumstances under which it was attempted, the enterprise could obviously attain only precarious results. But then, does it ever attain any that are definitive, and is it not necessary ceaselessly to reconsider them? And also, it is less important to succeed than to try. . . . The explanations of contemporary science are surer of being objective because they are more methodical and because they rest on more rigorously controlled observations, but they do not differ in nature from those which satisfy primitive thought.[21]

(4) The fourth position we are to consider is that of Lucien Lévy-Bruhl (until the time of writing *Les Carnets*). This is, as we shall see, crucially ambiguous on the point of concern to us.[22]

Lévy-Bruhl's central theme was to emphasise the differences between the content of two types of beliefs (seen as Durkheimian *représentations collectives*):[23] those characteristic of primitive societies and those characteristic of 'scientific' thinking. He tried to bring out those aspects in which these two types of belief differed; as he wrote: 'I intended to bring fully to light the mystical *aspect* of primitive mentality in contrast with the rational *aspect* of the mentality of our societies.'[24] Thus primitive beliefs were characteristically mystical, in the sense of being committed to 'forces, influences, powers imperceptible to the senses, and never the less real'.[24] Indeed,

the reality in which primitives move is itself mystical. There is not a being, not an object, not a natural phenomenon that appears in their collective representations in the way that it appears to us. Almost all that we see therein escapes them, or is a matter of indifference to them. On the other hand, they see many things of which we are unaware.[26]

Furthermore, their thought is (in his confusing but revealing term) 'prelogical':[27] that is '[it] is not constrained above all else, as ours is, to avoid contradictions. The same logical exigencies are not in its case always present. What to our eyes is impossible or absurd, it sometimes will admit without seeing any difficulty.'[28]

Lévy-Bruhl endorsed Evans-Pritchard's account of his viewpoint as seeking 'to understand the characteristics of mystical thought and to define these qualities and to compare them with the qualities of scientific thought';[29] thus it is 'not in accord with reality and may also be mystical where it assumes the existence of suprasensible forces'[30] and is not '"logical" in the sense in which a modern logician would use the term',[31] so that 'primitive beliefs when tested by the rules of thought laid down by logicians are found to contravene those rules'.[32] 'Objects, beings, phenomena' could be 'in a manner incomprehensible to us, at once both themselves and something other than themselves'.[33] Thus according to given criteria derived from 'scientific' thought, 'mystical' and 'pre-logical' thought was to be judged unsuccessful. Yet Lévy-Bruhl also wants to say that there are criteria which it satisfies. Hence, he wants to say that there is a sense in which the supra-sensible forces are 'real'. Thus, as we have seen, he writes of mystical forces as being 'never the less real'.[34] (On the other hand, he came to see that the primitive is not uniquely preoccupied with the mystical powers of beings and objects[35] and has a basic, practical notion of reality too.) Again, he explicitly endorses Evans-Pritchard's interpretation that 'primitive thought is eminently coherent, perhaps over-coherent. . . . Beliefs are co-ordinated with other beliefs and behaviour into an organised system.'[36] Yet he is crucially ambiguous about the nature of this coherence. On the one hand he writes that it is 'logical': '[t]he fact that the "*patterns of thought*" are different does not, once the premises have been given, prevent the "primitive" from reasoning like us and, in this sense, his thought is neither more nor less "logical" than ours'.[37] Yet, on the other hand, he appears to accept the propositions that mystical thought is 'intellectually consistent even if it is not logically consistent'[38] and that it is 'organised into a coherent system with a logic of its own'.[39]

Thus Lévy-Bruhl's position is an uneasy compromise, maintaining that primitive 'mystical' and 'prelogical' beliefs are on our standards irrational, but that on other (unspecified) standards they are about 'real' phenomena and 'logical'.[40]

(5) The fifth answer to our problem asserts that there is a strong case for assuming that, in principle, seemingly irrational belief-systems in primitive societies are to be interpreted as rational. It has been most clearly stated by Professor Peter Winch,[41] and it has been claimed that Evans-Pritchard's book *Nuer Religion* supports it.[42] According to Winch's view, when an observer is faced with seemingly irrational beliefs in a primitive society, he should seek contextually given criteria according to which they may appear rational.

Winch objects to Evans-Pritchard's approach in *Witchcraft, Oracles and Magic among the Azande* on the grounds that the criteria of rationality which he applies there are alien to the context. According to Evans-Pritchard:

> It is an inevitable conclusion from Zande descriptions of witchcraft that it is not an objective reality. The physiological condition which is said to be the seat of witchcraft, and which I believe to be nothing more than food passing through the small intestine, is an objective condition, but the qualities they attribute to it and the rest of their beliefs about it are mystical. Witches, as Azande conceive them, cannot exist.[43]

Winch objects to this position on the ground that it relies upon a notion of 'objective reality' provided by science: for Evans-Pritchard 'the scientific conception agrees with what reality actually is like, whereas the magical conception does not',[44] but, Winch maintains, it is a mistake to appeal to any such independent or objective reality. What counts as real depends on the context and the language used (thus 'it is *within* the religious use of language that the conception of God's reality has its place');[45] moreover, '[w]hat is real and what is unreal shows itself *in* the sense that language has ... we could not in fact distinguish the real from the unreal without understanding the way this distinction operates in the language'.[46] Thus European scepticism is misplaced and (we must suppose) Zande witchcraft is real.

Again, Winch objects to Evans-Pritchard's account of contra-dictions in the Zande belief-system. The Zande believe that a suspect may be proved a witch by post-mortem examination of his intestines for witchcraft-substance; they also believe that this is inherited through the male line. Evans-Pritchard writes:

> To our minds it appears evident that if a man is proven a witch the whole of his clan are *ipso facto* witches, since the Zande clan is a group of persons related biologically to one another through the male line. Azande see the sense of this argument but they do not accept its conclusions, and it would involve the whole notion of witchcraft in contradiction were they to do so. . . . Azande do not perceive the contradiction as we perceive it because they have no theoretical interest in the subject, and those situations in which they express their belief in witchcraft do not force the problem upon them.[47]

Winch's comment on this passage is that

> the context from which the suggestion about the contradiction is made, the context of our scientific culture, is not on the same level as the context in which the beliefs about witchcraft operate. Zande notions of witchcraft do not constitute a theoretical sytem in terms of which Azande try to gain a quasi-scientific understanding of the world. This in its turn suggests that it is the European, obsessed with pressing Zande thought where it would not naturally go – to a contradiction – who is guilty of misunderstanding, not the Zande. The European is in fact committing a category-mistake.[48]

Thus Winch's complaint against Evans-Pritchard's treatment of the Azande is 'that he did not take seriously enough the idea that the concepts used by primitive peoples can only be interpreted in the context of the way of life of these peoples';[49] thus we cannot legislate about what is real for them or what counts as a contradiction in their beliefs.[50] Moreover, Winch goes on to argue, rationality itself is context- or culture-dependent. 'We start', he writes, 'from the position that standards of rationality in different societies do not always coincide; from the possibility, therefore, that the standards of rationality current in S are different from our own . . . what we are concerned with are differences in *criteria of rationality*'.[51] He objects to the view, expressed by Professor MacIntyre, that 'the beginning of an explanation of why certain criteria are taken to be rational in some societies is that they *are* rational. And since this last has to enter into our explanation we cannot explain social behaviour independently of our own norms of rationality'.[52] Winch's case against this is that rationality in the end comes down to 'conformity to norms'; how this notion is to be applied to a given society 'will depend on our reading of their conformity to norms – what counts for them as conformity and what does not'.[53]

Let us see how Evans-Pritchard's *Nuer Religion* could be seen as an exemplification of Winch's approach. In the chapter entitled 'The Problem of Symbols' Evans-Pritchard attempts to show that the Nuer, although they *appear* to say contradictory and inconsistent things, do not really do so. Thus,

> It seems odd, if not absurd, to a European when he is told that a twin is a bird as though it were an obvious fact, for Nuer are not saying that a twin is like a bird, but that he is a bird. There seems to be complete contradiction in the statement; and it was precisely on statements of this kind recorded by observers of primitive peoples that Lévy-Bruhl based his theory of the prelogical mentality of these peoples, its chief characteristic being, in his view, that it permits such evident contradictions – that a thing can be what it is and at the same time something altogether different.[54]

However, 'no contradiction is involved in the statement which, on the contrary, appears quite sensible and even true, to one who presents the idea to himself in the Nuer language and within their system of religious thought'.[55]

According to Evans-Pritchard,

> the Nuer do not make, or take, the statement that twins are birds in any ordinary sense . . . in addition to being men and women they are of a twin-birth, and a twin-birth is a special revelation of Spirit; and Nuer express this special character of twins in the 'twins are birds' formula because twins and birds, though for different reasons, are both associated with Spirit and this makes twins, like birds, 'people of the above' and 'children of God', and hence a bird is a suitable symbol in which to express the special relationship in which a twin stands to God.[56]

Thus, it seems, Evans-Pritchard is claiming that according to Nuer criteria this statement is rational and consistent, indeed 'quite sensible and even true'. As he writes, towards the end of the book, 'It is in the nature of the subject that there should be ambiguity and paradox. I am aware that in consequence I have not been able to avoid *what must appear to the reader to be obscurities, and even contradictions, in my account.*'[57]

We shall return below to this example and to the question of whether in fact it is a practical application of Winch's views. Here let us merely restate the fifth answer to our problem: that it is likely in principle that beliefs that appear to be irrational can be reinterpreted as rational, in the light of criteria of rationality to be discovered in the culture in which they occur. (Of course, individual beliefs may fail according to these criteria, but Winch seems to hold that no reasonably large set of beliefs could do so.)

The use of the word 'rational' and its cognates has caused untold confusion and obscurity, especially in the writings of sociological theorists.[58] This, however, is not the best reason for seeking to break our problem down into different elements. There are strong reasons for suspecting that the first mistake is to suppose that there is a single answer to it; and this suspicion is only reinforced by the very plausibility of most of the statements cited in the foregoing section.

What is it for a belief or set of beliefs to be irrational? A belief may be characterised as a proposition accepted as true.[59] Beliefs, or sets of beliefs, are said to be irrational if they are inadequate in certain ways: (i) if they are illogical, for example, inconsistent or (self-) contradictory, consisting of or relying on invalid inferences, and so on; (ii) if they are, partially or wholly, false; (iii) if they are nonsensical (though it may be questioned whether they would then qualify as propositions and thus as beliefs); (iv) if they are situationally spcific or *ad hoc*, that is, not universalised because bound to particular occasions;[60] (v) if the ways in which they come to be held or the manner in which they are held are seen as deficient in some respect. For example: (*a*) the beliefs may be based, partially or wholly, on irrelevant considerations; (*b*) they may be based on insufficient evidence; (*c*) they may be held uncritically, that is, not held open to refutation or modification by experience, regarded as 'sacred' and protected by 'secondary elaboration' against disconfirming evidence;[61] (*d*) the beliefs may be held unreflectively, without conscious consideration of their assumptions and implications, relations to other beliefs, and so on (though here the irrationality may be predicated of the believer rather than the belief).

In addition, there are other well-used senses of 'rational' as applied to actions, such as (vi) the widest sense of simply goal-directed action;[62] (vii) the sense in which an action is said to be (maximally) rational if what is in fact the most efficient means is adopted to achieve a given end;[63] (viii) the sense in which the means that is believed by the agent to be the most efficient is adopted to achieve the agent's end (whatever it may be); (ix) the sense in which an action is in fact conducive to the agent's (expressed or unexpressed) 'long-term' ends; (x) the sense in which the agent's ends are the ends he ought to have.[64]

In this section I shall suggest that some criteria of rationality[65] are universal, that is relevantly applicable to all beliefs, in any context, while others are context-dependent, that is, are to be discovered by investigating the context and are only relevantly applicable to beliefs in that context. I shall argue (as against Winch) that beliefs are not only to be evaluated by the criteria that are to be discovered in the context in which they are held; they must also be evaluated by criteria of rationality that simply *are* criteria of rationality, as opposed to criteria of rationality in context *c*. In what follows universal criteria will be called 'rational (*1*) criteria' and context-dependent criteria 'rational (*2*) criteria'.

Let us assume we are discussing the beliefs of a society *S*. One can then draw a distinction between two sets of questions. One can ask, in the first place: (i) what for society *S* are the criteria of rationality *in general*? And, second, one can ask: (ii) what are the appropriate criteria to apply to a given class of beliefs within that society?

(i) In so far as Winch seems to be saying that the answer to the first question is culture-dependent, he must be wrong, or at least we could never know if he were right; indeed we cannot even conceive what it could *be* for him to be right. In the first place, the existence of a common *reality* is a necessary precondition of our understanding *S*'s language. This does not mean that we and the members of *S* must agree about all 'the facts' (which are the joint products of language and reality); any given true statement in *S*'s language may be untranslatable into ours and *vice versa*. As Whorf wrote, 'language dissects nature in many different ways'. What must be the case is that *S* must have our distinction between truth and falsity if we are to understand its language, for, if *per impossibile* it did not, we would be unable even to agree about what counts as the successful identification of public (spatio-temporally located) objects.[66] Moreover, any culture, scientific or not, which engages in successful prediction (and it is difficult to see how any society could survive which did not) must presuppose a given reality. Winch may write that '[o]ur idea of what belongs to the realm of reality is given for us in the language that we use'[67] and he may castigate Evans-Pritchard as 'wrong, and crucially wrong, in his attempt to characterise the scientific in terms of that which is "in accord with objective reality"'.[68] But, it is, so to speak, no accident that the predictions of both primitive and modern common sense and of science come off. Prediction would be absurd unless there were events to predict.[69] Both primitive and modern men predict in roughly the same ways; also they can learn each other's languages. Thus they each assume an independent reality, which they share.

In the second place, S's language must have operable logical rules and not all of these can be pure matters of convention. Winch states that 'logical relations between propositions . . . depend on social relations between men'.[70] Does this imply that the concept of negation and the laws of identity and non-contradiction need not operate in S's language? If so, then it must be mistaken, for if the members of S do not possess even these, how could we ever understand their thought, their inferences and arguments? Could they even be credited with the possibility of inferring, arguing or even thinking? If, for example, they were unable to see that the truth of p excludes the truth of its denial, how could they ever communicate truths to one another and reason from them to other truths? Winch half sees this point when he writes that

> the possibilities of our grasping forms of rationality different from ours in an alien culture . . . are limited by certain formal requirements centering round the demand for consistency. But these formal requirements tell us nothing about what in particular is to *count* as consistency, just as the rules of the propositional calculus limit, but do not themselves determine, what are to be proper values of p, q, etc.[71]

But this is merely a (misleading) way of saying that it is the content of propositions, not the logical relations between them, that is 'dependent on social relations between men'.

It follows that if S has a language, it must, minimally, possess criteria of truth (as correspondence to reality) and logic, which we share with it and which simply *are* criteria of rationality. The only alternative conclusion is Elsdon Best's, indicated in position (ii) above (p. 124), which seeks to state the (self-contradictory) proposition that S's thought (and language) operate according to quite different criteria and that it is literally incomprehensible to us. But if the members of S really did not have our criteria of truth and logic, we would have no grounds for attributing to them language, thought or beliefs and would *a fortiori* be unable to make any statements about these.

Thus the first two ways that beliefs may be irrational that are specified above (p. 132) are fundamental and result from the application of rational (*1*) criteria. Moreover, it can be shown that the other types of irrationality of belief indicated there are dependent on the use of such criteria. Thus nonsense (iii) and the failure to universalise (iv) may be seen as bad logic (for example: self-contradiction and bad reasoning). Whether this is the most *useful* way to characterise a particular belief in a given case is another question. Again, the types of irrationality relating to the ways of arriving at and of holding beliefs are dependent on rational (*1*) criteria. Thus (v) (*a*)–(*d*) are simply methodological inadequacies: they result from not following certain procedures that can be trusted to lead us to truths.[72] Again, in the sense of 'rational' relating to actions, senses (vii) and (ix) require the application of rational (*1*) criteria.

Thus the general standpoint of position (3) above (p. 124) is vindicated. In so far as primitive magico-religious beliefs are logical and follow methodologically sound procedures, they are, so far, rational (*1*); in so far as they are, partially or wholly, false, they are not. Also part of Lévy-Bruhl's position is vindicated. In so far as 'mystical' and 'prelogical' can be interpreted as false and invalid, primitive (and analogous modern) beliefs are irrational (*1*).

(ii) What, now, about the question of whether there are any criteria which it is appropriate to apply to a given class of beliefs within *S*? In the first place, the context may provide criteria specifying which beliefs may acceptably go together. Such criteria may or may not violate the laws of logic. Where they do, the beliefs are characteristically labelled 'mysterious'. Then there are contextually provided criteria of *truth*;[73] thus a study of Nuer religion provides the means for deciding whether 'twins are birds' is, for the Nuer, to be counted as 'true'. Such criteria may apply to beliefs (that is, propositions accepted as true) which do not satisfy rational (*1*) criteria in so far as they do not and could not correspond with 'reality': that is, in so far as they are *in principle* neither directly verifiable nor directly falsifiable by empirical means. (They may, of course, be said to relate to 'reality' in another sense;[74] alternatively, they may be analysed in terms of the coherence or pragmatist theories of truth.) This is to disagree with Leach and Beattie, who seek to discount the fact that beliefs are accepted as true and argue that they must be interpreted metaphorically. But it is also to disagree with the Frazer–Tylor approach, which would simply count them false because they are 'non-objective'.

There are (obviously) contextually provided criteria of *meaning*.

Again, there are contextually provided criteria which make particular beliefs *appropriate* in particular circumstances. There are also contextually provided criteria which specify the best way to arrive at and hold beliefs. In general, there are contextually provided criteria for deciding what counts as a 'good reason' for holding a belief.

Thus, reverting to our schema of ways that beliefs can be irrational (pp. 132–3), it will be seen that, for any or all of a particular class of beliefs in a society, there may be contextually provided criteria according to which they are 'consistent' or 'inconsistent', 'true' or 'false', meaningful or nonsensical, appropriate or inappropriate in the circumstances, soundly or unsoundly reached, properly or improperly held, and in general based on good or bad reasons. Likewise, with respect to the rationality of actions, the context may provide criteria against which the agent's reason for acting and even the ends of his action may be judged adequate or inadequate.

Thus the first position taken above (p. 122) is largely vindicated, in so far as it is really pointing to the need to allow for contextual (for example symbolic) interpretation, but mistaken in so far as it ignores the fact that beliefs purport to be *true*[75] and relies exclusively upon the non-explanatory notion of 'metaphor'.[76] The third position is mistaken (or inadequate) only in so far as it denies (or ignores) the relevance of rational (2) criteria. The fourth position foreshadows that advanced here, but it is misleading (as Lévy-Bruhl himself came to see) in so far as it suggests that rational (1) criteria are not universal and fundamental. The fifth position is ambiguous. In so far as Winch is claiming that there are no rational (1) criteria, he appears mistaken. In so far as he is claiming that there are rational (2) criteria, he appears correct. I take the quotations from *Nuer Religion* to support the latter claim.

One may conclude that all beliefs are to be evaluated by both rational (1) and rational (2) criteria. Sometimes, as in the case of religious beliefs, rational (1) truth criteria will not take the analysis very far. Often rational (1) criteria of logic do not reveal anything positive about relations between beliefs that are to be explicated in terms of 'provides a reason for'. Sometimes rational (1) criteria appear less important than 'what the situation demands'. In all these cases, rational (2) criteria are illuminating. But they do not make rational (1) criteria dispensable. They could not, for the latter, specify the ultimate constraints to which thought is subject: that is, they are fundamental and universal in the sense that any society which posesses what we may justifiably call a language must apply them *in general*, though particular beliefs, or sets of beliefs, may violate them.

If both sorts of criteria are required for the understanding of beliefs (for they enable us to grasp their truth conditions and their interrelations), they are equally necessary to the explanation of why they are held, how they operate and what their social consequences are. Thus only by the application of rational (*1*) criteria is it possible to see how beliefs which fail to satisfy them can come to be rationally criticised, or fail to be.[77] On the other hand, it is usually only by the application of rational (*2*) criteria that the point and significance that beliefs have for those that hold them can be grasped. Rational (*1*) and rational (*2*) criteria are necessary both to understand and to explain.

Chapter 7

On the Social Determination of Truth[1]

> I think that I gained some understanding of communist Russia by studying witchcraft among the Azande (E. E. Evans-Pritchard).[2]

The argument of this chapter may be stated abstractly as follows: (1) there are no good reasons for supposing that all criteria of truth and validity are (as many have been tempted to suppose) context-dependent and variable; (2) there are good reasons for maintaining that some are not, that these are universal and fundamental, and that those criteria which *are* context-dependent are parasitic upon them; (3) it is only by assuming such universal and fundamental criteria that a number of crucial sociological questions about beliefs can be asked, among them questions about differences between 'traditional' and 'modern' or 'pre-scientific' and 'scientific' modes of thought; and therefore (4) despite many possible difficulties and pitfalls, the sociologist or anthropologist need not prohibit, indeed he should be ready to make, cognitive and logical judgements (however provisional) with respect to the beliefs he studies.

It will be seen that this argument has four distinct stages: critical, philosophical, sociological and prescriptive. None of these is conclusive in itself, but hopefully they are more effective in combination than any of them taken singly. I take them to apply quite generally to the sociology of belief, and to be as relevant (see the quotation above) to the study of primitive religion and magic as to the study of ideology in contemporary industrial societies.

Critical

A wide range of thinkers in various traditions of thought have been tempted by the view that criteria of truth, or logic, or both, arise out of different contexts and are themselves variable. The temptation consists in an urge to see the rules specifying what counts as true and/or what counts as valid reasoning as themselves relative to particular groups, cultures or communities. (I shall leave aside purely philosophical attempts to establish relativism.)[3] Among those who have succumbed to the temptation in varying degrees have been a number of sociologists of knowledge (especially Mannheim), as well as philosophically minded social anthropologists and philosophers interested in the social sciences (from Lévy-Bruhl to Winch), linguists (most notably Whorf) and, most recently, historians and philosophers of science (notably Kuhn). Among those who have successfully resisted it are other sociologists of knowledge (including Durkheim), Marxist theorists (from Marx onwards), other social anthropologists (from Frazer and Tylor to Evans-Pritchard) and other philosophers of science (such as Popper). What forms has the temptation taken?

The various forms it has taken really amount to different ways of taking seriously Pascal's observation that what it truth on one side of the Pyrenees is error on the other.[4]

Thus Mannheim writes of revising 'the thesis that the genesis of a proposition is under all circumstances irrelevant to its truth'. For him the sociology of knowledge is an attempt to analyse the 'perspectives' associated with different social positions, to study the 'orientation towards certain meanings and values which inheres in a given social position (the outlook and attitude conditioned by the collective purposes of a group), and the concrete reasons for the different perspectives which the same situation presents to the different positions in it'. He holds that social or 'existential' factors are relevant, 'not only to the genesis of ideas, but penetrate into their forms and content and . . . decisively determine [*sic*] the scope and intensity of our experience and observation'. This, he claims, has decisive implications for epistemology:

The next task of epistemology, in our opinion, is to overcome its partial nature by incorporating into itself the multiplicity of relationships between existence and validity as discovered by the sociology of knowledge; and to give attention to the types of knowledge operating in a region of being which is full of meaning and which affects the truth value of the assertions.

Yet he also writes, as though trying to resist temptation, that it 'is, of course, true that in the social sciences, as elsewhere, the ultimate criterion of truth or falsity is to be found in the investigation of the object, and the sociology of knowledge is no substitute for this'.[5]

Likewise, Lévy-Bruhl, who followed Durkheim in many respects, diverged from him in this, arguing that primitive thought violates 'our most deeply rooted mental habits, without which, it seems to us, we could no longer think': it is 'mystical, that is oriented at every moment towards occult forces . . . pre-logical, that is indifferent for most of the time to contradiction' and committed to a view of causality 'of a type other than that familiar to us'. For Lévy-Bruhl (above all in his earlier writings), primitives literally 'live, think, feel, move and act in a world which at a number of points does not coincide with ours'[6] and 'the reality in which primitives move is itself mystical'.[7] Furthermore, he began from the hypothesis that societies with different structures had different logics;[8] what he came to call 'pre-logical' thinking might violate 'our' rules but it had its own 'structure', albeit 'strange and even hostile' to 'our conceptual and logical thought'.[9] But, in his latest writings, Lévy-Bruhl too struggled to resist the temptations of this position, acknowledging that the 'mystical mentality' only defined part of the primitives' world and that 'the logical structure of the mind is the same in all known human societies'.[10]

Winch gives a general philosophical rationale for giving in to temptation. For him 'our idea of what belongs to the realm of reality is given for us in the language that we use',[11] so that '[w]hat is real and what is unreal shows itself in the sense that language has. Further, both the distinction between the real and the unreal and the concept of agreement with reality themselves belong to our language.'[12] Similarly, 'criteria of logic . . . arise out of, and are only intelligible in the context of, ways of living or modes of social life': in fact, 'logical relations between propositions themselves depend on social relations between men'.[13] Indeed, for Winch, 'standards of rationality in different societies do not always coincide' and rationality itself comes down in the end to 'conformity to norms'.[14] Yet Winch too goes some way to qualifying this position, at least with respect to logic, when he speaks of 'certain [which?] formal requirements centering round the demand for consistency' – though he (mysteriously) thinks that these 'tell us nothing about what in particular is to *count* as consistency'.[15]

Whorf's linguistic relativity principle represents a relatively unqualified form of the view we are considering. For Whorf, 'all observers are not led by the same physical evidence to the same picture of the universe, unless their linguistic backgrounds are similar, or can in some way be calibrated'. We 'dissect nature along lines laid down by our native languages'; we 'cut up and organize the spread and flow of events as we do, largely because, through our mother tongue, we are parties to an agreement to do so, not because nature itself is segmented in exactly that way for all to see'. Whorf also speaks of 'possible new types of logic' and even claims that 'science CAN have a rational or logical basis even though it be a relativistic one', which 'may vary with each tongue'. Indeed,

> when anyone, as a natural logician, is talking about reason, logic, and the laws of correct thinking, he is apt to be simply marching in step with purely grammatical facts that have somewhat of a background character in his own language or family of languages but are by no means universal in all languages and in no sense a common substratum of reason.[16]

Finally, it is worth citing some of the statements of Kuhn, who has been strongly tempted by this view in relation to scientific paradigms, whose 'incommensurability' he stresses:

> Examining the record of past research from the vantage of contemporary historiography, the historian of science may be tempted to exclaim that when paradigms change, the world itself changes with them . . . paradigm changes do cause scientists to see the world of their research-engagement differently. In so far as their only recourse to that world is through what they see and do, we may want to say that after a revolution scientists are responding to a different world.[17]

From wanting to say it, Kuhn gradually induces himself to say it. Thus he writes that at 'the very least, as a result of discovering oxygen, Lavoisier saw nature differently' and 'in the absence of some recourse to that hypothetical fixed nature that he "saw differently", the principle of economy will urge us to say that after discovering oxygen Lavoisier worked in a different world'.[18] Then, more boldly, he expresses his conviction that 'we must learn to make sense of statements that at least resemble these'; and finally, he claims that in 'a sense that I am unable to explicate further, the proponents of competing paradigms practise their trades in different worlds'. Kuhn explicitly suggests that we may need to revise the traditional 'epistemological viewpoint that has most often guided Western philosophy for three centuries' as well as our conception of scientific progress; we may 'have to relinquish the notion, explicit or implicit, that changes of paradigm carry scientists and those who learn from them closer and closer to the truth'. In paradigm choice 'there is no standard higher than the assent of the relevant community'; in fact, the 'very existence of science depends upon vesting the power to choose between paradigms in the members of a special kind of community'.[19]

So far I have tried to show how a number of thinkers with an acute sense of the diversity of human thought (whether linked to social position, as in Mannheim, or culture, as in Lévy-Bruhl and Winch, or language, as in Winch and Whorf, or changing scientific paradigms, as in Kuhn) have allowed themselves to advance the further, crucial claim that truth and validity are similarly diverse. Do they advance any good arguments to support that claim?

Briefly, they appear, with varying degrees of explicitness, to offer two sorts of argument. The first is that since men's perception and understanding of the world is ineradicably theory-dependent, there is no theory-independent reference for terms like 'the world', 'nature', 'reality', and so on,[20] and therefore no theory-independent criterion of truth; and since theories differ, as between social positions, cultures, languages or scientific communities, standards of truth likewise differ. Similarly, since men's notion of what constitutes a valid move from p to q is theory-dependent, there is no theory-independent logic, and so, for parallel reasons, canons of validity are variable. The second sort of argument, found most explicitly in Mannheim, rests on a denial of the so-called genetic fallacy and asserts that identifying the social determinants of beliefs is not irrelevant to their truth and validity – on the ground that canons of truth and validity can thereby be shown to be socially variable.

The first argument is implausible for two reasons. In the first place, no reason is given for passing from the first step to the second. The influence, however deep, of theories upon men's perceptions and understanding is one thing; the claim that there are no theory-independent objects of perception and understanding is another. Similarly, the influence of theories upon what men may count as valid or consistent is one thing; the claim that validity and consistency are theory-dependent is another. In the second place, it does not follow from the diversity of theories, or indeed from the existence of different concepts or criteria of truth and validity in different contexts, that there may not be some such criteria which are invariable because universal and fundamental (see pp. 144–7 below).

As for the second argument, to assess it fully would require a detailed analysis of the possible interpretations of 'social', 'determination' and 'belief' (not to mention 'truth' and 'validity'). Let us, briefly, assume a range of definitions of 'social' extending from the purely material or morphological (for example physical size or spatial arrangement of groups) to the purely ideational or cultural.[21] Let us take 'determination' to mean any form of explanatory relation – whether causes; or reasons, motives, desires, purposes, aspirations or interests;[22] or structural identities or correspondences.[23] Let us take 'belief' to mean a proposition accepted as true. One can now ask: if beliefs are socially determined, are there any good reasons for seeing truth and validity as variable?

First, suppose a causal relation can be established between a social factor and a belief or set of beliefs: a certain social factor is shown to have a causal influence (whether weak or strong, partial or total) on the appearance or the adoption or the maintenance of a belief or set of beliefs or on their content or their form. This provides absolutely no ground for concluding that their truth or validity are relative – a point on which Marxists, maintaining that 'social being determines consciousness', have always been clear (since they count their own theories as non-relatively true). This is true even if all beliefs are causally determined – since some men may be lucky enough to be caused to believe what is true.[24] Causation may operate on both sides of the Pyrenees, but that does not commit us to French and Spanish truths and logics.

Second, it might be shown that a certain group of persons have certain good reasons or motives to adopt or adhere to certain beliefs because such beliefs accord with their desires, purposes, aspirations or interests: beliefs are imputed to them as expressing, whether in a transparent or distorted form, their aims or interests in a particular historical situation. They believe their beliefs because they have intelligible reasons for doing so, which can be explicated by an analysis of their situation. This might be shown for all beliefs, but still nothing would follow concerning the truth or consistency of what is believed by any particular category of persons (though, again, it might be shown, as Marx thought was the case, that a certain class of men had no good reason not to believe, and every good reason to believe, what is true).

Finally, the identification of structural identities or instances of conceptual fit between beliefs on the one hand and other social factors (including beliefs) on the other can show how these beliefs cohere with other beliefs and with other features of social life, but it will not in itself have any bearing on their truth or validity.

I conclude that, among the writers we have considered, no satisfactory reason has been given for supposing that there are no invariable and context-independent criteria of truth and valid reasoning.

Philosophical

Are there, then, any good reasons for supposing that there are such criteria? I have argued elsewhere that there are,[25] and will merely summarise those arguments here. Of course, any really hard-boiled relativist could just reject these arguments as themselves relative, but to do so he must realise the full implications of the pluralistic social solipsism his position entails; thus, he cannot speak, as Mannheim does, of 'perspectives' (on what?) or, as Whorf and Kuhn do, of different ways of dissecting nature and seeing the world. The consistent relativist must take the theory-dependence of his worlds seriously.

Let us suppose we are considering the beliefs of a group of persons *G* (which may be identified in any way – as occupying a particular social position, as sharing a culture or a language, as a scientific community, and so on). Are the truth of their beliefs and the validity of their reasoning simply up to them, a function of the norms to which they conform?

I maintain that the answer to this question is no – or at least that we could never know if it were yes; indeed, that we could not even conceive what it could *be* for it to be yes. For, in the first place, the existence of a common reality is a necessary precondition of our understanding *G*'s language. Though we need not agree about all 'the facts', the members of *G* must have our distinction between truth and falsity as applied to a shared reality if we are to understand their language, for if, *per impossibile*, they did not, we and they would be unable even to agree about the successful identification of public, spatio-temporally located objects. Moreover, any group which engages in successful prediction must presuppose a given reality, since there must be (independent) events to predict. Thus, if we can in principle learn G's language (and they ours) and we know that they engage in successful prediction, then we and they share a common and independent reality.

Second, G's language must have operable logical rules and not all of these can be pure matters of convention. Winch states that 'logical relations between propositions . . . depend on social relations between men'. Does this imply that the concept of negation and the laws of identity and non-contradiction need not operate in G's language? If so, then it must be mistaken, for if the members of G do not possess even these, how could we ever understand their thought, their inferences and their arguments? Could they even be credited with the possibility of inferring, arguing or even thinking? (Lévy-Bruhl came perilously near to maintaining this.)[26] If, for example, they were unable to see that the truth of p excludes the truth of its denial, how could they ever communicate truths to one another or reason from them to other truths?

I conclude that if G has a language in which it expresses its beliefs, it must, minimally, possess criteria of truth (as correspondence to a common and independent reality)[27] and logic — which are not and cannot be context-dependent. Suppose that G's language and belief-system operated according to quite different criteria. But then, if the members of G really did not have our criteria of truth and logic, we would have no adequate grounds for attributing to them a language expressing beliefs and would *a fortiori* be unable to make any statements about these.

The argument sketched here does not, however, entail that the members of G might not, against the background of what I claim are universal criteria of truth and logic, adhere systematically to beliefs which violate those criteria. This may happen unconsciously. Thus, according to Spiro, following Frazer and Roth, the Tully River Blacks 'are ignorant of physiological paternity, believing rather that conception is the result of four kinds of "magical" causation'.[28] Again, as Evans-Pritchard reports, Azande do not perceive contradictions in their beliefs, 'because they have no theoretical interest in the subject, and those situations in which they express their beliefs in witchcraft do not force the problem upon them'; indeed, 'it would involve the whole notion of witchcraft in contradiction' were they to pursue some arguments to their conclusions.[29] On the other hand, the violation of criteria of truth and logic may be quite conscious, as when contemporary theologians explain 'seeming' contradictions as mysteries. Again, it may be relatively harmless and socially insignificant, as when a religious sect engages in fantasy and inconsistency of thought; or it may be of the greatest social and political importance, as when the ideological controls over a society involve the systematic propagation of falsehoods and incompatible beliefs.

If, as I have claimed, there are universal criteria of truth and logic, why do I wish to call these criteria fundamental? I think it can be shown that they are fundamental in at least two senses. In the first place, they specify the ultimate constraints to which all thought is subject. Thus all societies, with languages expressing beliefs, must apply them in general (though they may violate them in particular); indeed, it could be argued that they represent basic adaptive mechanisms for any human society. But they are also, I think, fundamental in a second sense: namely, that it can probably be shown that those criteria of truth and validity which are at variance with them and *are* context-dependent are in fact parasitic upon them. That is, where there are second-order native beliefs about what counts as 'true' or 'valid' which are at odds with the basic criteria, those beliefs can only be rendered fully intelligible as operating against the background of such criteria.

For example, according to Franz Steiner,[30] the Chagga have a concept of 'truth' which is 'connected with the institution of the oath', and oath, vow and swearing are 'concerned in the formation of jural relationships and in legal procedure'. Steiner attempts to sketch 'an analysis of truth concepts and their relation to structural situations' among the Chagga. Their words *lohi* or *loi* mean 'a completely reliable statement'; *Ki lohi* means 'this is true' and *Kja lohi* means 'to speak true'. Witnesses, instead of acting as instruments of verification, are 'persons who, under oath, declare their solidarity with one of the parties and his statements'. The 'story to which they finally bind themselves is *lohi*' and a 'witness in court merely agrees to the words of the party under oath. He speaks *lohi*.' But Steiner's analysis shows that among the Chagga certain structural situations require *alternative* ways of guaranteeing the reliability of statements than verification (which is the basic way); as he says, the witness 'helps to establish a "truth" because no "verification" is possible'.[31] Again, it is clearly a parasitic notion of truth which is presupposed by Stalin's favourite ideological slogan during the last two decades of his rule: that in the dialectical unity of theory and practice, theory guides practice, but practice is the criterion of theoretical truth.[32] Here practice, as officially interpreted, served as a substitute for, and functional equivalent of, verification.

This last is, clearly, an empirical question. All I claim is that, while, as Steiner says, anthropologists (and sociologists) 'are interested in the social reality of "truth" rather than in its logical connexion with verification',[33] verification is likely to provide the basic paradigm against which other criteria of truth gain their sense.

Sociological

What consequences does the assumption of universal and fundamental criteria of truth and validity have for the sociology of belief? There are, I think, at least four sorts of questions which such an assumption opens up, and which denying it closes off.

In the first place, there are questions about the content and structure of a belief-system itself. A belief-system may consist in a number of ideas, theories and doctrines that are held to be plausible and naturally related partly because a number of distinctions have not been made or conclusions drawn. The good historian of ideas does not seek merely to reproduce a belief-system; he also aims to analyse it and thereby reveal its inner structure – a structure that may not have been perceptible to the believers. In order to do this, he must apply external and critical standards – not just the standards of his own culture or period, but the closest approximation he can make to standards of rational criticism.

Thus Lovejoy describes the first task of the historian of ideas as one of 'logical analysis – the discrimination *in* the texts, and the segregating *out* of the texts, of each of . . . the basic or germinal ideas, the identification of each of them so that it can be recognized wherever it appears, in differing contexts, under different labels or phrasings, and in diverse provinces of thought'. And his next task, according to Lovejoy, is 'to examine the relations between these ideas . . . logical, psychological and historical – and, especially, under the latter, genetic – relations'. By 'logical relations' Lovejoy says he means

> relations of implication or opposition between categories, or tacit presuppositions, or express beliefs or doctrines. When he has ascertained the currency and influence of a given idea in his period, the historian does well to ask himself, what does this idea logically presuppose, what does it imply, and with what other ideas is it implicitly incompatible – whether or not these logical relations were

recognised by those who embraced the idea. For if it should turn out that some of its implications were not recognised, this may become a highly important, though negative, historical fact. Negative facts are of much more significance for the intellectual historian than is usually appreciated. The things that a writer, given his premises, might be expected to say, but doesn't say – the consequences which legitimately and fairly evidently follow from his theses, but which he never sees, or persistently refuses to draw – these may be even more noteworthy than the things he does say or the consequences he does deduce. For they may throw light upon peculiarities of his mind, especially upon his biases and the non-rational elements in his thinking – may disclose to the historian specific points at which intellectual processes have been checked, or diverted, or perverted, by emotive factors. Negative facts of this kind are thus often indicia of positive but unexplicit or sub-conscious facts. So, again, the determination of not-immediately-obvious *in*compatibilities between ideas may lead to the recognition of the historically instructive fact that one or another writer, or a whole age, has held together, in closed compartments of the mind, contradictory preconceptions or beliefs. Such a fact – like the failure to see necessary positive implications of accepted premises – calls for psychological explanation, if possible; the historian must at least seek for a hypothesis to account for it.[34]

This leads directly to the second sort of question, intimately related to the first, that assuming non-context-dependent criteria makes possible – namely, why certain beliefs continue to be believed, or cease to be. It is only through the critical application of rational standards that one can identify the mechanisms that prevent men from perceiving the falsity or inconsistency of their beliefs, or the reasons which might lead some men at certain junctures to modify or reject accepted beliefs.

Only thus can one ask, as Evans-Pritchard does, why it is that Azande 'do not perceive the futility of their magic', or how ideological consensus may be maintained in the face of disconfirming evidence and internal incoherence. Only thus, for instance, can one identify the whole network of 'secondary elaborations' which protect 'sacred' beliefs against predictive failure and falsification. Such procedures are quite obviously not confined to primitive magic and witchcraft; they are part of the stock-in-trade of the professional ideologist (and Kuhn's work suggests that they are not absent from the practice of 'normal science'); it is, for example, highly instructive to examine critically the precise ways in which the seeming closure and internal coherence of Soviet ideology is maintained, how *a priori* assertions are substituted for, and hence preclude, empirical inquiry, and incompatibilities between different assertions are concealed.[35] And, finally, change in, and rejection of, prevailing ideas cannot be entirely explicable in terms of context-dependent criteria, above all where the criteria themselves are questioned or rejected. Only by assuming rational criteria applicable to all contexts can one fully explain why men abandon religious or magical beliefs, or scientific paradigms in the face of intolerable anomalies (what makes an anomaly intolerable? The answer to this question cannot be internal to the paradigm), or why intellectuals come to reject official myths.

This, in turn, leads to the third set of questions that assuming non-context-dependent criteria makes possible – namely, questions about the social role of ideology and false consciousness. These arise wherever men's beliefs about their own or other societies can be characterised as to some degree distorted or false and where, in virtue of this feature, such beliefs have significant social consequences. It is only by assuming that one has a reliable, non-relative means of identifying a disjunction between social consciousness or collective representations on the one hand and social realities on the other that one can raise certain questions about the ways in which belief-systems prevent or promote social change.

Only such an assumption, for instance, can enable an anthropologist to distinguish between, say, the 'conscious model' of a tribe's marriage-system and its actual structure,[36] or between 'real Kachin society' and its 'ideal structure'.[37] Only such an assumption could enable Marx to relate the 'insipid illusions of the eighteenth century', picturing society as made up of abstracted, isolated and 'natural' individuals, to '"bourgeois society"', which had been in course of development since the sixteenth century and made gigantic strides towards development since the eighteenth':

> the period in which this view of the isolated individual becomes prevalent, is the very one in which the inter-relations of society (general from this point of view) have reached the highest state of development.[38]

Similarly, only such an assumption could enable Lukács to speak of the 'incapacity' of 'bourgeois thought' to 'understand its own social bases' and of 'unmasking' the 'illusion of the reified fixity' of social phenomena.[39] And only this assumption could enable Ossowski to explore the consequences of certain conceptions of social structure in the social consciousness. Thus, in considering the concept of non-egalitarian classlessness, he shows how

> the objective reality with which these ways of viewing are concerned may impose an interpretation which is very far from that which a classless society would require. But from the viewpoint of the interests of privileged and ruling groups the utility of presenting one's own society in terms of a non-egalitarian classless society is apparent. In the world of today, both in the *bourgeois* democracies and the people's democracies, such a presentation affords no bases for group solidarity amongst the underprivileged; it inclines them to endeavour to improve their fortunes, and to seek upward social mobility by means of personal effort and their own industry, and not by collective action.

It is on this assumption that Ossowski can observe (with truth) that 'Marxian methods – and in general all sociological methods that threaten stereotypes and social fictions – are rarely found suitable from the viewpoint of the ruling or privileged groups for the analysis of their own society.'[40] The central point here is that to speak (non-rhetorically) of 'illusions' and 'social fictions' whose social functions one seeks to explain involves the critical application of criteria that are not merely relative to a particular social position.

Thus a student of Soviet ideology has recently observed, pursuing an argument interestingly parallel to that advanced here, that

> The only way to prove which ideological beliefs have performed what functions in the social process is to study the beliefs and the social process from the vantage point of genuine knowledge. Consider, for example, this belief, which was mandatory in the thirties: The land belongs to the people, and therefore collective farmers hold their land rent free. This . . . presents a specific, verifiable statement as a logical consequence of a vague but stirring principle.

The appropriate model for the historian of ideology should, it is argued, be

> not Voltaire's brilliant mocking of religious illogic, but the anthropologist's strenuous effort to discover the social functions of various types of thought. As the student of primitive religion begins

his analysis of rain-making ceremonies with the quiet assumption that they do not affect the weather, the student of Soviet ideology should begin his analysis with the observation that rent has existed in the Soviet Union, whether or not Soviet leaders have been aware of it.

Thus '[s]erious analysis begins when one asks how the systems of agricultural procurement have been distributing rent from the twenties to the present, and how beliefs and systems have been interacting and changing each other'. In this way one can examine the latent functions of the denial of rent in the context of forcible collectivisation – for example, 'to reassure "realistic" leaders that an insoluble problem, the result of their own wild action, did not exist'.[41]

Finally, the fourth set of questions which non-relative criteria open up relates to the differences between traditional or 'pre-scientific' and modern or 'science-orientated' modes of thought. Among the most central of such questions is: what factors have made possible the immensely superior cognitive powers of the latter? Another is: in what spheres are the former cognitively weak, or strong, and why? To see the matter in this way is not necessarily to make ethnocentric assumptions about 'the stupidity of savages'.[42] On the contrary, it is to acknowledge the underlying unity between pre-scientific and scientific world-views.

As Durkheim said, in criticism of Lévy-Bruhl, 'We believe . . . that these two forms of human mentality, however different they are, far from deriving from different sources, are born one from the other and are two moments of a single evolution.'[43] Both seek, among other things, to explain the natural and social world – so as 'not to leave the mind enslaved to visible appearances, but to induce it to master them and to connect what the senses separate'. Thus:

> The explanations of contemporary science are surer of being objective because they are more methodical and because they rest on more rigorously controlled observations, but they do not differ in nature from those which satisfy primitive thought. Today, as formerly, to explain is to show how one thing participates in one or several others. It has been said that the participations postulated by mythologies violate the principle of contradiction and are, for that reason, opposed to those implied by scientific explanations. Is not the statement that a man is a kangaroo, or that the sun is a bird, equal to identifying the two with each other? But our mode of thinking is no different when we characterize heat as movement, or light as a vibration of the ether, etc. Whenever we unite heterogeneous terms

by an internal bond, we necessarily identify contraries. Of course the terms we unite in this way are not those which the Australian aborigine connects together; we select them according to other criteria and for other reasons; but there is no essential difference in the process by which the mind relates them.[44]

From this standpoint, while conscious of the infinitely rich and various symbolic and expressive features of primitive and traditional thought and ritual (as Durkheim evidently was), one will be under no temptation to explain away false or inadequate attempts at explaining the world and reasoning about it as 'really' emotive, or expressive, or symbolic utterances, and thereby removed from the sphere of application of non-context-dependent criteria of truth and logic.

Prescriptive

The final section of this chapter can be brief, since it merely draws the practical moral of the previous three. The sociology of belief need not prohibit a critical cognitive and logical stance *vis-à-vis* the beliefs it studies; indeed, such a prohibition precludes its raising a whole range of problems which are, on the face of it, both genuine and important. On the other hand, there is a real danger involved in adopting such a stance which needs to be appreciated.

The danger lies in confusing the *current content* of Western beliefs with universal and fundamental criteria of truth and validity and in then proceeding to use this current content as a yardstick for classifying other people's beliefs. The English 'intellectualist' school so castigated by Lévy-Bruhl – above all Frazer and Tylor – certainly erred in this direction. Thus Tylor could speak confidently of 'occult science' – 'one of the most pernicious delusions that ever vexed mankind' – as 'mistaking an ideal for a real connexion'.[45] It could be argued that Evans-Pritchard, despite his own excellent criticisms of that school,[46] inherits the same tendency in his distinction between mystical and common-sense notions and his appeal to 'science' 'for a decision when the question arises whether a notion shall be classed as mystical or common-sense. Our body of scientific knowledge and logic are the sole arbiters of what are mystical, common-sense, and scientific notions' – even though he adds that their 'judgements are never absolute'.[47]

Indeed they are not, and it can be dangerous for the social anthropologist or sociologist to take his own assumptions for granted in classifying the beliefs of others. Above all is this so in the case of social and psychological matters, but it applies quite generally. A particularly striking instance of this is provided by Robin Horton in his discussion of the traditional African diagnosis of disease, which, though reference is made to spiritual agencies, usually identifies 'the human hatreds, jealousies, and misdeeds, that have brought such agencies into play'. Thus Victor Turner 'shows how, in diagnosing the causes of some bodily affliction, the Ndembu diviner not only refers to unseen spiritual forces, but also relates the patient's condition to a whole series of disturbances in his social field'. The idea of the social causation of disease, especially so-called 'organic' disease, was not scientifically respectable when Evans-Pritchard wrote his book on the Azande, and he accordingly classified such hypotheses as 'mystical'. Horton is surely right to urge 'the need to approach traditional religious theories of the social causation of sickness with respect'.[48]

Such respect is obviously methodologically sound and should be applied generally. It underlines the essentially provisional nature of all cognitive judgements. Which is to say that, without embracing any form of epistemological or logical relativism, the sociologist of belief should be as critical of his own beliefs as of the beliefs of others.

Chapter 8

Relativism: Cognitive and Moral

. . . on ne voit rien de juste ou d'injuste qui ne change de qualité en changeant de climat. Trois degrés d'élévation de pôle renversent toute la jurisprudence; un méridien décide de la vérité; en peu d'années de possession, les lois fondamentales changent; le droit a ses époques, l'entrée de Saturne au Lion nous marque l'origine d'un tel crime. Plaisante justice qu'une rivière borne? Vérité au deça des Pyrénées, erreur au delà![1]

In this chapter I want to consider how seriously these words of Pascal should be taken. How *far-reaching* are the implications of the relativism they express? Do they commit us simply to accepting the empirical claim that cultures and their components are remarkably diverse, or do they commit us further to some philosophical or normative doctrine? More specifically, are truth and logic, morality, even rationality itself, ultimately context- or culture- or theory-dependent, relative to particular and irreducibly various 'forms of life' or systems of thought? And how *wide-ranging* are their implications? In so far as they reach, do they do so equally to what we call knowledge and what we call morality – to 'truth' and to, say, 'justice'?

Relativism has had a considerable vogue in recent times, and many thinkers in different fields have, in varying degrees, yielded to its temptations. For Quine, 'Where it makes sense to apply "true" is to a sentence couched in the terms of a given theory and seen from within this theory, complete with its posited reality'.[2] For Wittgenstein, 'All testing, all confirmation and disconfirmation of a hypothesis takes place already within a system' and the system is 'the element in which arguments have their life'.[3] Under Wittgenstein's influence, Peter Winch applies this idea to the philosophy of social science and D. Z. Phillips to the philosophy of religion. For Winch, 'our idea of what belongs to the realm of reality is given for us in the language that we use' and 'logical relations between propositions themselves depend on social relations between men'.[4] According to Phillips, 'Religious language is not an interpretation of how things are, but determines how things are for the believer. The saint and the atheist do not interpret the same world in different ways. They see different worlds!'[5] In the history and philosophy of science, Kuhn and Feyerabend make similar claims. Kuhn says that 'in a sense that I am unable to explicate further, the proponents of competing paradigms practise their trade in different worlds': in paradigm choice, 'there is no standard higher than the assent of the relevant community'.[6] Feyerabend denies that it is 'possible to make a judgment of *verisimilitude* except within the confines of a particular theory',[7] and calls for an 'anarchistic epistemology'. Within linguistics, the so-called 'Sapir–Whorf hypothesis' posits 'the relativity of all conceptual systems, ours included, and their dependence upon language' and maintains that 'all observers are not led by the same physical evidence to the same picture of the universe, unless their linguistic backgrounds are similar, or can in some way be calibrated'.[8] Within social anthropology Lucien Lévy-Bruhl argued that primitives 'live, think, feel, move and act in a world which at a number of points does not coincide with ours': their reality is itself 'mystical', their logic is 'strange and even hostile' to 'our conceptual and logical thought' and they have a view of causality 'of a type other than that familiar to us',[9] while Ruth Benedict saw in different cultures 'equally valid patterns of life which mankind has created for itself from the raw materials of existence'.[10] And within the sociology of knowledge, Mannheim saw the identification of socially located perspectives as having a bearing on validity and the truth of what men believe.

The temptation of relativism is a powerful and all-embracing one. If forms of life or systems of thought are inescapably constitutive of men's perceptions and their understanding, then surely their moralities, their religious and their aesthetic principles will be as relative as their knowledge? Indeed, the social anthropologist Mary Douglas, a Durkheimian much influenced by Quine, links the social construction of reality with boundary-maintaining moral rules and the division between sacred and profane; conversely, she writes that 'the moral order and the knowledge which sustains it are created by social conventions. If their man-made origins were not hidden, they would be stripped of some of their authority.'[11] Thus knowledge, morality and religion are closely interlinked and mutually sustaining, and relative to particular social contexts. But equally, there are those who resist the temptation of such ideas by proclaiming objectivism in morality, religion and knowledge alike. Roger Trigg concluded his book *Reason and Commitment* by asserting that without the notion of objectivity,

> there could be no criteria to distinguish knowledge from ignorance, and human reason becomes impotent. With it, the claims of religion, the dicoveries of science, the assumptions of moral argument, and much else, take on the importance they deserve.[12]

The purpose of this chapter is to express a perplexing sense of intellectual discomfort at my inability to accept either of these all-embracing positions. To put the matter sharply, I can see good reasons for rejecting cognitive relativism but no overwhelmingly good reasons for rejecting moral relativism. This stance is, of course, not unfamiliar, among both social scientists and philosophers. Durkheim was firmly committed to the cognitive supremacy of science, while adhering to a certain kind of moral relativism, according to which a morality is a set of 'moral facts', that is socially given ideals and imperatives, characteristic of a given society of a given type at a given stage of development, which individuals can (cognitively) grasp more or less adequately. On the other hand, both Max Weber and most contemporary Anglo-Saxon philosophers tend towards upholding the cognitive supremacy of the scientific method and the non-cognitive status of moral judgement based on choice between principles or ideals that are irreducibly at war. I am inclined to this latter position, though it strikes me as certainly over-simple and perhaps ultimately untenable, for the sorts of reasons that are suggested later, (pp. 171–4). What follows, then, is a kind of dialogue between the case for combining cognitive anti-relativism with moral relativism, advanced in the first three sections, and two counter-arguments to that case, adumbrated in the fourth.

By cognitive relativism I do not mean the empirical thesis that there is a diversity of world-views, theories, forms of explanation, modes of classification and individuation, and so on, but rather the philosophical thesis that truth and logic are always relative to particular systems of thought or language; on this view, what is true and how successfully to ascertain it, and what is a valid or consistent argument, are always internal to a system, which is itself one among others and relative to a particular social group or context or historical period. I and others have argued the case against this view elsewhere[13] and I will here merely briefly recapitulate its main lines and implications.

First, and negatively, the influence, however deep, of theories, systems, paradigms, perspectives, and so on, upon men's perceptions and understanding is one thing; the relativist claim that there are no theory-independent objects of perception and understanding is another. Similarly, the influence of theories upon what men may count as valid or consistent is one thing; the relativist claim that validity and consistency are theory-dependent is another. Moreover, it does not follow from the diversity of theories, or indeed from the existence of different concepts and criteria of truth and validity, that there may not be some such concepts and criteria which are invariable because universal and fundamental.

(It is, incidentally, striking that few relativists seem able, in the end, to take the theory-dependence of their worlds, and the pluralistic social solipsism it entails, really seriously. A familiar pattern of retreat is discernible: witness Kuhn's 'Reflections on My Critics',[14] where, for instance, he speaks of the puzzles of normal science being 'directly presented by nature', or Mannheim's assertion that the 'ultimate criterion of truth or falsity is to be found in the investigation of the object',[15] or Winch's recent denial that he was ever arguing 'absurdly, that ways in which men live together can never be criticised, nor even that a way of living can never be characterised as in any sense "irrational"',[16] or Lévy-Bruhl's abandonment in his late notebooks of the notion of the all-pervasiveness of the 'mystical', and that of 'pre-logical mentality' on the ground that 'the logical structure of the mind is the same in all known human societies',[17] or Quine's recent claim that 'logical truth is guaranteed under translation' and his proposal to ban 'any manual of translation that would represent the foreigners as contradicting our logic (apart perhaps from corrigible confusions in complex sentences)', so that, for example, the Law of Excluded Middle is no longer seen as revisable.[18])

Second, and positively, there are grounds for supposing that there are concepts and criteria of truth and of logic that are not theory- or context-bound, but universal and fundamental. The truth of a community's beliefs and the validity of their reasoning cannot be entirely up to them, a function of the norms to which they conform, the language games they play, the linguistic dispositions they exhibit, the paradigms to which they subscribe.

Briefly (and exceedingly summarily), we can only justifiably claim that a community holds beliefs (propositions accepted as true) on the assumption that we can translate their language, and we can only do *that* (on the assumption that the meaning of a sentence is given by its truth conditions) if a number of circumstances hold. First, they must have beliefs about the world whose truth conditions are the same for them and for us, since only if this is so can we identify those beliefs. In other words, though we and they need not agree about all 'the facts', we must correctly assume that we and they share a reality which is independent of how it is conceived. Second, we and they must share certain forms of behaviour – specifically, the activities of asserting and describing, as opposed to, say, betting, objecting, questioning, and so on. Third, not all their logical rules can be matters of pure convention, since, unless they possess, say, the concept of negation and the laws of identity and non-contradiction, we could never understand their putative beliefs, inferences or arguments. Indeed, we could not then even credit them with the possibility of holding beliefs, inferring or arguing, and we could never find their equivalents of 'and', 'not', 'or', 'if ... then ...'. etc., whose meaning is in part given by the logical truths. Of course, they may violate the logical laws with which they ordinarily operate, say in ritual contexts, but the special mystery or paradox of what they then say gains its force from that very fact; and there may be certain limited logical divergences (for example they may be intuitionists who reject $p \vee \sim p$ as a logical truth), but these cannot go too far without incomprehensibility setting in.

I further maintain that there are criteria of rationality (specifically, principles specifying what counts as a good reason for believing something – especially what counts as verification and falsification) which simply *are* criteria of rationality, not merely criteria of rationality within a certain context or system, though there may well be alternative ways of arriving at truths (the oracle, for instance, may be wise). Only on that assumption is it possible to account for the reasons which justify commitment to a belief system as such. On the reverse assumption, there are no reasons which are not internal and relative to the system itself. The system determines what is a reason, and one cannot give a reason for accepting, or rejecting, the system. (What makes a Kuhnian 'anomaly' intolerable? The answer to this question cannot be internal to the paradigm.) To assert the existence of non-context-dependent criteria of rationality is not, however, to be ethnocentric, since *we* may well misconceive or misapply these criteria, and, within certain domains, such as the traditional diagnosis of disease, *they* (say, traditional or tribal societies) may in these respects be more rational than we are, or they may apply alternative criteria that are as successful as, or even more successful than, ours. Nevertheless, some ways are better (in a non-context-dependent sense of 'better') than others for arriving at truths – and, unless we assume this, we could not satisfactorily explain how belief systems hold together or how they change. Thus the web of Zande witchcraft beliefs holds together in part by shielding its adherents from the perception of falsification and contradiction ('a Zande cannot get out of its meshes because it is the only world he knows. He cannot think that his thought is wrong');[19] likewise, superstitions have been abandoned and scientific theories superseded in consequence, at least in part, of confrontation with evidence and logical criticism. The ultimate consequences of denying this view have been admirably expressed by Michael Dummett, in criticism of Quine's model of language, as follows:

At the worst, it is irremediably conservative, because there can be no base from which to criticise whatever is generally accepted: we do not really know any of the language unless we know all of the language; and we do not know the language until we accept as true everything that is so accepted by its speakers, since, until we do, we cannot have the same linguistic dispositions as they. At the best, it is simply defeatist: it renders in principle inscrutable the laws which govern the common acceptance of a statement as true or its later demotion. In either case it is, in effect though not in intention, anti-intellectual; for it stigmatizes as misguided any attempt either to discover or to impose such laws.[20]

In summary, then, I claim that there are conditions of truth, rules of logic and criteria of rationality which are universal and fundamental. They are universal, in that they exist and are operative within all languages and cultures. They are fundamental in two senses. First, they specify the ultimate constraints to which all thought is subject. Thus all societies, with languages expressing beliefs, must apply them in general, though they may violate them in particular; indeed, it could be argued that they are basic adaptive mechanisms for any human society. But they are also fundamental in a second sense: namely, that it can probably be shown that those concepts of truth, rules of reasoning and criteria of rationality which are at variance with these (above all, in ritual and ideological contexts), are in fact parasitic upon them. That is, where there are second-order native beliefs about what counts as true or valid or what counts as a good reason for holding a belief which are at odds with these basic principles, then those beliefs can only be rendered fully intelligible against the background of such principles.[21]

It has been argued against this general position that it altogether begs the question, since it assumes relativism to be incorrect: in particular, it assumes that we *can* successfully identify their beliefs, follow their reasoning and understand their reasons. To this there are three replies. First, to develop and press as far as they will go transcendental arguments such as those suggested here, which seek to establish the preconditions for transcultural (and, by extension, intracultural) communication. Second, if this still fails to convince the really hard-boiled relativist, stubbornly committed to philosophic doubt, then he must be made to acknowledge the solipsistic conclusions to which his doctrine, taken seriously, finally leads. Third, I would stress the sociological significance of denying cognitive relativism. Only such a denial makes it possible to examine – indeed acknowledge the possibility of – false consciousness, where men's beliefs about their own and other societies can be characterised as mistaken or distorted or empirically inadequate, and, in virtue of these features, have significant social and political consequences. Only by assuming that one has access to a reliable, non-relative means of identifying a disjunction between social consciousness, on the one hand, and social realities, on the other, is it possible even to raise questions about the ways in which misperceptions and misunderstandings of all kinds arise and play their part in preventing, or promoting, social change. (Of this, more later.) Similarly, only the application of non-context- or non-system-dependent rules of logic allow one to investigate the social rôle of absurdity.[22] Finally, only a denial of cognitive relativism allows one to raise questions about the differential cognitive success of different societies in different domains, and seek to explain these.[23]

I now turn to moral or ethical relativism. The following distinct doctrines have all been brought under this label.

(i) The empirical thesis that moral values and principles conflict in a fundamental way, that is, that they are not merely different, but incompatible: the conflict between them is not resolvable by being reduced to a factual dispute that is in turn resolvable, or by subsuming one principle under the other, or both under a third. When the conflict is seen as occurring across cultural lines between moral codes, this becomes the familiar doctrine of 'cultural relativism'. In general, it is an empirical thesis about the diversity of morals and the nature and distribution of moral conflict.

(ii) The philosophical thesis that there is in principle ultimately no rational way of resolving fundamental conflicts between moral values, beliefs, principles, codes, systems – that there is no warrant (or no warrant not itself internal and relative to a particular moral system) for counting a particular set of moral values, beliefs, etc. as true, valid, correct, objective, etc. As Westermarck wrote, this thesis implies

> that there is no objective standard of morality, and objectivity presupposes universality. As truth is one it has to be the same for any one who knows it, and if morality is a matter of truth and falsity, in the normative sense of the terms, the same must be the case with moral truth.[24]

The thesis that it is not has been variously called ethical subjectivism, meta-ethical relativism and axiological or value relativism: it is with this that I shall be concerned.

(iii) The normative thesis that an act is, say, right or wrong, good or bad, or a person, say, praise- or blame-worthy if and only if he so judges – or, in the cultural form, if his society so judges. This thesis amounts to the *making* of moral judgements, by systematically adopting the values and principles of the actor or his society. Bernard Williams calls a version of this 'the anthropologist's heresy, possibly the most absurd view to have been advanced even in moral philosophy' and characterises it 'in its vulgar and unregenerate form', which is also 'the most distinctive and the most influential', as advancing three propositions: 'that "right" means (can only be coherently understood as meaning) "right for a given society"; that "right for a given society" is to be understood in a functionalist sense; and that (therefore) it is wrong for people in one society to condemn, interfere with, etc., the values of another society'.[25] Williams easily shows the inconsistency of this composite doctrine: the third proposition uses a non-relative sense of 'wrong' not allowed for in the first proposition. But in a simpler and not inconsistent form, this version of relativism is just the first-order (ultraliberal or romantic) moral position of systematic acceptance: 'When in Rome judge as the Romans judge.' This is sometimes called *normative relativism*: it follows from neither of the other two theses and is certainly absurd.

These various theses must be distinguished from a further view, which is not relativist at all but often supposed to be: that moral judgements must take account of context and consequences. This is what John Ladd calls *applicational relativity*: it 'entails that a certain act which might be wrong in one set of circumstances could be right in other circumstances'[26] – or, one might add, that it might be (equally wrong, but) blame-worthy in the one and not in the other.

Now, it is clear that the first, negative, argument which I used when discussing cognitive relativism has an exact parallel in relation to moral relativism (by which I henceforth mean the second, philosophical, thesis distinguished above). The influence of moral codes, ethical systems, ways of life, and so on, on men's actual moral judgements and actions is one thing; the claim that there are no correct moral judgements or objectively right actions is another. It does not, in other words, follow from the diversity of morals, or indeed from the existence of different moral concepts and criteria, that there are no such concepts and criteria which are invariable because universal and fundamental. In other words, descriptive relativism does not entail meta-ethical relativism.

The problem is to discover analogous arguments of a positive nature which show that there *are* such invariable, universal and fundamental concepts and criteria. Without such arguments, meta-ethical relativism – the view that there are no extra- or trans-systemic grounds for criticising moral beliefs and actions or systems as a whole – appears convincing, or at least unrefuted. But, in the first place, it does not seem to be the case that we must assume a common set of objective moral truths in order to translate and identify alien moral beliefs. Can we not identify these, as John Ladd suggests,[27] by discovering the prescriptions for conduct that have an especial 'superiority and legitimacy' in a culture, such as those contained in 'the relatively formal discourses given by leaders to their people on the conduct expected of them', or 'in talks to children . . . conducted in a more serious atmosphere', or in the words and judgements of respected 'wise men' who give 'formal moral talks at important gatherings: at weddings, curing ceremonies, before and after a person's death, as well as during the airing of disputes'? Can we not ascertain a community's or group's moral concepts by discovering the regulative concepts which its members use to characterise and evaluate the activities and relations of central concern to them and to guide their actions in respect of those activities and relations? Some of these concepts may be identical to ours: others may be alternative, perhaps incompatible, interpretations of what are recognisably the same concepts, and therefore translatable, with caution, by our terms (Italian 'pride', Japanese 'honour', Baroste 'justice'); and yet others may be distinct concepts for which we have no equivalents in our own societies. The point is that there appear to be no determinable theoretical limits to what concepts a society or group, let alone an individual, can employ in this way. Some might suggest the requirements set by the need for societal survival. But it is not obvious that all societies, let alone groups and individuals within them, give priority to this need; and, in any case, as Colin Turnbull's *The Mountain People* horrifyingly shows,[28] a society of sorts can survive by following codes of behaviour that are far indeed from those to which we commonly attach value.

Nor, second, does there appear to be a distinctively moral logic, analogous to but distinct from the basic rules of logic discussed in the first section, which we must assume to exist in common between 'us' and 'them' in order that we should be able to identify their moral beliefs and arguments. And finally, there appear to be no distinctively moral criteria of rationality, that is, principles specifying what are to count as good reasons for moral judgements or actions, which are not internal to a particular moral belief system. There are, of course, those principles already considered under the heading of cognition – specifically the principles of logic and of verification and falsification. But these are not distinctive of moral thought, but rather of thought in general – which is not to deny that it is both possible and important to apply them in criticism of moral codes. Much social criticism within our societies takes the form of showing up inconsistencies between principles and attitudes or policies, as, for example, in the debate over capital punishment or the attack on racial discrimination in purportedly egalitarian societies.[29] Similarly, moral codes can be shown to be based on distorted or mistaken empirical beliefs (for example about race) or on false assumptions about the efficacy of certain practices (for example about the deterrent effects of certain forms of punishment).

But where are the further limits to what may count as a good reason for reaching moral conclusions? In a theocratic culture divine commands will provide such reasons, in a gerontocratic culture the authority of the elders and in a bibliocentric one that of the Book, under nationalism the higher ends of the collectivity and under official Communism those of the Party, in a market society individualistic utilitarian calculation, in a Mediterranean society the fear of shame or the desire for honour, and so on. Nevertheless, it is often suggested that there are certain universal rational principles which govern moral discourse – for example that moral judgements be universalisable, or impartial, or critical, or reflective, or that they be directed to the maximisation of human welfare, or that they minister to human needs or answer human interests, or that they respect human beings as persons or rational agents or ends in themselves, and so on. But it is not difficult to produce historical and ethnographic evidence of putative moral systems which violate each of these principles (and are these latter not, in many cases, empty, since what counts as, say, 'criticalness' or 'needs' or 'interests' will be largely, perhaps entirely, context-dependent?). And is it not too easy a solution to say that these are not then genuine moralities, since that is simply to refute moral relativism by definition? Still, it could be argued that some sub-set of the rational principles cited above, and others, must be appealed to by judgements or imperatives if they are to count as recognisably moral, though none need be common to all (that is, that there is a 'family resemblance' between moralities). But, even if this argument be accepted, there would still be very considerable scope, not merely for the interpretation of, but for the differential weighting of these supposedly distinguishing marks of morality.

Furthermore, this seemingly irresolvable polyarchy of moralities is an inherent feature of the moral world we inhabit; as Max Weber observed, 'the ultimately possible attitudes towards life are irreconcilable'.[30] Of course, as I have suggested above, the mere fact of moral diversity does not of itself entail that fundamental moral conflicts are not rationally resolvable: one of the contending moral principles or judgements may, after all, be 'correct' or 'valid', and others 'incorrect' or 'mistaken'. But in the absence of convincing arguments (that is, arguments that are not themselves rationally contestable) for this conclusion, or even for the pragmatic necessity of assuming it, the case for meta-ethical relativism survives.

Indeed, it may seem to be supported by a notable feature of moral concepts, at least in modern, morally polyarchic societies – that they are 'essentially contestable', inevitably involving 'endless disputes about their proper uses on the part of their users',[31] such that to engage in such disputes is itself to engage in moral argument. I think it is possible, and would be highly instructive, to identify distinct and systematically conflicting moralities within contemporary societies which are, in a Kuhnian sense, 'incommensurable' (this being an area of which both moral philosophers and sociologists are curiously shy). Recall Auden the Arcadian's response to the Utopian: 'between my Eden, and his New Jerusalem, no treaty is negotiable';[32] and consider the fundamental conflicts occurring at the present time within Britain over the permissible limits of social inequality and the requirements of social justice. These moralities are incommensurable in that adjudications in favour of one rather than another are themselves always rationally contestable and are always made from within a particular moral view, though of course moral views can themselves be changed from within, and indeed in the direction of what we call enlightenment and progress. But *that* judgement is itself system-dependent. It is one morality among others which counts universalisability, impartiality and concern with what it conceives as welfare, respect for persons, even criticalness or reflectiveness as commendable or important features. Despite the rationally contestable claims of that morality, such features appear to have a transcendental status only *from within* its perspective. As Westermarck showed, this is a claim characteristic of all moral systems, whose proponents 'believe that moral judgments possess an objective validity which none of them has been able to prove'.[33] In the absence of such proof, one can only conclude that in morality there is no Archimedean point.

I have argued that with respect to our knowledge of the world, truth is distinguishable from error because there are non-relative truth conditions, non-relative principles of reasoning and ways of justifying claims to such knowledge that are objectively better than other ways. By contrast, moral judgements may be incomptabile but equally rational, because the criteria of rationality and justification in morals are themselves relative to conflicting and irreconcilable perspectives. I now propose to illustrate these contentions by taking a much-discussed sociological topic, about which Mr Runciman has written an interesting and challenging book,[34] namely the question of social inequality.

If we ask, first, the question, 'What forms of inequality exist in a given society?', there will inevitably be a host of complex conceptual and methodological difficulties. Nevertheless, the question is in principle an answerable one. Given all the problems of how to classify and compare data, how to interpret official statistics, and so on, it is not impossible to document inequalities of income, wealth, education, status, and so on, though of course the sociological and political significance of these data and the interrelations between them will be matters of dispute. What is striking is that these sociological findings are at variance with the systematically patterned social perceptions of groups or strata within the society. Runciman seeks to show, among other things, that the reference groups with which people identify themselves strongly affect their perceptions of the social order, leading them to misperceive it in the sense of having empirically inadequate beliefs about it. Thus, Runciman writes:

> Given the actual distribution of wealth, the answer to the question ['What sort of people do you think are doing noticeably better than you and your family?'] which would most obviously and naturally accord with the facts of inequality would be a reference by both manual and non-manual workers to those in business or the professions. Although a few manual workers are earning more than some non-manual, the incomes of very many members of the non-manual stratum are far above those of even the most prosperous manual workers. But when asked a question directly tied to inequalities of class, few members of the manual stratum drew a comparison from the other side of the manual/non-manual line.[35]

'Not only', writes Runciman, 'are comparative reference groups not chosen in accordance with the facts of inequality, but such a correspondence with the facts is least likely of all among those who are in fact most unequally placed'.[36]

In other words, Runciman claims to have shown that manual workers, for historical reasons and specifically with respect to income and wealth, make comparisons which serve to limit and distort their awareness of the structured inequality of the social order as a whole. (This is, in fact, only one possible interpretation of Runciman's findings. Another is that they have the same awareness of inequalities, but only regard some as salient to them. Unfortunately the survey on which Runciman relies is too crude to distinguish between these two interpretations and he does not distinguish between them in his analysis.) This supposedly limited or distorted awareness is false consciousness in a very simple sense, though it is not for that reason sociologically or politically unimportant. To take another example, the Polish sociologist Stanislaw Ossowski writes of the 'difficulties with which Communist ideology has to cope in connexion with the changes which have taken place in the socialist society' as being 'no less than those which the American Creed has encountered in its collision with the American reality': in 'both countries the view of their own society is based on the assumption that even widely ranging shares in the national income are not sufficient to establish social stratification, nor do they necessarily cause either class antagonisms or other symptoms characteristic of a class structure'. But Ossowski clearly believed that such 'ways of viewing concrete societies' amount to 'stereotypes and social fictions' – to ideology in the Marxist sense. For

> the objective reality with which these ways of viewing are concerned may impose an interpretation which is very far removed from that which a classless society would require. But from the viewpoint of the interests of privileged and ruling groups the utility of presenting one's own society in terms of a non-egalitarian classless society is apparent. In the world of today, both in the *bourgeois* democracies and the people's democracies, such a presentation affords no bases for group solidarity amongst the underprivileged; it inclines them to endeavour to improve their fortunes, and to seek upward social mobility by means of personal effort and their own industry, and not by collective action.[37]

Here, then, are two relatively simple examples of false consciousness (which both have significant effects in helping to prevent social change). In Runciman's case it is a matter of a limited and distorted view of the pattern of inequalities; in Ossowski's case it is a systematically propagated ideological view, which is objectively mistaken (at variance with what 'objective reality imposes') about the causes and consequences of such inequalities. More complex forms of false consciousness, as found in the writings of Marx, involve an empirically inadequate understanding of the deeper structures and processes underlying social and economic relationships, and a consequent 'reification' of those relationships and blindness to historical possibilities of social change. Thus, for Marx, nineteenth-century political economy gave a superficial explanation of the workings of capitalism, and thereby precluded those convinced by it from conceiving of the possibility of capitalism's supersession by socialism.

Let us return to Runciman's book. In it he writes that once

the structure of a society has been examined and its pattern of inequalities mapped out, two questions at once arise, either of which leads in turn to the other: first, what is the relation between institutionalized inequalities and the awareness or resentment of them? And second, which, if any, of these inequalities ought to be perceived and resented – whether they are or not – by the standards of social justice?[38]

The last part of his book is devoted to trying to answer this second question. In it he uses Rawls's theory of social justice to 'classify feelings of relative deprivation as "legitimate" or "illegitimate" by the standards of social justice':[39] to demonstrate in principle what kinds of grievances could be vindicated as legitimate and what reference group choices could therefore be described by this standard as 'correct', and to reveal 'false consciousness' in the form of 'attitudes to social inequality' which are 'restricted or mistaken'.[40] This requires that one establish which inequalities are vindicated by 'the canons of justice'; these are established by a theory of justice which

can provide an adequate assessment of relative deprivation, and in so doing restate the 'false consciousness' argument in an appropriate form. Once given a theory of justice, there is a valid sense in which the perception or resentment of inequalities can be described as misguided over and above the sense of ignorance of observable facts, or expedient means. This is not because people's interests can be shown to be other than they think – because, for example, their location in society inhibits them from accepting the Marxist theory of history and thereby modifying their idea of what is to their advantage. The perception of inequalities can be shown to be misguided only in the different sense that if people resent inequalities which are not unjust, they are illegitimately resenting them; and if they accept or are unaware of inequalities which are unjust, they are waiving, as it were, a right to resent them.[41]

So Runciman tries to show

how the inequalities of class and status for which some empirical evidence has been presented could be assessed in the light of principles agreed under the conditions of Rawls's model. Are the inequalities which have been discussed such that the reference groups chosen represent a correct assessment of entitlement, or are these choices symptomatic of an inhibited or distorted recognition of how far the social structure is unjust? Ought more, or less, manual workers and their wives to feel that they are justly rewarded by comparison with others, or does the disapproval found among some members of the non-manual stratum express a legitimate grievance against narrowing differentials of class? Should manual and non-manual work be accorded equal prestige, or does justice permit certain kinds of talent or position to be more highly regarded than others?[42]

He concludes his discussion by sketching a picture of 'a just society with the social and economic lineaments of twentieth century Britain', in which there would be less inequality of wealth, no inherited privilege, no educational discrimination against social groups or the economically disadvantaged, no unearned income except on the basis of need, no inequalities of reward except those based on need, merit and contribution to the common good, equality of opportunity, no deference not based on praise, the authority of positions to be mutually agreeable in advance of their being occupied, maximum consultation before administrative decisions, and unlimited comparisons between social positions in the bringing of claims against one another.[43]

Now, one striking feature of this picture is its essential contestability. It may share with Rawls's own applications of his theory the feature of being in accord with what Rawls calls 'our' intuitions and 'our considered judgments' – namely, those embodied in a wide liberal-social-democratic consensus – but it is no less contestable for that. Ultra-conservatives, clerical authoritarians, Empire Loyalists, fascists, racial separatists, Saint-Simonian technocrats, individualist liberals, anarchists, radical egalitarians, all derive from 'the canons of justice' significantly different images of 'the just society'.

Yet Rawls's aim is, precisely, to eliminate this very contestability. The original position affords a standpoint that is 'objective and expresses our autonomy . . . to see our place from the perspective of this position is to see it *sub specie aeternitatis*: it is to regard the human situation not only from all social but also from all temporal points of view'.[44] In *A Theory of Justice* he claims to have found 'an Archimedean point for judging the basic structure of society' according to the principles of justice.[45] His central assumption is that these principles can be specified and rendered determinate through rational inquiry: that an intensive process of ratiocination based on 'knowledge of the general facts about human society'[46] can lead one to a single structured set of principles, which underlie 'our' sense of justice ('the unique solution to the problem set by the original position').[47] He seeks to validate his theory of justice by a controlled thought experiment which he believes can establish the 'basic principles' which determine our everyday judgements of what is just. But Rawls's thought experiment cannot establish the truth of the theory it advances. The materials used in that experiment are 'theoretically defined individuals'[48] rationally pursuing their potential interests under hypothetical constraints. These 'individuals' are supposedly abstracted from any social and historical context. But such abstract individuals are literally inconceivable; with all historically and socially specific determinants removed, they become what F. H. Bradley called 'a theoretical attempt to isolate what cannot be isolated'.[49] It is, therefore, not merely contingently but necessarily the case that, in practice, Rawls endows the 'individuals' in the Original Position with historically specific and socially located features. (And this is so with all social-contract theorists, and indeed all those who base their theories on the nature of abstract (pre-social, trans-social or non-social) 'individuals'. Such 'human nature' always turns out to belong to a particular kind of social man.)[50]

Thus the motivations, beliefs and indeed the very rationality of Rawls's 'individuals' are recognisably those of a sub-class of rather cautious, modern, Western, liberal, democratic, individualistic men. They are 'committed to different conceptions of the good',[51] so they 'put forward conflicting claims'[52] and are not prepared to abandon their interests,[53] they have 'general desires' for 'primary goods'[54] (which are clearly culture-specific), they 'tend to love, cherish, and support whatever affirms their own good',[55] they demand equality of opportunity, but regard unequal rewards as necessary incentives,[56] and their rationality consists in acquiring the means of furthering their ends, and, more specifically, in a safety-first policy of maximising the benefits of the worst possible outcome. They 'understand political affairs and the principles of economic theory; they know the bases of social organization and the laws of human psychology'[57] – but are these not culturally specific beliefs? And why, for example, should they, as Rawls maintains, rule out a hierarchical society as potentially just, or regard Aquinas's intolerance of heresy as irrational?[58] Because their values and their conceptions of rationality are distinctively those of certain modern Western men. In general, Rawls appeals to 'our' intuitions and claims that his theory is 'a theory of our moral sentiments as manifested by our considered judgments in reflective equilibrium'.[59] Yet 'we' mainfestly do not all agree and are in any case only a tiny segment of the human race. So, in the end, Rawls's Archimedean point for 'judging the basic structure of society' (necessarily) eludes him, and his achievement is narrower than and different from his aim – namely, to have produced a liberal-democratic theory of justice. Justice is an essentially contested concept and every theory of justice arises within and expresses a particular moral and political perspective.

As a matter of fact, Runciman makes little use of Rawls's thought experiment of the Original Position and seeks rather to treat the question of what set of arrangements would be regarded as just by disinterested persons 'in a deliberately empirical manner' by postulating what actual contemporary men, supposed 'temporarily amnesiac' about their interests, would be likely rationally to agree about: that is, he asks 'what principles would *in fact* have been selected . . . in such a situation?'[60] But without some implausible assumption of a shared 'moral sense', the hypothesis of such an agreement is quite arbitrary. More relevantly, it lacks even the surface plausibility of Rawls's heroic attempt to attain an Archimedean point with impossible hypothetical abstract 'individuals', since it involves postulating what actual concrete contemporary individuals would agree on under hypothetical conditions in the light of their given, specific moral perspectives.

Runciman seems to acknowledge at a number of points the essential contestability of the concept of justice. There are, he writes, 'rival theories of social justice' and 'alternative views of how [the relation between inequality and grievance] should be assessed by the standard of justice'.[61] But he also writes of that assessment as an 'answerable question',[62] and, as we have seen, characterises certain attitudes to inequalities as 'false consciousness', as 'incorrect', 'restricted', 'mistaken', and so on. But if the moral relativist position taken above is inescapably correct, then Runciman's attempt to assess feelings of relative deprivation in the light of social justice fails to reveal 'false consciousness'. It simply shows that from within a certain moral and political perspective such feelings will be evaluated according to certain principles. But that perspective has no privileged status.

I have argued that there is (or rather that we must assume there to be) an Archimedean point in matters of knowledge but that there appears to be no such Archimedean point in matters of morality. Why, then, do I find this double claim uncomfortable?

Because, in the first place, it appears to rest on too simple a distinction between fact and value. The problem here arises especially acutely with respect to the identification of social facts. Is it not possible that, within certain ranges, this is (perhaps must be) always done from within a particular moral and political perspective? If so, then, within those ranges, every description of a social phenomenon, every identification of a social fact will be value-laden, at least in the sense of ruling certain moral and political evaluations out of court. Perhaps, in other words, certain theory-laden identifications of social facts are inextricable fusions of description and evaluation, in the sense of presupposing a 'given framework' which 'restricts the range of value positions which can be defensibly adopted'.[63]

Let us take as an example the identification of an exercise of power within a society.[64] A concept of power very widely used in contemporary political science is the following: that *A* exercises power over *B* when *A* affects *B* in a manner contrary to *B*'s interests. Now the notion of 'interests' (like that of 'needs') is an irreducibly evaluative notion: if I say something is in your interests, I imply that you have a *prima facie* claim to it, and if I say that 'policy *x* is in *A*'s interest', this constitutes a *prima facie* justification for that policy. In general, talk of interests provides a licence for making judgements of a moral and political character. So it is not surprising that different conceptions of what human interests *are* are associated with different moral and political positions. One can distinguish (somewhat crudely) between the following three conceptions of what interests are: (i) the *liberal* conception, which relates men's interests to what they actually want or prefer, to their policy preferences as manifested by their political participation; (2) the *reformist* conception, which, deploring that not all men's wants are given equal weight within the political system, also relates their interests to what they actually want and prefer, but allows that this may be revealed in the form of deflected, submerged or concealed wants and preferences; and (3) the *radical* conception, which maintains that men's wants may themselves be a product of a system which works against their interests and, in such cases, relates the latter to what men would want and prefer, were they able to make the choice. In other words, each of these conceptions of interests picks out a certain range of the entire class of actual and possible wants as the relevant object of moral appraisal; and that selection is itself a matter of moral and political dispute.

In the light of this, and of the concept of power as defined above, it will be clear that different conceptions of what are to count as interests will yield different ways of identifying power. And this is indeed what one observes in practice. A political scientist operating with a purely liberal conception of interests, will only see power where there is a conflict of overt preferences between A and B, and A prevails. Another, who allows that B's preferences may be submerged, will cast his net wider. A third, who is ready to allow that power can be exercised against B's real interests (which may not be manifest in and many even conflict with his actual wants), will see power where neither of the other two see it. Moreover, these differences of empirical scope are essentially linked to different value assumptions; in each case these latter predetermine the concept's range of empirical application. From which I conclude that the concept of power too is essentially contested, and that what, on the face of it, looked like an empirically decidable matter (answering the question, 'Is this an exercise of power?') turns out on inspection to be ineradicably evaluative – and necessarily so, since it appears that any way of identifying power rests upon some normatively specific conception of interests, and conflicts, with others.

Thus the first cause for discomfort in being a cognitive anti-relativist but a moral relativist is that there may be, at least within certain ranges, no morally (and politically) neutral form of cognition of social facts: the concepts available for identifying them may be as essentially contested as I have claimed moral concepts to be.

The second reason for discomfort may be seen as arising from the fact that contests over the latter are, after all, contests over something: essentially contested concepts must have some common core; otherwise, how could we justifiably claim that the contests were about the same concept? Implicit in the position I have taken above is the idea that the concept of morality is itself essentially contestable: that the criteria determining what counts as 'moral', the objects of moral judgement, the forms of moral justification, and so on, are to be seen in a pluralistic manner as irreducibly and indefinitely diverse. But, how, in that case, can one identify a particular principle or judgement or belief as *moral* rather than something else? I cited with approval Ladd's suggestion that one can look for those prescriptions for conduct which have a special superiority and legitimacy in a culture and I also suggested looking for those regulative concepts which the members of a community apply to activities and relations of central concern to them. But how can we rule out the possibility of a given culture so applying non-moral concepts, according superiority and legitimacy to non-moral prescriptions, or at most to an attenuated and degraded morality? This seems, indeed, to be exactly the case of the Ik, the wretched starving tribe described in Turnbull's *The Mountain People*; as he says of them, they 'have successfully abandoned useless appendages, by which I refer to those "basic" qualities such as family, cooperative sociality, belief, love, hope and so forth, for the very good reason that in their context these militated against survival'.[65] Does not the very act of identifying a set of principles, judgements, actions, and so on, as *moral* commit us to making assumptions about the content of morality, its role in organising and regulating social life and its relation to human needs, wants, interests, purposes, virtues, excellences, defined somehow – but how? – independently of any particular moral perspective? And if *that* is so, are we not thereby committed to a non-contestable definition of morality, and thereby to setting limits – but how narrow? – to moral relativism by, at the very least, ruling out certain judgements and actions (such as those of the Ik) as candidates for morality?

I began this chapter by referring to the temptations of relativism. These can be overcome either by resisting them *in toto* or by giving in to them with abandon. The situations of the consistent Puritan and of the uninhibited voluptuary are at least unambiguous. It is the *partial* resistance to temptation that causes anxiety and a lingering sense of dissatisfaction.

Part 3

Aspects of Individualism

Chapter 9

Methodological Individualism Reconsidered[1]

In what follows I discuss and (hopefully) render harmless a doctrine which has a very long ancestry, has constantly reappeared in the history of sociology and still appears to haunt the scene. It was, we might say, begotten by Hobbes, who held that 'it is necessary that we know the things that are to be compounded before we can know the whole compound' for 'everything is best understood by its constitutive causes', the causes of the social compound residing in 'men as if but even now sprung out of the earth, and suddenly, like mushrooms, come to full maturity, without all kinds of engagement to each other'.[2] It was conceived by the thinkers of the Enlightenment, among whom, with a few important exceptions (such as Vico and Montesquieu) an individualist mode of explanation became pre-eminent, though with wide divergences as to what was included, in the characterisation of the explanatory elements. It was confronted by a wide range of thinkers in the early nineteenth century who brought to the understanding of social life a new perspective, in which collective phenomena were accorded priority in explanation. As de Bonald wrote, it is 'society that constitutes man, that is, it forms him by social education',[3] or, in Comte's words, a society was 'no more decomposable into individuals than a geometric surface is into lines, or a line into points'.[4] For others, however, such as Mill and the utilitarians, 'the Laws of the phenomena of society are, and can be, nothing but the actions and passions of human beings', namely 'the laws of individual human nature'.[5] This debate has recurred in many different guises – in the dispute between the 'historical' school in economics and the 'abstract' theory of classical economics, in endless debates among philosophers of history and between sociologists and psychologists,[6] and, above all, in the celebrated controversy between Durkheim and Gabriel Tarde.[7] Among others, Simmel[8] and Cooley[9] tried to resolve the issue, as did Gurvitch[10] and Ginsberg,[11] but it constantly reappears, for example in reactions to the extravagantly macroscopic theorising of Parsons and his followers[12] and in the extraordinarily muddled debate provoked by the wide-ranging methodological polemics of Hayek and Popper.[13]

AIM.

What I shall try to do here is, first, to distinguish what I take to be the central tenet of methodological individualism from a number of different theses from which it has not normally been distinguished; and second, to show why, even in the most vacuous sense, methodological individualism is implausible.

Let us begin with a set of truisms. Society consists of people. Groups consist of people. Institutions consist of people plus rules and roles. Rules are followed (or alternatively not followed) by people, and roles are filled by people. Also there are traditions, customs, ideologies, kinship systems, languages: these are ways people act, think and talk. At the risk of pomposity, these truisms may be said to constitute a theory (let us call it 'truistic social atomism') made up of banal propositions about the world that are analytically true, that is, in virtue of the meaning of words.

Some thinkers have held it to be equally truistic (indeed, sometimes, to amount to the same thing) to say that facts about society and social phenomena are to be explained solely in terms of facts about individuals. This is the doctrine of methodological individualism. For example, Hayek writes:

> There is no other way toward an understanding of social phenomena but through our understanding of individual actions directed toward other people and guided by their expected behaviour.[14]

Similarly, according to Popper,

> all social phenomena, and especially the functioning of all social institutions, should always be understood as resulting from the

decisions, actions, attitudes, etc. of human individuals, and . . . we should never be satisfied by an explanation in terms of so-called 'collectives'.[15]

Finally we may quote Watkins's account of 'the principle of methodological individualism':

> According to this principle, the ultimate constituents of the social world are individual people who act more or less appropriately in the light of their dispositions and understanding of their situation. Every complex social situation or event is the result of a particular configuration of individuals, their dispositions, situations, beliefs, and physical resources and environment.

It is worth noticing, incidentally, that the first sentence here is simply a (refined) statement of 'truistic social atomism'. Watkins continues:

> There may be unfinished or half-way explanations of large-scale social phenomena (say, inflation) in terms of other large-scale phenomena (say, full employment); but we shall not have arrived at rock-bottom explanations of such large-scale phenomena until we have deduced an account of them from statements about the dispositions, beliefs, resources and inter-relations of individuals. (The individuals may remain anonymous and only typical dispositions etc., may be attributed to them.) And just as mechanism is contrasted with the organicist idea of physical fields, so methodological individualism is contrasted with sociological holism or organicism. On this latter view, social systems constitute 'wholes' at least in the sense that some of their large-scale behaviour is governed by macro-laws which are essentially sociological in the sense that they are *sui generis* and not to be explained as mere regularities or tendencies resulting from the behaviour of interacting individuals. On the contrary, the behaviour of individuals should (according to sociological holism) be explained at least partly in terms of such laws (perhaps in conjunction with an account, first of individuals' roles within institutions, and secondly of the functions of institutions with the whole social system). If methodological individualism means that human beings are supposed to be the only moving agents in history, and if sociological holism means that some superhuman agents or factors are supposed to be at work in history, then these two alternatives are exhaustive.[16]

Methodological individualism, therefore, is a prescription for explanation, asserting that no purported explanations of social (or individual) phenomena are to count as explanations, or (in Watkins's version) as rock-bottom explanations, unless they are couched wholly in terms of facts about individuals.

It is now necessary to distinguish this theory from a number of others, from which it is usually not distinguished. It has been taken to be the same as any or all of the following.

(1) 'Truistic social atomism'. We have seen that Watkins, for example, seems to equate this with methodological individualism proper.

(2) A theory of meaning to the effect that every statement about social phenomena is either a statement about individual human beings or else it is unintelligible and therefore not a statement at all. This theory entails that all predicates which range over social phenomena are definable in terms of predicates which range over individual phenomena and that all statements about social phenomena are translatable without loss of meaning into statements that are wholly about individuals. As Jarvie has put it, '"Army" is merely a plural of soldier and *all* statements about the Army can be reduced to statements about the particular soldiers comprising the Army.'[17]

It is worth noticing that this theory is only plausible on a crude verificationist theory of meaning (to the effect that the meaning of p is what confirms the truth of p). Otherwise, although statements about armies are true only in virtue of the fact that other statements about individuals are true, the former are not equivalent in meaning to the latter, nor *a fortiori* are they 'about' the subject of the latter.

(3) A theory of ontology to the effect that in the social world only individuals are real. This usually carries the correlative doctrine that social phenomena are constructions of the mind and 'do not exist in reality'. Thus Hayek writes,

> The social sciences . . . do not deal with 'given' wholes but their task is to constitute these wholes by constructing models from the familiar elements — models which reproduce the structure of relationships between some of the many phenomena which we always simultaneously observe in real life. This is no less true of the popular concepts of social wholes which are represented by the terms current in ordinary language; they too refer to mental models.[18]

Similarly, Popper holds that 'social entities such as institutions or associations' are 'abstract models constructed to interpret certain selected abstract relations between individuals'.[19]

If this theory means that in the social world only individuals are observable, it is evidently false. Some social phenomena simply can be observed (as both trees and forests can); and, indeed, many features of social phenomena are observable (for example the procedure of a court) while many features of individuals are not (for example intentions). Both individual and social phenomena have observable and non-observable features. If it means that individual phenomena are easy to understand, while social phenomena are not (which is Hayek's view), this is highly implausible: compare the procedure of the court with the motives of the criminal. If the theory means that individuals exist independently of, for example groups and institutions, this is also false, since, just as facts about social phenomena are contingent upon facts about individuals, the reverse is also true. Thus, as we have seen, we can only speak of soldiers because we can speak of armies: only if certain statements are true of armies are others true of soldiers. If the theory means that all social phenomena are fictional and all individual phenomena are factual, that would entail that all assertions about social phenomena are false or else neither true nor false, which is absurd. Finally, the theory may mean that only facts about individuals are explanatory, which alone would make this theory equivalent to methodological individualism.

(4) A negative theory to the effect that sociological laws are impossible, or that law-like statements about social phenomena are always false. Hayek and Popper sometimes seem to believe this, but Watkins clearly repudiates it, asserting merely that such statements form part of 'half-way' as opposed to 'rock-bottom' explanations.

This theory, like all dogmas of the form 'x is impossible', is open to refutation by a single counter-instance. Since such counter-instances are readily available[20] there is nothing left to say on this score.

(5) A doctrine that may be called 'social individualism' which (ambiguously) asserts that society has as its end the good of individuals. When unpacked, this may be taken to mean any or all of the following: (a) social institutions are to be understood as founded and maintained by individuals to fulfil their ends (as in, for example, social-contract theory); (b) social institutions in fact satisfy individual ends; (c) social institutions ought to satisfy individual ends. (a) has undergone a revival recently (see chs 10 and 11); (b) is certainly held by Hayek with respect to the market, as though it followed from methodological individualism;

and (*c*), which, interpreting 'social institutions' and 'individual ends' as a non-interventionist state and express preferences, becomes political liberalism, is clearly held by Popper to be uniquely consonant with methodological individualism.

However, neither (*b*) nor (*c*) is logically or conceptually related to methodological individualism, while (*a*) is a version of it.

What I hope so far to have shown is what the central tenet of methodological individualism is and what it is not. It remains to assess its plausibility.

It asserts (to repeat) that all attempts to explain social and individual phenomena are to be rejected (or, for Watkins, rejected as rock-bottom explanations) unless they refer exclusively to facts about individuals. There are thus two matters to investigate: (1) what is meant by 'facts about individuals'?; and (2) what is meant by 'explanation'?

(1) What is a fact about an individual? Or, more clearly, what predicates may be applied to individuals? Consider the following examples:

(i) genetic make-up; brain-states,
(ii) aggression; gratification; stimulus–response,
(iii) co-operation; power; esteem,
(iv) cashing cheques; saluting; voting.

What this exceedingly rudimentary list shows is at least this: that there is a continuum of what I shall henceforth call individual predicates from what one might call the most non-social to the most social. Propositions incorporating only predicates of type (i) are about human beings *qua* material objects and make no reference to and presuppose nothing about consciousness or any feature of any social group or institution. Propositions incorporating only individual predicates of type (ii) presuppose consciousness but still make no reference to and presuppose nothing about any feature of any social group or institution. Propositions incorporating only predicates of type (iii) do have a minimal social reference; they presuppose a social context in which certain actions, social relations and/or mental states are picked out and given a particular significance (which makes social relations of certain sorts count as 'co-operative', which makes certain social positions count as positions of 'power' and a certain set of attitudes count as 'esteem'). They still do not presuppose or entail any particular propositions about any particular form of group or institution. Finally, propositions incorporating only individual predicates of type (iv) are maximally social, in that they presuppose and sometimes directly entail propositions about particular types of group and institution. ('Voting Labour' is at an even further point on the continuum.)

Methodological individualism has frequently been taken to confine its favoured explantions to any or all of these sorts of individual predicates. We may distinguish the following four possibilities.

(i) Attempts to explain in terms of type (i) predicates. A good example is H. J. Eysenck's *Psychology of Politics*.[21] According to Eysenck, 'Political actions are actions of human beings; the study of the direct cause of these actions is the field of the study of psychology. All other social sciences deal with variables which affect political action indirectly.'[22] (Compare this with Durkheim's famous statement that 'every time that a social phenomenon is directly explained by a psychological phenomenon, we may be sure that the explanation is false'.)[23] Eysenck sets out to classify attitudes along two dimensions – the Radical – Conservative and the Tough-minded – Tender-minded — on the basis of evidence elicited by carefully constructed questionnaires. Then, having classified the attitudes, his aim is to *explain* them by reference to antecedent conditions and his interest here is centred upon the modifications of the central nervous system.

(ii) Attempts to explain in terms of type (ii) predicates. Examples are Hobbes's appeal to appetites and aversions, Pareto's residues and those Freudian theories in which sexual activity is seen as a type of undifferentiated activity that is (subsequently) channelled in particular social directions.

(iii) Attempts to explain in terms of type (iii) predicates. Examples are those sociologists and social psychologists (from Tarde to Homans)[24] who favour explanations in terms of general and 'elementary' forms of social behaviour, which do invoke some minimal social reference but are unspecific as to any particular form of group or institution.

(iv) Attempts to explain in terms of type (iv) predicates. Examples of these are extremely widespread, comprising all those who appeal to facts about concrete and specifically located individuals in order to explain. Here the relevant features of the social context are, so to speak, built into the individual. Open almost any empirical (though not theoretical) work of sociology, or history, and explanations of this sort leap to the eye.

Merely to state these four alternative possibilities is to suggest that their differences are more important than their similarities. What do they show about the plausibility of methodological individualism? To answer this it is necessary to turn to the meaning of 'explanation'.

(2) To explain something is (at least) to overcome an obstacle – to make what was unintelligible intelligible. There is more than one way of doing this.

It is important to see, and it is often forgotten, that to *identify* a piece of behaviour, a set of beliefs, and so on, is sometimes to explain it. This may involve seeing it in a new way, picking out hidden structural features. Consider an anthropologist's interpretation of ritual or a sociological study of (say) bureaucracy. Often explanation resides precisely in a successful and sufficiently wide-ranging identification of behaviour or types of behaviour (often in terms of a set of beliefs). Again, to take an example from Mandelbaum,[25] a Martian visiting earth sees one man mark a piece of paper that another has handed to him through some iron bars; on his being told that the bank-teller is certifying the withdrawal slip he has had the action explained, through its being identified. If the methodological individualist is saying that no explanations are possible (or rock-bottom) except those framed exclusively in terms of individual predicates of types (i), (ii) and (iii), that is, those not presupposing or entailing propositions about particular institutions and organisations, then he is arbitrarily ruling out (or denying finality to) most ordinarily acceptable explanations, as used in everyday life, but also by most sociologists and anthropologists for most of the time. If he is prepared to include individual predicates of type (iv), he seems to be proposing nothing more than a futile linguistic purism. Why should we be compelled to talk about the tribesman but not the tribe, the bank-teller but not the bank? And let no one underestimate the difficulty or the importance of explanation by identification. Indeed, a whole methodological tradition (the phenomenological) holds this to be the characteristic mode of explanation in social science.

Another way of explaining is to deduce the specific and particular from the general and universal. If I have a body of coherent, economical, well-confirmed and unfalsified general laws from which, given the specifications of boundary and initial conditions, I predict (or 'retrodict') x, and x occurs, then, in one very respectable sense, I have certainly explained x.[26] This is the form of explanation which methodological individualists characteristically seem to advocate, though they vary as to whether the individual predicates which are uniquely to constitute the general laws and specifications of particular circumstances are to be of types (i), (ii), (iii) or (iv).

If they are to be of type (i), either of two equally unacceptable consequences follow. Eysenck writes,

> It is fully realised that most of the problems discussed must ultimately be seen in their historical, economic, sociological, and perhaps even anthropological context, but little is to be gained at the present time by complicating the picture too much.[27]

But the picture is already so complicated at the very beginning (and the attitudes Eysenck is studying are only identifiable in social terms); the problem is how to simplify it. This could logically be achieved either by developing a theory which will explain the 'historical, economic, sociological . . . anthropological context' exclusively in terms of (for example) the central nervous system, or by demonstrating that this 'context' is simply a backdrop against which quasi-mechanical psychological forces are the sole causal influences at work. Since, apart from quaint efforts that are of interest only to the intellectual historian, no one has given the slightest clue as to how either alternative might plausibly be achieved, there seems to be little point in taking it seriously, except as a problem in philosophy. Neuro-physiology may be the Queen of the Social Sciences, but her claim remains entirely speculative.

If the individual predicates are to be of type (ii), there is again no positive reason to find the methodological individualist's claim plausible. Parallel arguments to those for type (i) predicates apply: no one has yet provided any plausible reason for supposing that, for example, (logically) pre-social drives uniquely determine the social context or that this context is causally irrelevant to their operation. As Freud himself saw, and many neo-Freudians have insisted, the process of social channelling is a crucial part of the explanation of behaviour, involving reference to features of both small groups and the wider social structure.

If the individual predicates are to be of type (iii), there is still no positive reason to find the methodological individualist's claim plausible. There may indeed be valid and useful explanations of this type, but the claim we are considering asserts that all proper, or rock-bottom, explanations must be. Why rule out as possible candidates for inclusion in an *explicans* (statement of general laws *plus* statement of boundary and initial conditions) statements that are about, or that presuppose or entail other statements that are about, social phenomena? One reason for doing so might be a belief that, in Hume's words, 'mankind [is] . . . much the same in all times in all places'.[28] As Homans puts it, the characteristics of 'elementary social behaviour, far more than those of institutionalised behaviour, are shared by all mankind':

> Institutions, whether they are things like the physician's role or things like the bureaucracy, have a long history behind them of development within a particular society; and in institutions societies differ greatly. But within institutions, in the face-to-face relations between individuals . . . characteristics of behavior appear in which mankind gives away its lost unity.[29]

This may be so, but then there are still the differences between institutions and societies to explain.

Finally, if the claim is that the individual predicates must be of type (iv), then it appears harmless, but also pointless. Explanations, both in the sense we are considering now and in the sense of identifications, may be wholly couched in such predicates but what uniquely special status do they possess? For, as we have already seen, propositions incorporating them presuppose and/or entail other propositions about social phenomena. Thus the latter have not really been eliminated; they have merely been swept under the carpet.

It is worth adding that since Popper and Watkins allow 'situations' and 'interrelations between individuals' to enter into explanations, it is difficult to see why they insist on calling their doctrine 'methodological individualism'. In fact the burden of their concerns and their arguments is to oppose certain sorts of explanations in terms of social phenomena. They are against 'holism' and 'historicism', but opposition to these doctrines does not entail acceptance of methodological individualism. For, in the first place, 'situations' and 'interrelations between individuals' can be described in terms which do not refer to individuals without holist or historicist implications. And, second, it may be impossible to describe them in terms which do refer to individuals,[30] and yet they may be indispensable to an explanation, either as part of an identifying explanation in the statement of a general law, or of initial and boundary conditions.

Chapter 10

No Archimedean Point

(A Review of John Rawls's *A Theory of Justice*)[1]

This vast book has been long awaited and lavishly praised. It has been called 'the most substantial and interesting' work of English-speaking moral philosophy since the war, and 'the most notable contribution' to English-speaking political philosophy since Sidgwick and Mill. This generous praise is not surprising. For it claims to have found 'an Archimedean point for judging the basic structure of society' according to the principles of social justice.

   Principles of social justice assign rights and duties and distribute benefits and burdens among men whose conflicting interests require resolution in a morally acceptable manner. The central assumption of Professor Rawls's remarkable book is that these principles can be specified and rendered determinate through rational inquiry: that an intensive process of ratiocination based on knowledge of 'the general facts about human society' can lead one to a single, structured set of principles which underlie our sense of justice. A theory of justice, on this view, is an attempt to identify the deep structure which determines our everyday judgements of what is just. If successful, it will 'match our convictions of justice or extend them in an acceptable way'.

   The principles of Rawls's theory contrast sharply with alternative concepts of justice, above all with the utilitarian view, which has been so influential in our philosophical tradition. By contrast, Rawls offers a 'contract theory' of what he calls 'justice as fairness'. In doing this, he sees himself as attempting to 'generalise and carry to a higher order of abstraction the traditional theory of the social contract as represented by Locke, Rousseau and Kant'.

The central idea underlying this theory is very simple. It amounts to a thought experiment on a heroic scale. How, Rawls asks, should society be arranged if it is to conform to principles which would be chosen by rational persons uninfluenced by knowledge of their own social situation, their natural endowments or even their individual life-plans? He imagines such persons in the situation of a social contract, setting up a society, deciding on principles which will specify the basic structure of its political and economic arrangements that will in turn determine the basic rights and duties of its members and the distribution of social benefits between them. They are to decide this behind a 'veil of ignorance' about their own eventual prospects and purposes in such a society. The point of this is to secure fairness by removing 'the effects of specific contingencies which put men at odds and tempt them to exploit social and natural circumstances to their own advantage'. They also have no knowledge of the particular political, economic and cultural circumstances of their society, so as to secure fairness between generations.

What, then, are the principles which such rational persons would choose? They would not, Rawls argues, choose the utilitarian principle of maximising either total or average satisfactions, since this might involve any one of them ending up with lower life chances for the benefit of others – which would be irrational. On the contrary, Rawls argues that his hypothetical men would agree on a scheme which benefits all and in which inequality is to the advantage of those who are worst off. The principles they would agree on are, in order of priority, first, that 'Each person is to have an equal right to the most extensive total system of equal basic liberties compatible with a similar liberty for all', and, second, that 'social and economic inequalities are to be arranged so that they are both: (a) to the greatest benefit of the least advantaged, consistent with the just savings principle, and (b) attached to offices and positions open to all under conditions of fair equality of opportunity.'

These principles are, of course, abstract, and the second part of the book seeks to show what kind of 'basic structure' of society ideally satisfies them. The answer is a 'constitutional democracy' which preserves equal basic liberties, with a government which promotes equality of opportunity and guarantees a social minimum, and an economic system based on the market. In fact, Rawls claims that 'the choice between a private-property economy and socialism is left open', but his treatment of the latter is perfunctory – which is curious for a book on social justice. He also applies his theory in a moderate defence of civil disobedience in a 'nearly just democratic regime' (where does he have in mind?), arguing that it is 'one of the stabilising devices of a constitutional system'. The final, least satisfactory part of the book attempts to relate the theory of justice to a theory of goodness as rationality. Here he tries to show, according to 'the principles of moral psychology', how the sense of justice would ideally be acquired, and in conclusion argues that an ideally just society would allow for individual autonomy, encourage the realisation of community, mitigate the propensity to envy and spite, and 'enable human beings to express their nature as free and equal moral persons'.

Rawls's book is truly impressive in its boldness and its scope. Yet its achievement is, perhaps necessarily, narrower than and different from its aim, which is to uncover *the* essential principles of justice in society. For the thought experiment on which it rests does not, and cannot, establish the truth of the theory it advances. The materials used in that experiment are 'theoretically defined individuals', rationally pursuing their potential interests under hypothetical constraints. But who exactly *are* these individuals? It has long been a standard criticism of this mode of reasoning that man is a social being who cannot be abstracted from a particular social and historical context. As F. H. Bradley once put it, if we abstract from a man all those features which result from his social context, he becomes 'a theoretical attempt to isolate what cannot be isolated'.

And indeed, it turns out that the motivation, beliefs and indeed the very rationality of Rawls's 'individuals' are recognisably those of some modern, Western, liberal, individualistic men. They are 'committed to different conceptions of the good', they 'put forward competing claims' and are 'not prepared to abandon their interests', they 'tend to love, cherish and support whatever affirms their own good', they demand equality of opportunity, but regard unequal rewards as necessary incentives, and their rationality consists in acquiring the means to further their ends and, importantly, in a safety-first policy of planning for the worst possible outcome. They allegedly 'understand political affairs and the principles of economic theory; they know the basis of social organisation and the laws of human psychology' – but are these not merely culturally specific beliefs? And why should they rule out a hierarchical society as potentially just, or regard Aquinas's intolerance of heresy as irrational? Because their values and their conceptions of rationality are those of modern Western men. In general, Rawls appeals to 'our' intuitions and claims that his theory is 'a theory of our moral sentiments as manifested by our considered judgments'. Yet 'we' are only a tiny segment of the human race.

So, in the end, the 'Archimedean point for judging the basic structure of society' that Rawls seeks eludes him. Every political theory, and every theory of justice, expresses a particular political and moral perspective. Rawls's achievement, which is considerable, is indeed to have produced *a* theory of justice – a theory of liberal democratic justice.

Chapter 11

State of Nature

(A Review of Robert Nozick's *Anarchy, State and Utopia*)[1]

This brilliant and strange book's method and its conclusions are absurd, but to see why is profoundly enlightening. It is brilliant in most of the O.E.D.'s senses – 'bright, sparkling . . . striking; talented, showy'. It is strange because it addresses fundamental issues of political theory and ethics (Is the state justified and what are its proper limits? What is justice? How does it relate to equality? What is the good society?) in the accents of the seventeenth and eighteenth centuries, and more particularly of Locke, as though oblivious of the nineteenth-century critiques of abstract individualism and of most of twentieth-century social science. It is innocent of history, psychology, political science, sociology and ethnography – though not of 'the most developed theories dealing with the choice of rational agents (namely, decision theory, game theory, and economic analysis)'. Its principal method is 'state of nature theory', drawing substantive political conclusions from how abstractly conceived 'rational' individuals, removed from any specific social context, would behave in imagined situations. And these conclusions are that

    a minimal state, limited to the narrow functions of protection against

force, theft, fraud, enforcement of contracts, and so on, is justified;
that any more extensive state will violate persons' rights not to be
forced to do certain things, and is unjustified; and that the minimal
state is inspiring as well as right.

Thus the state may not legitimately seek (what some will call) justice
through redistribution, coercing some to aid others, nor may it prohibit
people's activities for their own good or protection.

The book's first part seeks to justify the minimal state as against the
individualist anarchist, who condemns the state as immoral. It proceeds
by a thought experiment: imagine individuals in a state of nature, with
rights ('various boundaries that may not be crossed without another's
consent'), who act in their own interests and generally (but not always)
do 'what they are morally required to do'; trace the story of how
associations would arise to protect their rights and how a dominant
association within a territory would emerge which would have two
essential features of the state – it would exercise a monopoly over the
use of force and afford universal protection of rights in the territory. The
beauty of this story for Professor Nozick is that the state 'grows by an
invisible-hand process and *by morally permissible means*, without
anyone's rights being violated': hence the minimal state is morally
legitimate and the anarchist's principled objections refuted.

The second part of the book defends the *minimal* state against
arguments for a more extensive state by seeking to refute 'those
generally acknowledged to be most weighty and influential'. The first is
that the state is necessary or the best instrument to achieve distributive
justice. Against this Nozick advances his own 'entitlement theory' of
justice, according to which a person's holdings are just if acquired
through just original acquisition or just transfer (as a voluntary
exchange or a gift) or through the rectification of injustice in the first
two senses: if 'each person's holdings are just, then the total set
(distribution) of holdings is just'. In the light of this 'theory', Nozick
concludes that no state is justified in applying some principle or
principles which aim at some end-result and specify some patterned
distribution: the 'entitlement theory', by contrast, is historical ('whether
a distribution is just depends on how it came about') and most likely in
practice to upset any pattern, through the voluntary actions of
individuals. He then seeks to demolish the case for state action to
promote equality, whether of opportunity or of self-esteem, arguing that
in all cases the state should confine itself to enforcing contracts and

prohibiting theft, and so on, thereby securing (unequally distributed) holdings to those entitled to them.

The third part of the book offers a speculative Utopia, consisting in 'a system of diverse communities, organised along different lines and perhaps encouraging different types of character, and different patterns of abilities and skills' – voluntary and diverse experiments in living in which people 'do their own thing' and between which they freely move. It will by now be no surprise to learn that, for such a system, the minimal state is the only possible framework and 'best realises the utopian aspirations of untold dreamers and visionaries'.

The central flaw in all these arguments is the *abstractness* of the individualism they presuppose. Consider the state of nature. Who are the individuals in Nozick's thought experiment? What is the *content* of their rights, of their motivations and of their interests? Why do they 'generally . . . do what they are morally required to do'? Why *generally* (rather than never or always) and what *are* they required to do? To these questions Nozick has no answer; he simply assumes that his 'rational' and partly moral individuals will act as his model and conclusions require, and he even says that if they do not, then they manifest 'special psychologies which thwart the operation of the invisible-hand process we have described'.

The crucial point is that this circularity is no accident. All psychologies are 'special' in this sense, for the identity of the individual is, in part, constituted by his social and cultural environment, so that to abstract him from it is, in a deep sense, incoherent. For this reason, all state of nature theories (with a social contract or, as in this case, without) are thought experiments involving 'individuals' whose motivations, interests and behaviour always, *and necessarily*, turn out to be historically and socially specific, thereby generating the results expected. Indeed, Nozick is involved in a double incoherence (or absurdity). For if, as is plausibly the case, the social context which actually serves to constitute the individuals of his theory is inconceivable without a state, then to try to imagine them independently of the state amounts to a further conceptual impossibility. As Marx, summing up a whole range of nineteenth-century arguments on this point, succinctly observed, '*man* is not an abstract being, squatting outside the world. Man is *the human world*, the state, society'.

This abstract individualism – common to state of nature theory and to classical and neoclassical economics, and presupposing pre-social, trans-social or non-social 'individuals' – is a distorting lens which satisfies the intellect while simplifying the world. Nozick's world not only excludes the ever-growing role of the state within contemporary capitalism; it is also radically pre-sociological, without social structure, or social and cultural determinants of, and constraints upon, the voluntary acts and exchanges of its component individuals. Thus, for example, the distribution of resources in society is merely 'the product of many individual decisions which the different individuals involved are entitled to make': inequality of opportunity is to be understood as just 'different persons separately giving other persons different things'; rights exist in an institutional vacuum and are simply 'particular rights over particular things held by particular persons, and particular rights to reach agreements with others'; and Utopia can grow 'spontaneously from the individual choices of many people over a long period of time'.

Hence there are some extraordinary instances of sociological and political naivety: the minimal state, combined with an alert citizenry, supposedly minimises the chances of the economically advantaged acquiring political power; the 'free operation of the market, some people's voluntary uniting (kibbutzim, and so on), private philanthropy, and so on, greatly reduces private destitution'; the 'free operation of a market system will not actually run foul of the Lockean proviso', which limits acquisition to there being 'enough and as good left in common for others'; and voluntary communities could 'overcome the whole thrust of the society' and bring about Utopia.

Hence, finally, there are some extraordinary gaps in the argument: no theory of the basis or content of rights; no discussion of how the minimal state is to be controlled, and kept minimal; no account of what 'original acquisition' of holdings can possibly *mean* in an already settled, let alone industrial, society, or of the principles of just transfer (norms of reciprocity and gift giving), or of how to apply the 'principle of rectification' of injustice. Indeed, Nozick even suggests, oddly, that 'past injustices might be so great as to make necessary . . . a more extensive state in order to rectify them' – but, even more oddly, only 'in the short run'.

Anarchy, State and Utopia invites comparison with John Rawls's *A Theory of Justice* – to the considerable advantage of the latter. Both see the world through the individualist lens that has always been popular in the United States, although Nozick's world is far more thorough-going in its individualism than that of Rawls. He has, of course, firm allies outside Harvard's philosophy department, among economists such as Milton Friedman and F. A. Hayek, publicists such as Ayn Rand, and even psychiatrists such as Thomas Szasz. It is, however, particularly helpful that a very clear-sighted philosopher should polish the lens with such care and look very determinedly through it. For he brilliantly reveals the absurdity of doing so if we wish to interpret the world, let alone change it.

Notes and References

Chapter 1

1. Karl Marx, Preface to *A Contribution to the Critique of Political Economy* in Karl Marx and Frederick Engels, *Selected Works* (Moscow: Foreign Languages Publishing House, 1962), vol. I, pp. 362–3.

2. See R. E. Neustadt, *Presidential Power: The Politics of Leadership* (New York: Wiley, 1960); and 'The Constraining of the President: The Presidency after Watergate', *British Journal of Political Science*, 4, 4 (1974) pp. 383–97.

3. See Richard Crossman, *The Diaries of a Cabinet Minister*, vol. I (London: Cape, 1975). Note the interesting and suggestive ambiguity of the word 'determined', as shown by the phrase 'I am determined not to be determined.' This is discussed by Raymond Williams in his *Keywords* (London: Croom-Holm, 1976) pp. 90–1.

4. See Stephen Cohen, *Bukharin and the Bolshevik Revolution* (London: Wildwood House, 1974).

5. See Immanuel Wallerstein, 'The State and Social Transformation: Will and Possiblity', *Politics and Society*, 1, 3 (1971) pp. 359–64 and Paul Streeten, 'Alternatives in Development', *World Development*, vol. 2, 2 (Feb 1974) pp. 5–8.

6. See F. Parkin, *Class, Inequality and Political Order* (London: Paladin, 1971) ch. 4.

7. See Lewis A. Coser, 'Structure and Conflict', in *Approaches to the Study of Social Structure*, ed. Peter M. Blau (London: Open Books, 1976).

8. See D. M. White, 'The Problem of Power', *British Journal of Political Science*, 2 (1972) pp. 479–90.

9. W. B. Gallie, 'Essentially Contested Concepts', *Proceedings of the*

Aristotelian Society, 56 (1955–6) p. 169. For a further development of this argument, see the author's *Power: A Radical View* (London: Macmillan, 1974).

10. B. Russell, *Power: a New Social Analysis* (London: Allen & Unwin, 1960) p. 25. Cf. Denis Wrong, 'Some Problems in Defining Social Power', *American Journal of Sociology*, 73 (1967–8) p. 676: 'I do not see how we can avoid restricting the term "power" to intentional and effective control by particular agents.'

11. H. H. Gerth and C. Wright Mills (eds), *From Max Weber: Essays in Sociology* (London: Routledge & Kegan Paul, 1948) p. 180.

12. H. Lasswell and A. Kaplan, *Power and Society* (Yale University Press, 1950) p. 76.

13. T. Parsons, 'On the Concept of Political Power', in his *Sociological Theory and Modern Society* (New York: Free Press, 1967), pp. 331, 308.

14. N. Poulantzas, *Political Power and Social Classes* (London: New Left Books, 1973) p. 104.

15. See J. Rawls, *A Theory of Justice* (Oxford University Press, 1972) pp. 5–6.

16. In saying this, I am accepting the position advanced by Anthony Kenny in his recent book, *Will, Freedom and Power* (Oxford: Blackwell, 1976). Kenny rightly argues that voluntary actions include 'the unintentional bringing about of foreseen consequences and concomitant and side effects of intentional actions' (p. 58). He further argues that the sense of 'want' in which all voluntary actions are wanted actions is minimal. It is enough that the agent acts willingly, knowing that he need not so act: 'all voluntary action must be action that is performed willingly in the sense that it must be accompanied with at least consent' (p. 59). I would say that some cases of power exercise may not even meet this criterion, for example the neglect of politically 'invisible' poverty; it would fail to be voluntary in Kenny's terms, yet it would still be the exercise of a 'two-way' human power.

17. Ibid. 'To say that an agent brought about a certain result because he wanted to is . . . to say . . . that the agent was free from certain types of causal influence, such as constraint . . . If there were a causal link between the want and the action, the action would cease to be voluntary' (p. 120).

18. Ibid.

19. Raymond Boudon, *The Uses of Structuralism* (London: Heinemann, 1971) p. 46.

20. Weber writes of this 'masterless slavery in which capitalism enmeshes the worker or the debtor', arguing that 'the personal conduct of those who participate, on either the side of the rulers or the ruled . . . is essentially prescribed by objective situations'; similarly, he argues that the individual bureaucrat 'cannot squirm out of the apparatus to which he is harnessed . . . he is only a single cog in an ever-moving mechanism which prescribes to him an essentially fixed route of march': cited in Gerth and Wright Mills (eds), *From Max Weber*, pp. 58, 228.

21. A. R. Radcliffe-Brown, *Structure and Function in Primitive Society* (London: Cohen & West, 1952) p. 11.

22. S. F. Nadel, *The Theory of Social Structure* (London: Routledge, 1957).

23. Godfrey and Monica H. Wilson, *The Analysis of Social Change, Based on Observations in Central Africa* (Cambridge University Press, 1945, 1965) p. 49.

24. C. Lévi-Strauss, *Structural Anthropology*, trans. C. Jakobson and B. G. Schoepf (London: Allen Lane, 1968) p. 298.

25. R. K. Merton, *Social Theory and Social Structure* (New York: Free Press, 1957) pp. 52–3.

26. T. Parsons, *The Social System* (London: Routledge, 1951) p. 36.

27. P. Blau, 'Parameters of Social Structure', in P. Blau (ed.), *Approaches to the Study of Social Structure* (London: Open Books, 1976) p. 221.

28. A. Stinchcombe, 'Merton's Theory of Social Structure', in *The Idea of Social Structure*, ed. Lewis A. Coser (New York: Harcourt Brace, 1975); cited in ibid. pp. 34–5.

29. E. Durkheim, *Moral Education* (New York: Free Press, 1961) p. 54.

30. For example, Michel Foucault's 'episteme', which defines 'the epistemological space specific to a particular period', determining that period's possibilities of thought, and practice, such as a 'money reform, a banking custom, a trade practice. . . . In any given culture and at any given moment, there is always one episteme that defines the conditions of possibility of all knowledge, whether expressed in a theory or silently invested in a practice': M. Foucault, *The Order of Things* (London: Tavistock, 1970) p. 168.

31. Merton, *Social Theory and Social Structure*, pp. 160, 134.

32. For this view of totalitarianism, see the writings of Hans Buchheim, Leonard Schapiro and Franz Neumann – for whom totalitarian dictatorship was the absolute negation of 'the major institutional principles of modern liberalism' because 'the main repressive agencies are not courts and administrative bodies, but the secret police and the party': F. Neumann, *The Democratic and the Authoritarian State* (New York: Free Press, 1964) p. 246.

33. Crossman, *Diaries of a Cabinet Minister*, p. 268.

34. Ibid. p. 416.

35. Ibid. p. 149.

36. Joel Feinberg, *Social Philosophy* (Englewood Cliffs, N. J.: Prentice-Hall) p. 13.

37. Ibid. pp. 12–13.

38. Although it may be irrational or unreasonable to do so.

39. See C. Lévi-Strauss, *The Elementary Structures of Kinship*, trans. J. Bell, J. von Sturmer and R. Needham (London: Tavistock, 1969).

40. J.-P. Sartre, *L'Existentialisme est un Humanisme* (Paris: Nagel, 1959) pp. 22, 78, 59–62, trans. Steven Lukes. These views of the early Sartre arose out of the experience of the Resistance when 'there appeared to be a possiblity of free decision . . . a man is always free to be a traitor or not': hence Sartre's conclusion that 'in any circumstances, there is always a possible choice'; however, after the war came 'the true experience, that of *society*'. The later Sartre takes a more dialectical view of the relation between individual and society ('the individual interiorizes his social determinations: he interiorizes the relations of production, the family of his childhood, the historical past, the contemporary institutions, and he then re-exteriorizes these in acts and options which necessarily refer us back to them') and of the relation between agency

200   *Notes and References*

and structure, though always seeing the first as prior to the second ('Structures are created by activity which has no structure, but suffers its results as a structure.') However, 'the idea which I have never ceased to develop is that in the end one is always responsible for what is made of one': J.-P. Sartre, 'Itinerary of a Thought', *New Left Review*, 58 (Nov–Dec 1969) pp. 44, 45, 60, 45.

41. K. R. Popper, *The Open Society and its Enemies* 4th edn (London: Routledge, 1962) vol. 2, p. 197.

42. Karl Popper, 'Normal Science and its Dangers', in *Criticism and the Growth of Knowledge*, ed. I. Lakatos and A. Musgrave (Cambridge University Press: 1970) p. 56.

43. Ibid. As a logical rather than an empirical thesis against cognitive relativism, Popper's case is much more acceptable.

44. For a mild English version, cf. G. D. H. Cole in his Guild Socialist period, writing: 'If the workers want to destroy capitalism, and are ready to take its place and to assume its power, there is absolutely nothing to stop them from doing so . . . what is wrong with Labour today is not nearly so much lack of power as lack of will and imagination': *Workers Control in Industry* (Independent Labour Party, 1919) pp. 14, 15.

45. Louis Althusser and Etienne Balibar, *Reading Capital*, trans. B. Brewster (London: New Left Books, 1970) p. 180. It is striking how references to human beings in Althusserian writings almost always appear within quotation marks. It is also noteworthy that Althusser in his recent *Autocritique* appears to have recanted somewhat, now taking a less extreme position: 'Marx employs very regularly the concept of places and function and the concept of *Träger* (supports) as the support of *relations*: but that is not to evacuate concrete reality, to reduce real men to the pure functions of supports': *Éléments d'Autocritique* (Paris, 1974) p. 62.

46. *Reading Capital*, pp. 253, 252.

47. Poulantzas, *Political Power and Social Classes*, pp. 62, 63.

48. N. Poulantzas, 'The Problem of the Capitalist State', *New Left Review*, 58 (Nov–Dec 1969) p. 70.

49. N. Poulantzas, 'The Capitalist State: A Reply to Miliband and Laclau', *New Left Review*, 95 (Jan–Feb 1976) pp. 82, 71.

50. N. Poulantzas, *Classes in Contemporary Capitalism*, trans. D. Fernbach (London: New Left Books, 1975) pp. 183, 176.

51. See, for example, ibid. pp. 10, 14–15, 16, 29, 129–30, 175, 180, 187–8, 203, 287–8, 298, 313.

52. 'The Capitalist State: A Reply to Miliband and Laclau', p. 70.

53. This is particularly true of *Political Power and Social Classes*, and, although he (like Althusser) now criticises himself for having laid insufficient stress on the primary of the class struggle, his *Classes in Contemporary Capitalism*, though it contains some discussion of agency, alternatives and strategy, continues to stress 'the structural determination of class, i.e. . . . . the existence within class practices of determination by the structure – by the relations of production, and by the places of political and ideological domination/subordination' (p. 14).

54. *Political Power and Social Classes*, p. 104.

55. Ibid. p. 99.

56. Ibid. p. 101.

57. E. Laclau, 'The Specificity of the Political: the Poulantzas–Miliband Debate', *Economy and Society* (Feb 1975) p. 98.

58. 'The Problem of the Capitalist State', p. 70.

59. R. Miliband, 'The Capitalist State: Reply to Nicos Poulantzas', *New Left Review*, 59 (Jan–Feb 1970) p. 57.

60. 'The Specificity of the Political', pp. 93, 95.

61. Cohen, *Bukharin and the Bolshevik Revolution*, p. 325.

62. Quoted in E. H. Carr, 'The Legend of Bukharin', *Times Literary Supplement*, 8, 785 (20 Sept 1974) p. 990.

63. Alexander Solzhenitsyn, *The Gulag Archipelago 1918–1956*, vol. 1, trans. T. P. Whitney (London: Fontana, 1974) pp. 414, 409.

64. *Bukharin and the Bolshevik Revolution*, pp. 323, 324, 325, 335, 381. This explanation is perhaps hinted at by Bukharin himself when he spoke of his own 'pecular duality of mind' or 'dual psychology', resulting from objectionable Stalinist methods and shared Bolshevik goals: ibid. p. 351.

65. M. Liebman, 'Bukharinism, Revolution and Social Development', in *Socialist Register 1975*, ed. R. Miliband and J. Saville (London: Merlin Press, 1975) pp. 82–5.

66. Carr, 'The Legend of Bukharin, p. 990.

67. Ibid.

68. Ibid.

69. See, for example, Cohen, *Bukharin and the Russian Revolution*, pp. 323, 335, 350, This is also the view taken by Leonard Schapiro in his review of Cohen: 'Bukharin's Way', *New York Review of Books* (7 Feb 1974) pp. 3–7.

70. R. Skidelsky, *Politicians and the Slump. The Labour Government of 1929–1931* (London: Macmillan, 1967) p. xii.

71. Ibid.

72. R. McKibbin, 'The Economic Policy of the Second Labour Government 1929–1931', *Past and Present*, 68 (August 1975) pp. 95–123.

73. Ibid. pp. 102, 120–1.

74. Ibid. pp. 121–3.

75. Ibid. p. 114.

76. *Political Quarterly*, III (1932) pp. 323–45.

77. R. Harrison, 'Labour Government: Then and Now', *Political Quarterly*, XLI (1970) p. 73.

78. 'The Choice Before the Labour Party', pp. 326, 324–5.

79. I use the notion of 'action' here extremely widely, to include wanting, thinking, feeling, and so on, and to embrace both *positive* and *negative* action: cf. Bentham – 'to strike is a positive act, not to strike on a certain occasion a negative one. Positive acts are styled also acts of commission, negative acts of omission or forbearance', in *An Introduction to the Principles of Morals and Legislation* (1789) ch. VII, section VIII. See my 'Reply to Bradshaw', *Sociology*, 10 (January 1976) pp. 129–32.

80. 'The Legend of Bukharin', p. 990.

81. *The Gulag Archipelago*, pp. 411–12.

82. Skidelsky, *Politicians and the Slump*, p. 394.

83. 'The Economic Policy of the Second Labour Government', p. 102.

84. Iris Murdoch, 'Against Dryness: A Polemical Sketch', *Encounter* 88 (Jan 1961) p. 18. For further discussion of this picture of the individual, see the present author's *Individualism* (Oxford: Blackwell, 1973).

85. Iris Murdoch, *The Sovereignty of Good* (London: Routledge, 1970) pp. 8–9.

86. Murdoch, 'Against Dryness', p. 17.

87. R. Miliband, 'The Labour Government and Beyond', in *The Socialist Register 1966*, ed. R. Miliband and J. Saville (London: Merlin Press, 1966) p. 23.

88. See Erving Goffman, *The Presentation of Self in Everyday Life* (New York: Doubleday, 1956) p. 253.

89. Perhaps indeed there can occur a disjunction between what a correct analysis tells us and what law and morality may require. Perhaps Eichmann – the 'real' Eichmann – *was* unable to resist orders; perhaps also it is just, in legal and moral contexts, to see 'Eichmann' as the representative moral agent in that situation and in consequence punish the real Eichmann. In doing so, one restructures the moral context in which future agents act, instilling in them the belief that, in cases such as this, the plea of inability is not legally or morally acceptable, thereby perhaps rendering future Eichmanns more able to resist.

90. See Saul Kripke, 'Naming and Necessity', in *Semantics of Natural Language*, ed. G. Harman and D. Davidson, 2nd edn (Dordrecht: Reidel, 1972) pp. 253–355.

91. Compare Chomsky's critique of the behaviourism of B. F. Skinner.

Chapter 2

1. The general position was well put by Charles Merriam: 'Politics, in short, faces the common problem of passing from rule of thumb to more precise measurement, from the art to the science', quoted in H. Eulau, J. G. Eldersveld, and M. Janowitz (eds.), *Political Behaviour, a Reader in Theory and Research* (Glencoe: The Free Press, 1956) p. 274. This view is evident throughout this work. For discussion of it, see B. Crick, *The American Science of Politics* (London: Routledge, 1959).

Some writers have a practical and simple view of political theory, as in this statement from William A. Glazer; 'Many of the problems now besetting the world arise from the fact that physicists and engineers know how to combine theory and fact more efficiently than do political scientists and policy makers'. 'The Types and Uses of Political Theory', *Social Research* (Autumn 1955) p. 252. The general methodological questions raised by these views and by some of the claims of the voting-behaviour researchers, for example, Lazarsfeld, are not, however, the subject of this chapter.

2. We are mainly concerned with those who give detailed consideration to empirical findings in reformulating democratic theory. The main references are B. Berelson, P. F. Lazarsfeld, and W. McPhee, *Voting* (University of Chicago Press, 1954), especially ch. 14; B. Berelson, 'Democratic Theory and Public Opinion', *Public Opinion Quarterly* vol. 16 (Autumn 1952) and reprinted in Eulau *et al.*, *Political Behaviour*, pp. 107–15; Milne and Mackenzie, *Marginal*

Seat, 1955 (The Hansard Society for Parliamentary Government, 1958) ch. 13; S. M. Lipset, *Political Man* (London: Heinemann, 1960) *passim*; and R. A. Dahl, 'Hierarchy, Democracy and Bargaining in Politics and Economics', reprinted in Eulau *et al.*, *Political Behaviour*, pp. 83–90. See also Talcott Parsons, '*Voting* and the Equilibrium of the American Political System', and Eugene Burdick, 'Political Theory and the Voting Studies', in *American Voting Behaviour*, ed. Burdick and Brodbeck (Glencoe: The Free Press, 1960), chs. 4 and 6; J. A. Schumpeter, *Capitalism, Socialism and Democracy* (London: Allen & Unwin, 1950) 3rd edn, pt IV; J. P. Plamenatz, 'Electoral Studies and Democratic Theory', *Political Studies*, vol. VI (1958) pp. 1–9; and W. H. Morris-Jones, 'In Defence of Apathy', *Political Studies*, vol. II (1954) pp. 25–37.

3. *Voting*, p. 306.

4. There are of course dangers in generalising in this way, and we hope to bring out some of the differences as our argument develops. The main works considered are Rousseau's *Social Contract*, James Mill's *Essay on Government* and J. S. Mill's *Representative Government*.

5. Participation was not always limited to specifically political activities. Mill, in particular, wrote in *The Political Economy* that 'all classes of the community, down to the very lowest, should have much to do for themselves and should be encouraged to manage as many as possible of their joint concerns by voluntary co-operation'.

6. *Representative Government* in John Stuart Mill, *Utiliarianism, Liberty and Representative Government* (London: J. M. Dent, Everyman's Library, 1910) p. 217.

7. This is not an exhaustive list of the arguments which have been urged in support of democracy. Others might be added, for example, that the vote is a good means of informing the government of specific areas of dissatisfaction, that the expertise of administrators can be controlled by the wisdom of the plain man, that the election allows the government to calculate the limits to its possible acivity, and so on.

8. Political sociology has not eliminated the tendency to argue the case for democracy in the old terms, though some space may be given to *elite* theorists, for example, Mosca and Pareto, in passing. Cf. J. H. Hallowell, *The Moral Foundation of Democracy* (University of Chicago Press, 1954); N. Micklem, *The Idea of Liberal Democracy* (London: Johnson, 1957), A. Ross, *Why Democracy?* (Harvard U. P., 1952), for a restatement of some of the traditional arguments. Christian beliefs are important in the first two of these.

9. James Mill, *Essay on Government* (Cambridge University Press, 1937) p. 6.

10. *Representative Government*, p. 209.

11. *The Social Contract* (London, Everyman, 1947) p. 88.

12. *Representative Government*, p. 300.

13. See especially P. F. Lazarsfeld, B. Berelson, and H. Gaudet, *The People's Choice* (New York: Duell, Sloan & Pearce, 1944); Berelson *et al.*, *Voting*; H. Campbell, G. Gurin, and W. E. Miller, *The Voter Decides* (Evanston: Row, Peterson & Co., 1954); Campbell *et al.*, *The American Voter* (New York: Wiley, 1960); Milne and Mackenzie, *Marginal Seat, 1955*; M. Benney,

A. P. Gray, and R. H. Pear, *How People Vote* (London: Routledge & Kegan Paul, 1956). For a convenient survey of the findings, see Lipset, *Political Man*, though this tends to be somewhat cavalier in interpretation and generalisation.

14. Berelson, 'Democratic Theory and Public Opinion', p. 109.

15. However, for an elaborate critique of the Anglo–American treatment of this problem see H. Daudt, *Floating Voters and the Floating Vote* (Leiden: Stenfert Kroese, 1961).

16. Schumpeter attacks Wallas on precisely these grounds; see Schumpeter, *Capitalism, Socialism and Democracy*, p. 256, n. 7. He declares that Wallas's analysis should have led to a more drastic revision of the classical doctrine than it in fact did.

17. This point is made by Key, 'The Politically Relevant in Survey', *Public Opinion Quarterly* (1960).

18. Schumpeter, *Capitalism, Socialism and Democracy*, p. 259, n. 11.

19. 'Electoral Studies and Democratic Theory'.

20. Berelson, *Voting*, p. 306.

21. Dahl, 'Hierarchy, Democracy and Bargaining in Politics and Economics', p. 87 (our emphasis).

22. Ibid. p. 86 (our emphasis). Robert A. Dahl's *A Preface to Democratic Theory* (Chicago University Press, 1956) is, however, a more sophisticated formulation.

23. 'any clear-headed theory of politics requires discrimination between states of fact, causal connections, formal implications, and the values or ends that a policy is designed to achieve. In any political philosophy all these factors are combined, but no combination can alter the fact that they are logically different and that conclusions about them are differently warranted.' G. H. Sabine, *A History of Political Theory* 2nd edn (New York: Holt, 1950) p. ix.

24. *Representative Government*, p. 206. Mill devoted a great deal of attention to the possible dangers to good government resulting from the extension of the franchise to the working class, for example in 'Democracy in America' in *Dissertations and Discussions*, vol. II (1867–75) pp. 1–83 *passim*. He wrote that a labouring class prematurely given political power might easily interfere with contracts, introducing 'unenlightened legislation for the supposed interests of the many; laws founded on mistakes in political economy': ibid. p. 37.

25. For a very illuminating discussion of this problem and with particular reference to our concerns see W. G. Runciman, 'Sociological Evidence and Political Theory', in *Philosophy, Politics and Society: Second Series*, ed. P. Laslett and W. G. Runciman (Oxford: Blackwell, 1962).

26. Campbell *et al.*, *The American Voter*, p. 544.

27. Schumpeter, *Capitalism, Socialism and Democracy*, p. 269.

28. Ibid. p. 254.

29. 'Competitive Pressure and Democratic Consent' in Eulau *et al.*, *Political Behaviour*, pp. 275–85, which is based on a larger study with the same title (Michigan: Institute of Public Administration, 1956).

30. Ibid. p. 280.

31. Berelson, *Voting*, p. 312.

32. Ibid. p. 311.

33. Ibid. p. 314.

34. Ibid. p. 316.

35. Ibid. p. 320.

36. See in this connection an interesting paper by David Easton called 'Limits of the Equilibrium Model in Social Research', *Chicago Behavioral Sciences Publications*, no. 1 (1953), reprinted in Eulau *et al.*, *Political Behaviour*.

37. Parsons, '*Voting* and the Equilibrium of the American Political System', p. 114 (our emphasis). For general criticism of Parsons's functional theories see R. Dahrendorf, 'Out of Utopia', *American Journal of Sociology* (1958) pp. 115–27.

38. Berelson, *Voting*, p. 323.

39. Berelson 'Democratic Theory and Public Opinion', p. 114.

40. Parsons, '*Voting* and the Equilibrium of the American Political System', p. 114.

41. Herbert Tingsten, *Political Behaviour* (London: P. S. King & Son, 1937).

42. Ibid. p. 226.

43. Lipset, *Political Man*, p. 32, n. 20. Lipset claims on the same page that 'the belief that a very high level of participation is always good for democracy is not valid'. This statement is true but misleading. In supporting participation the classical democrats were thinking mainly in terms of a stable, liberal society, in which people accepted the good faith of their opponents and were prepared to work within the system.

44. *Political Studies*, voi. II (1954) pp. 25–37.

45. Ibid. p. 25.

46. Ibid. p. 36.

47. Ibid. p. 37.

48. D. N. Hogan, *Election and Representation* (Cork University Press and Oxford: Blackwell, 1945).

49. J. L. Talmon, *The Origins of Totalitarian Democracy* (London: Mercury Books, 1961). See especially pp. 46–7.

50. Sir I. Berlin, *Two Concepts of Liberty* (Oxford University Press, 1958).

51. Ibid. pp. 15–16. Berlin, however, does not support the view that apathy preserves democracy and liberty. His position is that positive liberty can lead to totalitarian consequences when the meaning of the word 'self' is extended.

52. Hogan, *Election and Representation*, p. 276.

53. Talmon, *The Origins of Totalitarian Democracy*, p. 232.

Chapter 3

1. This is a well-travelled paper. It began life as a seminar paper at Oxford and was subsequently presented at Harvard, Nanterre and the Free University of Berlin. I hope it has benefited from the interestingly different reactions it provoked and also from the helpful critical comments of David Apter, Hans-Peter Dreitzel, Graeme Duncan, Anthony Heath, R. W. Johnson, Frank Parkin, and Dan Sperber.

2. Max Gluckman, 'Les Rites de Passage', in *Essays on the Ritual of Social Relations*, ed. Gluckman (Manchester University Press, 1962) p. 48.

3. W. J. M. Mackenzie, *Politics and Social Science* (Harmondsworth: Penguin, 1967) p. 212.

4. Mary Douglas, *Purity and Danger. An Analysis of Concepts of Pollution and Taboo* (London: Routledge & Kegan Paul, 1966). p. 65.

5. Edmund R. Leach, 'Ritual', in *International Encyclopedia of Social Sciences* (New York: Macmillan and The Free Press, 1968) vol. 13, p. 526.

6. Monica Wilson, *Rituals of Kinship among the Nyakyusa* (Oxford University Press for the International African Institute, 1957) p. 9; Max Gluckman, *Politics, Law and Ritual in Tribal Society* (Oxford: Blackwell, 1965) p. 251; Raymond Firth, *Elements of Social Organization* (London: Watts, 1951) p. 222; and *Notes and Queries in Anthropology*, revised and rewritten by a committee of the Royal Anthropological Institute of Great Britain and Ireland, 6th edn (London: Routledge & Kegan Paul, 1951). p. 175.

7. S. F. Nadel, *Nupe Religion* (London: Routledge & Kegan Paul, 1954) p. 99.

8. J. Goody, 'Religion and Ritual: The Definitional Problem', *British Journal of Sociology*, vol. 12 (1961) p. 159.

9. Dan Sperber, *Le symbolisme en général* (Paris: Hermann, 1974) p. 16.

10. John Beattie, 'Ritual and Social Change', *Man*, vol. 1 (1966) p. 60, and 'On Understanding Ritual', in *Rationality*, ed. Bryan R. Wilson (Oxford: Blackwell, 1970) p. 240.

11. Leach, 'Ritual', pp. 523, 524; and E. R. Leach, *Political Systems of Highland Burma: A Study of Kachen Social Structure* (London: Bell, 1954) p. 13.

12. A. R. Radcliffe-Brown, *Structure and Function in Primitive Society* (London: Cohen & West, 1952).

13. Those objects may, of course, be multiple and occur at different levels of meaning. As Turner writes, ritual symbols 'condense many references, uniting them in a single cognitive and affective field': Victor W. Turner, *Dramas, Fields and Metaphors. Symbolic Action in Human Society* (Cornell University Press, 1974) p. 55. They are '*multivocal* or *polysemous*, i.e. they stand for many things at once. Each has a "fan" or "spectrum" of referents, which tend to be interlinked by what is usually a simple mode of association, its very simplicity enabling it to interconnect a wide variety of *significata*': Victor W. Turner, 'Three Symbols of *Passage* in Ndembu Circumcision Ritual', in *Essays On the Ritual of Social Relations*, ed. Gluckman, p. 125. Moreover, these 'are drawn from many domains of social experience and ethical evaluation' – Victor W. Turner, *The Ritual Process: Structure and Anti-Structure* (London: Routledge & Kegan Paul, 1969) p. 52 – including physiological and 'normative' or moral phenomena, including principles of organisation.

14. Leach, 'Ritual', p. 523.

15. Turner, 'Three Symbols of *Passage*' and *The Ritual Process*.

16. Sperber, *Le symbolisme en général*, p. 78.

17. Emile Durkheim, *The Elementary Forms of the Religious Life*, trans. J. W. Swain (London: Allen & Unwin, 1915) p. 225.

18. Ibid. p. 225.

19. Ibid. pp. 220, 358, 379, 381.

20. Ibid. p. 375.

21. Ibid. p. 427.

22. Ibid. p. 428; amended translation by Steven Lukes.

23. For an incisive critique, see Norman Birnbaum, 'Monarchs and Sociologists: A Reply to Professor Shils and Mr Young', *Sociological Review*, n.s. vol. 3 (1955) pp. 5–23; and also Robert Bocock, *Ritual in Industrial Society* (London: Allen & Unwin, 1974) pp. 102–4.

24. Edward Shils and Michael Young, 'The Meaning of the Coronation', *Sociological Review*, n.s. vol. 1 (1953) p. 67.

25. Ibid. p. 67.

26. Ibid. p. 67.

27. Ibid. pp. 70–1.

28. Ibid. p. 72.

29. Ibid. p. 74.

30. Ibid. pp. 78–9.

31. Ibid. p. 80.

32. J. G. Blumler, J. R. Brown, A. J. Ewbank and T. J. Nossiter, 'Attitudes to the Monarchy: Their Structure and Development during a Ceremonial Occasion', *Political Studies*, vol. 19 (1971) pp. 149–71.

33. Ibid. pp. 170, 171.

34. W. Lloyd Warner, *The Living and the Dead: A Study of the Symbolic Life of Americans* (Yale University Press, 1959), and *American Life: Dream and Reality*, rev. edn (University of Chicago Press, 1962).

35. *American Life*, p. 30.

36. *The Living and the Dead*, p. 278.

37. *American Life*, p. 16.

38. Ibid. p. 18.

39. Ibid. p. 8.

40. *The Living and the Dead*, p. 273.

41. *American Life*, p. 8.

42. Ibid. p. 7.

43. See, for example, ibid. and *The Living and the Dead*, p. 277.

44. Robert N. Bellah, 'Civil Religion in America', in *Religion in America*, ed. William G. McLoughlin and Robert N. Bellah (Boston: Houghton Mifflin, 1968).

45. Ibid. p. 21.

46. Ibid. p. 4.

47. Ibid. pp. 5–6.

48. Ibid. p. 10.

49. Ibid. p. 20.

50. Ibid. p. 15.

51. Sidney Verba, 'The Kennedy Assassination and the Nature of Political Commitment', in *The Kennedy Assassination and the American Public: Social Communication in Crisis*, ed. B. S. Greenberg and E. B. Parker (Stanford University Press, 1965). For a persuasive critique, see Lewis Lipsitz, 'If, As Verba Says, The State Functions As Religion, What Are We To Do Then To Save Our Souls?', *American Political Science Review*, vol. 62 (1968)

pp. 527–35. See also Verba's reply, 'If, as Lipsitz Thinks, Political Science is To Save Our Souls, God Help Us!', *American Political Science Review*, vol. 62 (1968) pp. 576–7, with reply by Lipsitz (pp. 577–8).

52. 'The Kennedy Assassination', pp. 353, 354.

53. Ibid. pp. 354–5.

54. Ibid. p. 358.

55. Ibid. p. 358.

56. Ibid. pp. 359–60.

57. Ibid. p. 359.

58. Ibid. p. 353.

59. 'The Meaning of the Coronation', p. 65.

60. For a very useful spelling-out of some the complexities embedded in this question, see Percy S. Cohen, *Modern Social Theory* (London: Heinemann, 1968).

61. See David Lockwood, 'Social Integration and System Integration', in *Explanations in Social Change*, eds. K. Zollschan and Walter Hirsch (London: Routledge & Kegan Paul, 1964).

62. Michael Mann, 'The Social Cohesion of Liberal Democracy', *American Sociological Review*, vol. 35 (1970) pp. 423–39. Cf John Goldthorpe, 'Social Inequality and Social Integration in Modern Britain', in *Poverty, Inequality and Class Structure*, ed. Dorothy Wedderburn (Cambridge University Press, 1974), which plausibly characterises British *economic* life as in 'a situation of anomie', with '"disorderly" industrial relations, the "wages jungle" and general economic "free for all"' and 'little consensus on the principles which *ought* to apply' (pp. 222, 223, 226).

63. See Herbert McCloskey, 'Consensus and Ideology in American Politics', *American Political Science Review*, vol. 58 (1964) pp. 361–82.

64. Mann, 'The Social Cohesion of Liberal Democracy', p. 437.

65. *The Times* (13 April 1972).

66. Compare the role of cricket in the West Indies, and the riots which matches against the English teams provoke (when the home team loses). As Orlando Patterson argues, in 'The Cricket Ritual in the West Indies', *New Society*, no. 352 (26 June 1969) pp. 988–9: 'In the West Indies, a test match is not so much a game as a collective ritual – a social drama in which almost all the basic conflicts within the society are played out symbolically. At certain moments this ritual acquires a special quality which reinforces its potency and creates a situation that can only be resolved in violence.' Cricket is the Englishman's game, and yet it also gives the West Indian masses 'a weapon against their current aggressors, the carriers of the dominant English culture in local society'. Indeed,

A test match is in fact one of the few exceptional occasions when the West Indian lower classes feel solidarity. The atomism created by poverty, conflicting values, and charismatic politics loses its divisiveness in the presence of the game. Here at last – in the medium of genuine heroes – the only heroes in a land barren of other heroes or a heroic tradition – the masses respond as one, share a common experience, bite their nails in a common war of nerves against a common enemy – against 'Them' (pp. 988–9).

Patterson's all-too-brief analysis strikes me as a model of how such rituals should be analysed, displaying sensitivity to different interpretations of the same ritual among different social groups.

67. 'The Nature of Mass Demonstrations', *New Society*, no. 295 (May 1968) pp. 754–5.

68. Ibid. pp. 754–5.

69. Richard Rose, *Governing Without Consensus: An Irish Perspective* (London: Faber & Faber, 1971) p. 258.

70. Murray Edelman, *The Symbolic Uses of Politics* (University of Illinois Press, 1964) p. 20.

71. See Abner Cohen, *Two Dimensional Man: An Essay on the Anthropology of Power and Symbolism in Complex Society* (London: Routledge & Kegan Paul, 1974); and Steven Lukes, 'A Way of Seeing', *New Society*, no. 620 (22 August 1974) pp. 495–6.

72. Turner, *The Ritual Process* and *Dramas, Fields and Metaphors*; and Bocock, *Ritual in Industrial Society*, ch. 8.

73. Thurman Arnold, *The Symbols of Government* (New York: Harcourt, Brace & World, 1962) p. 45.

74. Ibid. pp. 34–5.

75. Walter Bagehot, *The English Constitution*, Introduction by R. H. S. Crossman (London: Fontana, 1963) p. 61. A role which is, moreover, made the more effective by the occasional, overt and successful performance of their instrumental functions. The occasional success of backbenchers in checking or even reversing government policies greatly enhances the symbolic effectiveness of Parliament as a mobiliser of consent.

76. Edelman, *The Symbolic Uses of Politics*, p. 56.

77. Ibid. p. 17.

78. Albert Salomon, 'Symbols and Images in the Constitution of Society', in *Symbols and Society*, ed. L. Bryson, L. Finkelstein, H. Hoagland and R. M. MacIver, 14th Symposium of Conference on Science, Philosophy and Religion in their Relation to the Democratic Way of Life, Harvard University (New York: Harper, 1955) p. 100.

79. Compare Edelman: '[Participation in elections] is participation in a ritual act, however; only in a minor degree is it participation in policy formation. Like all ritual, whether in primitive or modern societies, elections draw attention to common social ties and to the importance and apparent reasonableness of accepting the public policies that are adopted . . . elections could not serve this vital social function if the common belief in direct popular control over governmental policy through elections were to be widely questioned.' *The Symbolic Uses of Politics*, p. 3. Cf. Edelman, *Politics as Symbolic Action: Mass Arousal and Quiescence*, Institute for Research on Poverty Monograph Series (Chicago: Markham, 1971). See Richard Hamilton, *Class and Politics in the United States* (New York: Wiley, 1974) ch. 3, for a valuable discussion and suggested explanations of the considerable gap in the United States between popular wants, on the one hand, and executive accomplishment, on the other.

80. E. E. Schattschneider, *The Semi-Sovereign People* (New York: Holt, Rinehart & Winston, 1960) p. 71.

81. Peter Bachrach and Morton S. Baratz, *Power and Poverty. Theory and*

Practice (New York: Oxford University Press, 1970) p. 43. There are, of course, considerable difficulties in using the concept of the 'mobilisation of bias' – now much discussed in the literature of community power, and examined by the present writer in *Power: A Radical View* (London: Macmillan, 1974). But these difficulties are certainly no less serious than those generated by the notion of 'value-consensus'; and it is the contention of this chapter that the use of the former concept opens up a whole range of significant empirical questions which the use of the latter closes off.

Chapter 4

1. My thanks are especially due to Dr S. Avineri, Sir I. Berlin and the late Professor J. P. Plamenatz for their kind and helpful comments on an earlier draft of this chapter.

2. For other discussions of these concepts, treating them together but in ways rather different both from one another and from that adopted here, see J. Horton, 'The Dehumanisation of Anomie and Alienation', *British Journal of Sociology*, xv, 4 (December 1964), and E. H. Mizruchi, 'Alienation and Anomie', in *The New Sociology: Essays in Social Science and Social Theory*, ed. I. L. Horowitz (Oxford University Press, 1964).

3. Robert Nisbet writes: 'The hypothesis of alienation has reached an extraordinary degree of importance. It has become nearly as prevalent as the doctrine of enlightened self-interest was two generations ago': *The Quest for Community* (Oxford University Press, 1953) p. 15. There is even an 'alienation reader': E. and M. Josephson, *Man Alone* (New York, 1962).

4. R. K. Merton, *Social Theory and Social Structure*, rev. edn (New York: Free Press, 1957) ch. IV.

5. According to a recent article on the subject (H. McClosky and J. H. Schaar, 'Psychological Dimensions of Anomy', *American Sociological Review*, 30 (1965)) there have been since Merton's paper first appeared about thirty-fiver papers on 'anomy'. 'In addition, the concept has been used in a large number of books and essays and applied to discussions of an astonishing variety of topics, ranging from delinquency among the young to apathy among the old, and including along the way such matters as political participation, status aspirations, the behaviour of men in prisons, narcotics addiction, urbanization, race relations, social change, and suicide' (p. 14).

6. G. Nettler, 'A Measure of Alienation', *American Sociological Review*, 22 (1957); M. Seeman, 'On the Meaning of Alienation', *American Sociological Review*, 24 (1959); M. B. Scott, 'The Social Sources of Alienation', *Inquiry*, 6 (1963); and L. Srole, 'Social Integration and Certain Corollaries', *American Sociological Review*, 21 (1956).

7. *Social Theory and Social Structure*, ch. v, p. 162.

8. R. Williams, *American Society* (New York: Knopf, 1951) p. 537; D. Riesman, *The Lonely Crowd* (Yale University Press, 1950) p. 287; R. MacIver, *The Ramparts We Guard* (New York: Macmillan, 1950) pp. 84–5; H. Lasswell, 'The Threat to Privacy', in R. MacIver (ed.), *Conflict of*

Loyalities, ed. R. MacIver, (New York: Harper, 1952); and Srole, 'Social Integration and Certain Corollaries', p. 712.

9. G. Lukacs, *Histoire de classe et conscience de classe* (Paris, 1960) p. 230.

10. L. Feuer, 'What is Alienation? The Career of a Concept', *New Politics* (1962) p. 132.

11. C. Lefort in 'Marxisme et Sociologie', *Les cahiers du centre d'etudes socialistes*, 34–5 (1963) p. 24.

12. E. Fromm, *The Sane Society* (New York: Rinehart, 1955) p. 120.

13. MacIver, *The Ramparts We Guard*, p. 84.

14. Emile Durkheim, *Professional Ethics and Civic Morals*, trans. C. Brookfield (London: Routledge & Kegan Paul, 1957) p. 12. It has been argued that, despite Durkheim's attempt to distinguish 'anomie' from 'egoism' in *Suicide*, they are not in the end conceptually distinct. See B. D. Johnson, 'Durkheim's One Cause of Suicide', *American Sociological Review*, 30, 6 (1965) pp. 882–6.

15. But Durkheim obviously did not want to see men treated as commodities or as appendages to machines. (See *Division of Labour*, New York: Free Press, 1933, pp. 371–3), and Marx had much to say, especially in vol. III of *Capital*, about avarice and unregulated desires prevalent under capitalism (see also his account of 'raw communism' in the 1844 manuscripts).

16. See, for example, B. F. Dohrenwend, 'Egoism, Altruism, Anomie and Fatalism: A Conceptual Analysis of Durkheim's Types', *American Sociological Review*, 24 (1959) p. 467, where anomie is described as 'ambiguous . . . indistinct . . . and infused with value judgments about what is "good" and "bad"', and Seeman, 'On the Meaning of Alienation'.

17. Cf. the famous passage from the *German Ideology* in which Marx writes of 'communist society, where no one has one exclusive sphere of activity but each can become accomplished in any branch he wishes' and where it is 'possible for me to hunt in the morning, fish in the afternoon, rear cattle in the evening, criticize after dinner, just as I have a mind, without ever becoming hunter, fisherman, shepherd or critic'. See also *Capital* (Moscow: Foreign Languages Publishing House, 1959) I, pp. 483–4 and Engels, *Anti-Dühring* (Moscow: Foreign Languages Publishing House, 1959), pp. 403 and 409. On the other hand, Marx seems to have changed his attitude at the end of his life to a concern with leisure in the 'realm of freedom'.

18. J.-J. Rousseau, *The Social Contract*, trans. G. D. H. Cole (London: Everyman, 1913) p. 12.

19. These possibilities are distinguished for analytical purposes. Clearly, in most actual cases they are combined. Rousseau, for instance, combines (1) and (2), while Pareto combines (2) and (4). I shall in the end argue that Marx and Durkheim combine (4) and (5).

20. As Marx says: 'The history of *industry* and industry as it *objectively* exists is an *open* book of the *human faculties*': *Early Writings*, ed. T. B. Bottomore (London: Watts, 1963) p. 162; and, as Durkheim says, 'society is, or tends to be, essentially industrial': *Divisions of Labour*, ed. G. Simpson (New York: Free Press, 1933) p. 3, and what characterises its morality is 'that there is something more human, and therefore more rational' about modern, organised societies (p. 407).

21. This image is, I would argue, ultimately Romantic in origin. Compare the following from Schiller's *Briefe ueber die aesthetische Erziehung des Menschen*: 'enjoyment is separated from labour, the means from the end, exertion from recompense. Eternally *fettered* only to a single little fragment of the whole, man fashions himself only as a fragment; ever hearing only the monotonous whirl of the wheel which he turns, he never displays the full harmony of his being' (*Sixth Letter*). For Schiller, and, I believe, for Marx, it is 'the aesthetic formative impulse' which 'establishes . . . a joyous empire . . . wherein it releases man from all the fetters of circumstance, and frees him, both physically and morally, from all that can be called constraint' (ibid. *Twenty-Seventh Letter*).

22. *Division of Labour*, p. 63. Whereas Marx's model of disalienated work is artistic creation, Durkheim writes that 'art is a game. Morality, on the contrary, is life in earnest' and 'the distance separating art and morality' is 'the very distance that separates play from work': *Moral Education* (New York: Free Press, 1961) p. 273. This is the Protestant Ethic transposed into Kantian terms: 'the categorical imperative is assuming the following form: Make yourself usefully fulfil a determinate function': *Divison of Labour*, p. 43. As to self-realisation, Durkheim writes: 'As for a simultaneous growth of all the faculties, it is only possible for a given being to a very limited degree': *Division of Labour*, p. 237, amended translation by Steven Lukes.

23. R. Blauner, *Alienation and Freedom: The Factory Worker and his Industry* (Chicago University Press, 1964) pp. 182 and 122.

24. M. Morse, *The Unattached* (Harmondsworth: Penguin, 1965) pp. 75–6 and 28–9.

25. G. Friedmann, *Fin du peuple juif?* (Paris: Gallimard, 1965) pp. 95, 99, 96.

26. E. Mayo, *The Human Problems of an Industrial Civilisation* (New York: Macmillan, 1933) pp. 152–3.

27. I am particularly indebted in the discussion of this example to the pages on this subject in S. S. Wolin, *Politics and Vision* (London: Allen & Unwin, 1961) pp. 407–14.

28. D. J. Roethlisberger and W. J. Dickson, *Management and the Worker* (Harvard University Press, 1939) p. 551.

29. Wolin, *Politics and Vision*, p. 412.

30. E. W. Bakke, *Bonds of Organization*, quoted in ibid., p. 506.

31. P. Selznick, *Leadership in Administration*, quoted in ibid. p. 413.

Chapter 5

1. James S. Coleman, 'Equality of Opportunity and Equality of Results', *Harvard Educational Review*, 43 (February 1973) p. 137.

2. C. Taylor, 'Socialism and Weltanschauung', in *The Socialist Idea: A Reappraisal*, ed. L. Kolakowski and S. Hampshire (London: Weidenfeld & Nicolson, 1974) p. 56.

3. Though equality is an objective central to socialism, socialists have not, in general, been very explicit about its content or the values on which it rests. I

have (perhaps surprisingly) found the ideas of certain English egalitarians and socialists (Arnold, Morris, Tawney, Cole, Orwell) especially helpful.

4. Babeuf came perhaps the nearest to doing so, proclaiming: 'Let there be no other difference between people than that of age or sex. Since all have the same needs and the same faculties, let them henceforth have the same education and the same diet. They are content with the same sun and the same air for all; why should not the same portion and the same quality of nourishment not suffice for each of them?' *Manifeste des égaux* (1796) in *Les précurseurs français du socialisme de Condorcet à Proudhon*, ed. M. Leroy (Paris: Editions du temps présent, 1948) pp. 67–8 (trans. S. Lukes).

5. See A. B. Atkinson, *Unequal Shares: Wealth in Britain* (London: Allen Lane, 1972) pp. 80ff.

6. H. Dalton, *Some Aspects of Inequality of Incomes in Modern Communities* (London: Routledge, 1925) cited in ibid. p. 84.

7. Christopher Jencks *et al.*, *Inequality. A Reassessment of the Effects of Family and Schooling in America* (London: Allen Lane, 1974) pp. 9–10.

8. The argument which follows, spelling out the principle of equal respect, is taken from the present author's *Individualism* (Oxford: Blackwell, 1973) pt III.

9. Condorcet, *Sketch for the Progress of the Human Mind* (1793), trans. June Barraclough (London: Weidenfeld & Nicolson, 1955) p. 184.

10. R. H. Tawney, *Equality*, 4th edn (London: Allen & Unwin, 1952) p. 260.

11. Ibid. p. 153.

12. William Godwin, *Enquiry Concerning Political Justice and its Influence on Morals and Happiness* (1793), 3rd edn. vol. I (London: Rolinson, 1798) pp. 214–15.

13. William Morris, *Letters on Socialism* (1888), privately printed (London, 1894) letter I, p. 5.

14. *Equality*, p. 254.

15. George Orwell, *Homage to Catalonia* (London: Secker & Warburg, 1938; Harmondsworth: Penguin, 1962) p. 66.

16. Bernard Williams, 'The Idea of Equality', in *Philosophy, Politics and Society*, ed. P. Laslett and W. G. Runciman (Oxford: Blackwell, 1962) pp. 117, 118.

17. Ibid. pp. 119–20.

18. Friedrich A. Hayek, *Individualism*, True and False (Oxford: Blackwell, 1946) p. 24.

19. Tawney, *Equality*, p. 87.

20. *Inequality*, p. 135.

21. Matthew Arnold, 'Democracy' (1861) in *The Portable Matthew Arnold*, ed. Lionel Trilling (New York: Viking Press, 1949) pp. 442–3.

22. *Equality*, p. 49.

23. Ibid. pp. 35–6.

24. Ibid. p. 47.

25. Ibid. p. 108.

26. C. A. R. Crosland, *The Future of Socialism* (London: Cape, 1956) pp. 150–1.

27. See J. H. Goldthorpe, 'Social Stratification in Industrial Society', reprinted in *Class, Status and Power: Social Stratification in Comparative*

Perspective, 2nd edn. R. Bendix and S. M. Lipset (London: Routledge, 1967).

28. Frank Parkin, *Class, Inequality and Political Order* (London: MacGibbon & Kee, 1971) p. 39.

29. P. M. Blau and O. D. Duncan, *The American Occupational Structure* (New York: Wiley, 1967) p. 7.

30. See H. F. Lydall, *The Structure of Earnings* (Oxford University Press, 1968).

31. Cited in David Lane, *The End of Inequality? Stratification under State Socialism* (Harmondsworth: Penguin, 1971) p. 81.

32. See, for example, H. Gordon Skilling and Franklyn Griffiths (eds) *Interest Groups in Soviet Politics* (Princeton University Press, 1971).

33. P. J. D. Wiles and S. Markowski, 'Income Distribution under Communism and Capitalism: Some Facts about Poland, the UK, the USA and the USSR', *Soviet Studies*, 22 (1971) p. 344.

34. Ibid. p. 353.

35. Atkinson, *Unequal Shares*.

36. See John Westergaard and Henrietta Resler, *Class in a Capitalist Society: A Study of Contemporary Britain* (London: Heinemann, 1975) p. 110 and ch. 7 *passim*. I was grateful to the authors for their permission to read the text of this extremely valuable study in advance of publication.

37. Atkinson, *Unequal Shares*, pp. 37–8.

38. Ibid. p. 251.

39. Ibid. p. 77.

40. See Westergaard and Resler, *Class in a Capitalist Society*, ch. 4; and Parkin, *Class, Inequality and Political Order* pp. 125–6.

41. Parkin, ibid., p. 127.

42. See Goldthorpe, 'Social Stratification in Industrial Society', p. 653.

43. D. Wedderburn and C. Craig, 'Relative Deprivation in Work', paper presented at the British Association for the Advancement of Science (Exeter, 1969), cited in Parkin, *Class, Inequality and Political Order* p. 26.

44. C. Kerr *et al.*, *Industrialism and Industrial Man* (Harvard University Press, 1960).

45. See Westergaard and Resler, *Class in a Capitalist Society*, pt 3; and the present author's *Power: a Radical View* (London: Macmillan, 1974), and 'Political Ritual and Social Integration', *Sociology*, 9 (1975) pp. 289–308 (see above, Chapter 3).

46. Lane, *The End of Inequality?*, p. 69.

47. See Parkin, *Class, Inequality and Political Order*, p. 144; and his article, 'Class Stratification in Socialist Societies', *British Journal of Sociology* (December 1969).

48. Lane, *The End of Inequality?*, pp. 72–4.

49. Parkin, *Class, Inequality and Political Order*, p. 146.

50. Ibid. p. 147; cf. Lane, *The End of Inequality?* p. 78.

51. Ibid. p. 149.

52. P. Machonin, 'Social Stratification in Contemporary Czechoslovakia', *American Journal of Sociology*, 75 (1970) pp. 725–41. For an English summary of Machonin and his associates' full-scale study of this subject, see

Ernest Gellner, 'The Pluralist Anti-levellers of Prague', *European Journal of Sociology*, xii (1971) pp. 312–25.

53. Wiles and Markowski, 'Income Distribution under Communism and Capitalism', p. 344.

54. Ibid.

55. See Atkinson, *Unequal Shares*, p. 77 and Lydall, *The Structure of Earnings*.

56. See Michalina Vaughan, 'Poland', in *Contemporary Europe. Class, Status and Power*, ed. Margaret Scotford Archer and Salvador Giner (London: Weidenfeld & Nicolson, 1971).

57. Lane, *The End of Inequality?*, pp. 129–37.

58. H. J. Eysenck, *The Inequality of Man* (London: Temple Smith, 1973) p. 224.

59. Ibid. p. 270.

60. Ibid. pp. 159, 224.

61. Ibid. p. 224.

62. R. Herrnstein, *IQ in the Meritocracy* (London: Allen Lane, 1973).

63. Arthur R. Jensen, *Educability and Group Differences* (London: Methuen, 1973) p. 363.

64. Jencks, *Inequality*, p. 315.

65. Ibid. p. 71.

66. *The Inequality of Man*, p. 111.

67. See Jencks, *Inequality*, appendix A.

68. Ibid.

69. Ibid. ch. 3, pt ii.

70. Ibid. p. 72.

71. K. Davis and W. E. Moore, 'Some Principles of Stratification', in *Class, Status and Power*, ed. Bendix and Lipset, p. 47.

72. Ibid. p. 48.

73. Ibid. p. 48.

74. See G. A. Huaco, 'The Functionalist Theory of Stratification: Two Decades of Controversy', *Inquiry*, 9 (Autumn 1966) pp. 215–40.

75. Ralf Dahrendorf, 'On the Origin of Social Inequality', in *Philosophy, Politics and Society*, second series, ed. Laslett and Runciman, p. 107.

76. Ibid. p. 103.

77. Ibid. p. 103.

78. Ibid. p. 102.

79. Parkin, *Class, Inequality and Political Order*, pp. 181–2.

80. Ibid. p. 183.

81. Ibid. p. 184.

Chapter 6

1. I am most grateful to Martin Hollis, John Beattie, Rodney Needham, Jean Floud, John Torrance and Vernon Bogdanor, among others for their very kind and helpful criticisms of an earlier draft of this chapter.

2. Some have argued that its solution bears directly on anthropological

practice. (See, for example, P. Winch, 'Understanding a Primitive Society', *American Philosophical Quarterly*, I (1964) pp. 307–24, where Evans-Pritchard's account of witchcraft among the Azande is held to be partly vitiated by his supposedly mistaken answer to it.) I agree with this position, but in this chapter I do not seek to substantiate it.

3. E. Leach, *Political Systems of Highland Burma* (London: Athlone Press, 1954) pp. 13–14.

4. Ibid. p. 182.

5. R. Firth, *Essays on Social Organisation and Values* (London: Athlone Press, 1964) p. 237.

6. Ibid. pp. 238–9.

7. See J. Beattie, *Other Cultures* (London: Cohen & West, 1964) chs v and xii; and 'Ritual and Social Change', *Man*, I (1966) pp. 60–74.

8. Beattie, 'Ritual and Social Change', p. 68. Thus, magic is 'the acting out of a situation, the expression of a desire in symbolic terms, it is not the application of empirically acquired knowledge about the properties of natural substances': Beattie, *Other Cultures*, p. 206. Cf. T. Parsons, *The Structure of Social Action* (London: Allen & Unwin, 1937) p. 431: 'Ritual actions are not . . . either simply irrational, or pseudo rational, based on prescientific erroneous knowledge, but are of a different character altogether and as such not to be measured by the standards of intrinsic rationality at all' – cited in Beattie, 'Ritual and Social Change'. Parsons wrongly attributes this position to Durkheim; as I shall show, Durkheim did not see religion as *merely* symbolic.

9. Beattie, 'Ritual and Social Change', p. 72. For Beattie magic and religion 'both imply ritual, symbolic ideas and activities rather than practical "scientific" ones': Beattie, *Other Cultures*, p. 212. For an example of the procedures Beattie advocates, see V. Turner, 'Symbols in Ndembu Ritual', in *Closed Systems and Open Minds*, ed. M. Gluckman (Edinburgh: Oliver and Boyd, 1964) pp. 20–51.

10. Beattie appeals to the authority of Suzanne Langer ('Ritual and Social Change', p. 66), but I am unsure how far his allegiance to her views goes. I do not know whether he would wish to argue, as she does, that rationality and even logic can be ascribed to expressive symbolism and whether he would subscribe to the general view that '[r]ationality is the essence of mind and symbolic transformation its elementary process. It is a fundamental error, therefore, to recognise it only in the phenomenon of systematic, explicit reasoning. That is a mature and precarious product. Rationality, however, is embodied in every mental act' – Langer, *Philosophy in a New Key* (Harvard University Press, 1942) p. 99. Miss Langer's is in any case a special sense of 'rationality'. As I hope to show, the fundamental meaning of rationality is essentially linked to the phenomenon of systematic, explicit reasoning.

11. 'Macri Medical Lore', *Journal of Polynesian Society*, XIII (1904) p. 219, cited in L. Lévy-Bruhl, *Les Fonctions mentales dans les sociétés inférieures* (Paris: Alcan, 1910) p. 69.

12. C. G. and B. Z. Seligman, *Pagan Tribes of the Nilotic Sudan* (London: Routledge, 1932) p. 25, cited in E. E. Evans-Pritchard, 'Lévy-Bruhl's Theory of Primitive Mentality', *Bulletin of the Faculty of Arts*, Egyptian University (Cairo), II (1934) pp. 1–36.

13. E. E. Evans-Pritchard, 'The Intellectualist (English) Interpretation of

Magic', *Bulletin of the Faculty of Arts*, Egyptian University (Cairo), I (1933) pp. 282–311; see also his *Theories of Primitive Religion* (Oxford University Press, 1965) ch. II.

14. Cf. E. Leach, 'Frazer and Malinowski', *Encounter*, xxv (1965) pp. 24–36: 'For Frazer, all ritual is based in fallacy, either an erroneous belief in the magical powers of men or an equally erroneous belief in the imaginary powers of imaginary deities' (p. 29).

15. R. Horton, 'African Traditional Thought and Western Science', *Africa* xxxvii (1967) pp. 50–71 and 155–87. Cf. also his 'Destiny and the Unconscious in West Africa', *Africa*, xxxi (1961) pp. 110–16; 'The Kalabari World View: an Outline and Interpretation', *Africa*, xxxii (1962) pp. 197–220; 'Ritual Man in Africa', *Africa*, xxxiv (1964) pp. 85–104. (For a symbolist critique of Horton, see Beattie, 'Ritual and Social Change'.) For other neo-Frazerian' writings, see J. Goody, 'Religion and Ritual: the Definitional Problem', *British Journal of Sociology*, xii (1961) pp. 142–64; I. C. Jarvie, *The Revolution in Anthropology* (London: Routledge & Kegan Paul, 1964); and I. C. Jarvie and J. Agassi, 'The Rationality of Magic', *British Journal of Sociology*, xviii (1967) pp. 55–74.

16. Horton, 'African Traditional Thought and Western Science', pp. 50–71.

17. Ibid. p. 53.

18. Ibid. p. 58.

19. Ibid.

20. Ibid. pp. 155–6.

21. E. Durkheim, *Les Formes élémentaires de la vie religieuse* (Paris: Alcan, 1912) pp. 339–41.

22. See *Les Carnets de Lucien Lévy-Bruhl* (Paris: Presses Universitaires de France, 1949) *passim*, where it is made explicit and partially resolved.

23. It is worth noting that Durkheim differed crucially from Lévy-Bruhl, emphasising the continuities rather than the differences between primitive and modern scientific thought; see Durkheim, *Les Formes élémentaires de la vie religieuse*, pp. 336–42, and 'Review of L. Lévy-Bruhl, *Les Fonctions mentales dans les sociétés inférieures*, and E. Durkheim, *Les Formes élémentaires de la vie religieuse*', *Année sociologique*, xii (1913) pp. 33–7.

24. L. Lévy-Bruhl, 'A Letter to E. E. Evans-Pritchard', *British Journal of Sociology*, iii (1952) pp. 117–23.

25. L. Lévy-Bruhl, *Les Fonctions mentales dans les sociétés inférieures* (Paris: Alcan, 1910) p. 30.

26. Ibid. pp. 30–1.

27. He eventually abandoned it; see *Les Carnets*, pp. 47–51, 60–2, 69–70, 129–35, etc.

28. L. Lévy-Bruhl, *La Mentalité primitive*, Herbert Spencer Lecture (Oxford: Clarendon, 1931) p. 21.

29. Evans-Pritchard, 'Lévy-Bruhl's Theory of Primitive Mentality'. Lévy-Bruhl's general endorsement of this article is to be found in Lévy-Bruhl, 'A Letter to E. E. Evans-Pritchard'.

30. Evans-Pritchard, 'Lévy-Bruhl's Theory of Primitive Mentality'.

31. Ibid.

32. Ibid.

33. Lévy-Bruhl, *Les Fonctions mentales*, p. 77.

34. This position he did not abandon; see *Les Carnets*, pp. 193–8, for example, where it is strongly reaffirmed.

35. Evans-Pritchard, 'Lévy-Bruhl's Theory of Primitive Mentality'.

36. Ibid.

37. Lévy-Bruhl, 'A Letter to E. E. Evans-Pritchard', p. 121.

38. Evans-Pritchard, 'Lévy-Bruhl's Theory of Primitive Mentality'.

39. Ibid. Cf. *Les Carnets*, p. 61, where he recalls that he had begun from the hypothesis that societies with different structures had different logics. The theory of the 'prelogical' was a modified version of this hypothesis, which he only finally abandoned much later, when he came to hold that the 'logical structure of the mind is the same in all known human societies' (p. 62).

40. Lévy-Bruhl's final position was as follows: 'there is no primitive mentality which is distinguished from the other by *two* characteristic features (being mystical and prelogical). There is one mystical mentality that is more marked and more easily observable among "primitives" than in our societies, but present in every human mind': *Les Carnets*, p. 131.

41. Winch, 'Understanding a Primitive Society', pp. 307–24.

42. E. Gellner, 'Concepts and Society', *Transactions of the Fifth World Congress of Sociology* (Washington: International Sociological Association, 1963) I (1962) pp. 153–83; and A. MacIntyre, 'Is Understanding Religion Compatible with Believing?', in *Faith and the Philosopher*, ed. J. Hick (London: Macmillan, 1964).

43. E. E. Evans-Pritchard, *Witchcraft, Oracles and Magic among the Azande* (Oxford University Press, 1937) p. 63.

44. Winch, 'Understanding a Primitive Society', p. 308.

45. Ibid. p. 309.

46. Ibid.

47. Evans-Pritchard, *Witchcraft*, pp. 24–5.

48. Winch, 'Understanding a Primitive Society', p. 315.

49. Ibid.

50. The philosophical basis for this position is to be found in P. Winch, *The Idea of a Social Science and its Relation to Philosophy* (London: Routledge, 1958). Cf. in particular the following passage: 'criteria of logic are not a direct gift from God, but arise out of, and are only intelligible in the context of, ways of living and modes of social life. It follows that one cannot apply criteria of logic to modes of social life as such. For instance, science is one such mode and religion is another; and each has criteria of intelligibility peculiar to itself. So within science or religion, actions can be logical or illogical: in science, for example, it would be illogical to refuse to be bound by the results of a properly carried-out experiment; in religion it would be illogical to suppose that one could pit one's own strength against God's, and so on' (pp. 100–1).

51. Winch, 'Understanding a Primitive Society', p. 317.

52. A. MacIntyre, 'A Mistake about Causality in Social Science', in *Philosophy, Politics and Society*, second series, ed. P. Laslett and W. G. Runciman (Oxford: Blackwell, 1962) p. 61. This formulation suffers from its emphasis on the location of these norms rather than on their nature.

53. Winch, 'Understanding a Primitive Society', p. 318.

54. E. E. Evans-Pritchard, *Nuer Religion* (Oxford University Press, 1956) p. 131.

55. Ibid.

56. Ibid. pp. 131–2.

57. Ibid. p. 318; emphasis mine. Professor Gellner's comment on this approach is that it 'absolves too many people of the charge of systematically illogical or false or self-deceptive thought'. Moreover, 'The trouble with such all-embracing logical charity is, for one thing, that it is unwittingly quite *a priori*: it may delude anthropologists into thinking that they have *found* that no society upholds absurd or self-contradictory beliefs, whilst in fact the principle employed has ensured in advance of any inquiry that nothing may count as prelogical, inconsistent or categorically absurd though it may be. And this, apart from anything else, would blind one to at least one socially significant phenomenon: the social role of absurdity.' See Gellner, 'Concepts and Society', p. 171.

58. I think Max Weber is largely responsible for this. His use of these terms is irredeemably opaque and shifting.

59. Philosophers have disputed over the question of whether 'belief' involves reference to a state of mind. I agree with those who argue that it does not; thus I would offer a dispositional account of 'acceptance'. As will be evident, I take it that belief is by definition propositional. As to the philosophical status of propositions, this does not affect the argument.

60. This is the sense of rationality stressed by Professor R. Hare, *Freedom and Reason* (Oxford University Press, 1963).

61. Cf. Horton, 'African Traditional Thought and Western Science', pp. 50–71, and 155–87, especially pp. 167–9. For numerous examples of this, see Evans-Pritchard, *Witchcraft*.

62. See, for example, Jarvie and Agassi, 'The Rationality of Magic'.

63. Cf., for example, Parsons, *The Structure of Social Action*, pp. 19, 698–9.

64. Cf., for example, G. C. Homans, *Social Behaviour: Its Elementary Forms* (London: Routledge, 1961) p. 80 for senses (ix) and (x). It is perhaps worth adding here that I do not find Mr Jonathan Bennett's stipulative definition of rationality germane to the present discussion: whatever it is that humans possess which marks them off, in respect of intellectual capacity, sharply and importantly from all other known species' – *Rationality* (London: Routledge, 1964) p. 5.

65. I take 'criterion of rationality' to mean a rule specifying what would count as a reason for believing something (or acting). I assume that it is only by determining the relevant criteria of rationality that the question 'Why did X believe p?' can be answered (though, of course, one may need to look for other explanatory factors. I merely claim that one must first look here).

66. Cf. P. Strawson, *Individuals* (London: Methuen, 1959); and S. Hampshire, *Thought and Action* (London: Chatto & Windus, 1959) ch. I.

67. Winch, *The Idea of a Social Science*, p. 15.

68. Winch, 'Understanding a Primitive Society', p. 308.

69. I owe this argument to Martin Hollis. I have profited greatly from his two papers, 'Reason and Ritual', in *Rationality*, ed. B. R. Wilson (Oxford: Blackwell, 1970), and 'Witchcraft and Winchcraft', *Philosophy of the Social Sciences*, vol. 2 (1972) pp. 89–103.

70. Winch, *The Idea of a Social Science*, p. 126.

71. Winch, 'Understanding a Primitive Society', p. 318.

72. Though, as Horton shows, they may be unnecessary; see 'African Traditional Thought and Western Science', p. 58.

73. Cf. *Les Carnets*, pp. 80–2, 193–5.

74. Ibid. p. 194.

75. Beattie and Firth see the sense of this argument but do not accept its conclusion; see quotation in text above and Beattie, *Other Cultures*, pp. 206–7.

76. Cf. Goody, 'Religion and Ritual', pp. 142–64, especially pp. 156–7, 161. As Evans-Pritchard (somewhat unfairly) says: 'It was Durkheim and not the savage who made society into a god' – *Nuer Religion*, p. 313.

77. Cf. Evans-Pritchard, *Witchcraft*, pp. 475–8, where twenty-two reasons are given why the Azande 'do not perceive the futility of their magic'.

Chapter 7

1. I wish to thank Robin Horton, Martin Hollis, Jerry (G. A.) Cohen, Michael Inwood, Bill Newton-Smith and David Wood for their criticisms of an earlier draft of this chapter.

2. E. E. Evans-Pritchard, *Social Anthropology* (London: Cohen & West, 1951) p. 129.

3. They have been interestingly made, and combated, within the Polish philosophical tradition and subsequently among Polish Marxists (for example Schaff and Kolakowski). See H. Skolimowski, *Polish Analytical Philosophy* (London: Routledge, 1967) and Z. Jordan, *Philosophy and Ideology* (Dordrecht: Reidel, 1963). Also relevant is the American pragmatist tradition, and, especially, the work of Quine.

4. *Pensées*, v, 294, quoted in P. L. Berger and T. Luckmann, *The Social Construction of Reality* (New York: Anchor Books, 1967) p. 5.

5. K. Mannheim, *Ideology and Utopia* (London: Routledge, 1960) pp. 262–3, 255–6, 240, 264, 4.

6. L. Lévy-Bruhl, *La Mentalité primitive* (Paris: Alcan, 1922) pp. 48, 85, 47.

7. L. Lévy-Bruhl, *Les Fonctions mentales dans les sociétés inférieures* (Paris: Alcan, 1910) p. 30.

8. See *Les Carnets de Lucien Lévy-Bruhl* (Paris: Presses Universitaires de France, 1949) p. 61.

9. *La Mentalité primitive*, p. 520.

10. *Les Carnets*, p. 62.

11. P. Winch, *The Idea of a Social Science and its Relation to Philosophy* (London: Routledge, 1958) p. 15.

12. P. Winch, 'Understanding a Primitive Society', *American Philosophical Quarterly*, 1, 4 (1964) p. 309.

13. Winch, *The Idea of a Social Science*, pp. 100, 126.

14. 'Understanding a Primitive Society', pp. 317, 318.

15. Ibid. p. 318.

16. *Language, Thought and Reality: Selected Writings of Benjamin Lee Whorf*, ed. with intro. by J. B. Carroll (M.I.T. Press, 1964) pp. 214, 213, 240, 241, 239, 211.

17. T. S. Kuhn, *The Structure of Scientific Revolution* (University of Chicago Press, 1964) p. 110. For Kuhn's more recent statements concerning these issues, see his postscript to the second edition (1970), and his contributions to *Criticism and the Growth of Knowledge*, ed. I. Lakatos and A. Musgrave (Cambridge University Press, 1970).

18. Ibid. p. 117. I owe to Jerry Cohen the observation that it is an odd principle of economy which favours a policy of multiplying entire worlds.

19. Ibid. pp. 120, 149, 125, 169, 93, 166.

20. Thus, for example, for Kuhn, paradigms are 'constitutive of nature' (ibid. p. 109) and for Winch 'there is no way of getting outside the concepts in terms of which we think of the world': *The Idea of a Social Science*, p. 15.

21. For an interesting discussion of different definitions of 'social', see W. L. Wallace, *Sociological Theory* (London: Heinemann, 1969).

22. I leave aside the controversial question of whether, or to what extent, this set of relations can be regarded as causal.

23. The term 'structural identity' comes from Max Scheler. I have in mind a wide range of such relations, ranging from Durkheim's and Mauss's attempts to relate symbolic classification and social structure, on the one hand, to Sorokin's attempts to identify structural relations between particular ideas with a given *Weltanschauung*, on the other.

24. This is evidently Lukács's view: see G. Lukács, *Histoire et conscience de classe* (1923) trans. into French by K. Axelos and J. Bois (Paris: Editions de Minuit, 1960) esp. pp. 189–256. See also English translation by Rodney Livingstone, (London: Merlin Press, 1971).

25. S. Lukes, 'Some Problems about Rationality', *European Journal of Sociology*, 8 (1967) reprinted in *Rationality*, ed. B. R. Wilson (Oxford: Blackwell, 1970).

26. For example: '[primitive thought] is not oriented, like our thought, towards knowledge properly so-called. It does not know the joys and the usefulness of knowledge. Its collective representations are always in large part of an emotional nature. Its thought and language remain scarcely conceptual': *La Mentalité primitive*, p. 50.

27. Cf. Russell's definition: 'when a sentence or belief is "true", it is so in virtue of some relation to one or more facts; but the relation is not always simple, and varies both according to the structure of the sentence concerned and according to the relation of what is asserted to experience:' B. Russell, *My Philosophical Development* (London: Allen & Unwin, 1959) p. 189.

28. M. E. Spiro, 'Religion: Problems of Definition and Explanation', in *Anthropological Approaches to the Study of Religion*, ed. M. Banton (London: Tavistock, 1966) p. 111. I do not see that E. Leach, 'Virgin Birth', *Proceedings of the Royal Anthropological Institute for 1966* (1967), has in any way cast doubt on this interpretation.

29. E. E. Evans-Pritchard, *Witchcraft, Oracles and Magic among the Azande* (Oxford: Clarendon Press, 1937) pp. 25, 24.

30. F. Steiner, 'Chagga Truth', *Africa*, 24 (1954).

31. Ibid. pp. 364, 368, 366, 365, 368, 367, 364.

32. See D. Joravsky, 'Soviet Ideology', *Soviet Studies*, 18, 1 (1966) pp. 2–19, esp. p. 10.

33. Steiner, 'Chagga Truth', p. 304.

34. A. O. Lovejoy, 'The Meaning of Romanticism for the Historian of Ideas', *Journal of the History of Ideas*, 2 (1941) pp. 262, 264–5.

35. See G. Wetter, *Soviet Ideology Today*, trans. P. Heath (London: Heinemann, 1966); D. Bell, 'Soviet Ideology', *Slavic Review*, 24 (1965); and the present writer's review article about the former in *New Society* (16 June 1966).

36. See, for example, P. Rivière, *Marriage among the Trio* (Oxford: Clarendon Press, 1970).

37. E. Leach, *Political Systems of Highland Burma* (London: Bell, 1954) p. 106.

38. K. Marx, *Introduction to the Critique of Political Economy* (1857), in *A Contribution to the Critique of Political Economy*, trans. N. I. Stone (Chicago: Kerr, 1913) pp. 226–8.

39. Lukács, *Histoire et conscience de classe*, French edn, pp. 229, 253.

40. S. Ossowski, *Class Structure in the Social Consciousness*, trans. S. Patterson, (London: Routledge, 1963) pp. 154, 116. Ossowski treated the 'official image of contemporary Soviet society' as in crucial ways at variance with social realities (he attempted the same for 'the American Creed') and he wrote optimistically of 'the Polish October of 1956' as leading to 'the destruction of the official myths which concealed our reality' (pp. 112, 193).

41. Joravsky, 'Soviet Ideology', pp. 11, 13, 14. 'The outside observer', Joravsky writes, 'has easily identified an illogical argument and an unverified belief by reference to his own genuine knowledge of logic and economics' (p. 12).

42. Leach, 'Virgin Birth', p. 46. This article constitutes something of a credo for the opposite view to that which I am advancing. For a splendid defence and application of the latter, see R. Horton, 'African Traditional Thought and Western Science', *Africa*, 37 (1967) and his earlier papers referred to therein.

43. E. Durkheim, 'Review of Lévy-Bruhl, *Les Fonctions mentales . . .* and his own *Formes élémentaires de la vie religieuse'*, *Année sociologique*, 12 (1909–12) p. 35.

44. E. Durkheim, *Les Formes élémentaires de la vie religieuse* (Paris: Alcan, 1912) pp. 340, 340–1.

45. E. B. Tylor, *The Origins of Culture*, pt 1 of *Primitive Culture* (1871) (New York: Harper, 1958) pp. 112, 116.

46. E. E. Evans-Pritchard, 'The Intellectualist (English) Interpretation of Magic', *Bulletin of the Faculty of Arts*, Egyptian University (Cairo), 1, 2 (1933).

47. Evans-Pritchard, *Witchcraft*, p. 12.

48. Horton, 'African Traditional Thought and Western Science', pp. 53, 54, 56. The reference to Turner is to his *Ndembu Divination*, Rhodes-Livingstone Papers, 31 (1962) and 'An Ndembu Doctor in Practice', in *Magic, Faith and Healing*, ed. A. Kiev (London: Collier-Macmillan, 1964).

Chapter 8

1. Pascal, *Pensées*, v, 294.

2. *Word and Object* (New York: Wiley, 1960) p. 24.

3. *On Certainty* (Oxford: Blackwell, 1969) section 105.

4. *The Idea of a Social Science* (London: Routledge, 1958) pp. 15, 126.

5. *Faith and Philosophical Enquiry* (London: Routledge, 1970) p. 132.

6. *The Structure of Scientific Revolutions* (University of Chicago Press, 1964) pp. 149, 93.

7. 'Consolations for the Specialist', in *Criticism and the Growth of Knowledge*, ed. I. Lakatos and A. Musgrave (Cambridge University Press, 1970) pp. 227–8.

8. J. B. Carroll (ed.), *Language, Thought and Reality* (M.I.T. Press, 1964) p. 214.

9. *La Mentalité primitive* (Paris: Alcan, 1922) pp. 47, 520, 85.

10. *Patterns of Culture* (London: Routledge, 1935) p. 201.

11. *Rules and Meanings* (Harmondsworth: Penguin, 1973) p. 15.

12. *Reason and Commitment* (Cambridge University Press, 1973) p. 168.

13. See especially Steven Lukes, 'Some Problems about Rationality' (Chapter 6 in this book) and Martin Hollis, 'The Limits of Irrationality' and 'Reason and Ritual', in *Rationality*, ed. Bryan Wilson (Oxford: Blackwell, 1970); Martin Hollis, 'Witchcraft and Winchcraft', *Philosophy of Social Science*, 2 (1972) pp. 89–103; and the present author's, 'On the Social Determination of Truth' (Chapter 7 in this book), in *Modes of Thought: Essays on Thinking in Western and Non-Western Societies*, ed. Robin Horton and Ruth Finnegan (London: Faber, 1973).

14. In *Criticism and the Growth of Knowledge*, ed. Lakatos and Musgrave.

15. *Ideology and Utopia* (London: Routledge, 1960) p. 4.

16. *Ethics and Action* (London: Routledge, 1972) p. 3.

17. *Les Carnets de Lucien Lévy-Bruhl* (Paris: P.U.F., 1949) p. 61.

18. *Philosophy of Logic* (Englewood Cliffs, N.J.: Prentice-Hall, 1970) pp. 83ff.

19. E. E. Evans-Pritchard, *Witchcraft, Oracles and Magic among the Azande* (Oxford: Clarendon Press, 1937) p. 194.

20. *Frege* (London: Duckworth, 1973) p. 627.

21. See Chapter 7 of this book; also in *Modes of Thought*, ed. Horton and Finnegan, pp. 240–1.

22. See Ernest Gellner, 'Concepts and Society', in *Rationality*, ed. Wilson.

23. See the essays in *Modes of Thought*, ed. Horton and Finnegan, especially that by Horton, and also his essay 'African Traditional Thought and Western Science' in *Rationality*, ed. Wilson.

24. *Ethical Relativity* (London: Kegan Paul, 1932) p. 183.

25. *Morality* (Harmondsworth: Penguin, 1973) p. 34.

26. *The Structure of a Moral Code* (Harvard University Press, 1957) p. 327.

27. Ibid. pp. 107–8.

28. *The Mountain People* (London: Cape, 1973).

29. See, for example, Gunnar Myrdal, *An American Dilemma: The Negro Problem and Modern Democracy*, 2 vols (New York: Harper, 1944).

30. *From Max Weber*, ed. H. H. Gerth and C. Wright Mills (London: Routledge, 1943), p. 152.

31. W. B. Gallie, 'Essentially Contested Concepts', *Proceedings of the Aristotelian Society*, 56 (1955–6) p. 169.

32. 'Vespers', in *Collected Shorter Poems* (London: Faber, 1966) p. 334.

33. *Ethical Relativity*, pp. 44–5.

34. *Relative Deprivation and Social Justice* (London: Routledge, 1966).

35. Ibid. p. 196.

36. Ibid. p. 210.

37. *Class Structure in the Social Consciousness* (London: Routledge, 1963) pp. 115–17, 154.

38. Runciman, *Relative Deprivation*, pp. 3–4.

39. Ibid. p. 284.

40. Ibid. p. 292.

41. Ibid. pp. 251–2.

42. Ibid. p. 260.

43. Ibid. p. 291.

44. *A Theory of Justice* (Oxford: Clarendon Press, 1972). p. 587.

45. Ibid. p. 584.

46. Ibid. p. 137.

47. Ibid. p. 119.

48. Ibid. p. 147.

49. *Ethical Studies* (Oxford: Clarendon Press, 1927) P. 171.

50. For a fuller development of this argument, see the present author's *Individualism* (Oxford: Blackwell, 1973) chs 11, 20.

51. *A Theory of Justice*, p. 327.

52. Ibid. p. 128.

53. Ibid. p. 129.

54. Ibid. p. 92.

56. Ibid. p. 177.

56. See ibid. p. 315.

57. Ibid. p. 137.

58. See ibid. p. 215.

59. Ibid. p. 120.

60. 'False Consciousness', in *Sociology in its Place and Other Essays* (Cambridge University Press, 1970) pp. 220–1.

61. *Relative Deprivation*, pp. 295, 8.

62. Ibid. p. 295.

63. Charles Taylor, 'Neutrality in Political Science', in *Philosophy, Politics and Society*, 3rd series, ed. Peter Laslett and W. G. Runciman (Oxford: Blackwell, 1967) pp. 56–7.

64. The argument of this and the next paragraph is more fully set out in the present author's *Power: A Radical View* (London: Macmillan, 1974).

65. *The Mountain People*, p. 289.

Chapter 9

1. The author thanks Martin Hollis of the University of East Anglia for his comments on this chapter.

2. *The English Works of Thomas Hobbes*, ed. Sir William Molesworth (London: Bohn, 1839) i 67; ii xiv; ii 109.

3. L. de Bonald, *Théorie du pouvoir* (Paris: Adrien le Clere 1854) i 103.

4. A Comte, *Système de politique positive* (Paris: Mathias 1851) ii 181.

5. J. S. Mill, *A System of Logic* 9th edn (London: Longman, Green & Co., 1875) ii 469. 'Men are not', Mill continues, 'when brought together, converted into another kind of substance, with different properties'.

6. See D. Essertier, *Psychologie et sociologie* (Paris: Alcan 1927).

7. Cf. E. Durkheim, *Les Règles de la méthode sociologique*, 2nd edn (Paris: Alcan 1901); and G. Tarcle, *Les Lois sociales* (Paris: Alcan 1898).

8. See *The Sociology of Georg Simmel*, trans. and ed. with intro. by K. H. Wolff (New York: Free Press, 1950) esp. chs i, ii and iv. For example: 'Let us grant for the moment that only individuals "really" exist. Even then, only a false conception of science could infer from this "fact" that any knowledge which somehow aims at synthesizing these individuals deals with merely speculative abstractions and unrealities' (pp. 4–5).

9. See C. H. Cooley, *Human Nature and the Social Order* (New York: Scribner, 1901). For Cooley, society and the individual are merely 'the collective and distributive aspects of the same thing' (pp. 1–2).

10. See G. Gurvitch, 'Les faux problèmes de la sociologie au XIXe siècle', in *La Vocation actuelle de la sociologie* (Paris: Presses Universitaires 1950) esp. pp 25–37.

11. See M. Ginsberg, 'The Individual and Society', in *On the Diversity of Morals* (London: Heinemann, 1956).

12. See G. C. Homans, 'Bringing Men Back In', *American Sociological Review* (1964); and D. H. Wrong, 'The Oversocialised Conception of Man in Modern Sociology', *American Sociological Review* (1961).

13. See the following discussions: F. A. Hayek, *The Counter-Revolution of Science* (New York: Free Press, 1952) chs 4, 6 and 8; K. R. Popper, *The Open Society and its Enemies* (London: Routledge, 1945) ch 14 and *The Poverty of Historicism* (London: Routledge, 1957) chs 7, 23, 24 and 31; J. W. N. Watkins, 'Ideal Types and Historical Explanation', *British Journal for the Philosophy of Science* (1952) (reprinted in *Readings in the Philosophy of Science*, ed. H. Feigl and M. Brodbeck (New York, 1953)) 'Methodological Individualism' (note) ibid., 'Historical Explanation in the Social Sciences', ibid. (1957); M. Mandelbaum, 'Societal Laws', ibid. (1957). L. J. Goldstein, 'The Two Theses of Methodological Individualism' (note) ibid. (1958); Watkins, 'The Two Theses of Methodological Individualism' (note) ibid. (1959); Goldstein, 'Mr Watkins on the Two Theses' (note) ibid. (1959), Watkins 'Third Reply to Mr Goldstein' (note) ibid. (1959); R. J. Scott, 'Methodological and Epistemological Individualism' (note) ibid. (1961); M. Mandelbaum, 'Societal Facts', *British Journal of Sociology* (1955); E. Gellner, 'Explanations in History', *Proceedings of the Aristotelian Society* (1956) these last two articles together with Watkins's 1957 article above are reprinted in *Theories of History*, ed. P. Gardiner (New York: Free Press, 1959) together with a reply to Watkins by Gellner. Gellner's paper is here retitled 'Holism and Individualism in History and Sociology'; M. Brodbeck, 'Philosophy of Social Science', *Philosophy of Science* (1954); Watkins, 'Methodological Individualism: A

Reply' (note) ibid. (1955); Brodbeck, 'Methodological Individualisms: Definition and Reduction', ibid. (1958); Goldstein, 'The Inadequacy of the Principle of Methodological Individualism', *Journal of Philosophy* (1956); Watkins 'The Alleged Inadequacy of Methodological Individualism' (note) ibid. (1958); C. Taylor, 'The Poverty of the Poverty of Historicism', *Universities and Left Review* (Summer 1958) followed by replies from I. Jarvie and Watkins, ibid. (Spring 1959); J. Agassi, 'Methodological Individualism', *British Journal of Sociology* (1960); E. Nagel, *The Structure of Science* (London: Routledge, 1961) pp. 535–46; A. C. Danto, *Analytical Philosophy of History* (Cambridge University Press, 1965) ch xii; and W. H. Dray, 'Holism and Individualism in History and Social Science' in *The Encyclopedia of Philosophy*, ed. P. Edwards (New York: Free Press, 1967).

14. *Individualism and Economic Order* (Chicago University Press, 1949) p. 6.

15. *The Open Society*, 4th edn, ii 98.

16. 'Historical Explanation in the Social Sciences' in *Theories of History*, ed. Gardiner, p. 505. Cf. 'large-scale *social* phenomena must be accounted for by the situations, dispositions and beliefs of *individuals*. This I call methodological individualism'; Watkins, 'Methodological Individualism: A Reply', *Philosophy of Science* (1955) p. 58 (see n. 13 above).

17. *Universities and Left Review* (Spring 1959) p. 57.

18. *The Counter-Revolution of Science*, p. 56.

19. *The Poverty of Historicism*, p. 140.

20. Popper himself provides some; see ibid. pp. 62–3.

21. *Psychology of Policies* (London, 1960).

22. Ibid. p. 10.

23. *Les règles de la méthode sociologique*, p. 103.

24. See Homans, *Social Behaviour* (London: Routledge, 1961).

25. 'Societal Facts'.

26. For example Hempel calls this 'deductive-nomological explanation'. For a defence of this type of explanation in social science, see R. Rudner, *Philosophy of Social Science* (Englewood Cliffs, N.J.: Prentice-Hall, 1965). I have not discussed 'probabilistic explanation', in which the general laws are not universal and the *explicans* only makes the *explicandum* highly probable, in the text; such explanations pose no special problems for my argument.

27. *Psychology of Politics*, p. 5.

28. D. Hume, *Essays Moral and Political*, ed. T. H. Green, and T. H. Grose (London: Longmans, Green & Co., 1875) ii 68.

29. *Social Behaviour*, p. 6.

30. For example, in the cases of rules and terminologies of kinship or of language generally.

Chapter 10

1. John Rawls, *A Theory of Justice* (Oxford: Clarendon Press, 1972).

Chapter 11

1. Robert Nozick, *Anarchy, State and Utopia* (Oxford: Blackwell, 1974).